Frommer's® W9-BHJ-881

irreverent guide to London

other titles in the

irreverent guide

series

Frommer's®

irreverent guide to London

3rd Edition

By
Kate Sekules

A BALLIETT & FITZGERALD BOOK
IDG BOOKS WORLDWIDE, INC.

a disclaimer

Prices fluctuate in the course of time, and travel information changes under the impact of the varied and volatile factors that influence the travel industry. Neither the author nor the publisher can be held responsible for the experiences of readers while traveling. Readers are invited to write to the publisher with ideas, comments, and suggestions for future editions.

about the authors

Native Londoner **Kate Sekules** writes about travel, food, and fitness for magazines, including *The New Yorker, Travel and Leisure, Health and Fitness, Time Out,* and *Vogue,* and for the *Condé Nast* website *Epicurious.*

Ben Illis is an actor and writer living in London.

Balliett & Fitzgerald Inc.

Editorial director: Will Balliett / Executive editor: Tom Dyja / Managing editor: Alexis Lipsitz / Production editor: Michael Walters

IDG Books Worldwide, Inc.

An International Data Group Company
919 E. Hillsdale Blvd., Suite 400
Foster City, CA 94404

ISBN 0-02-863787-9
ISSN 1085-4789

Interior design contributed to by Tsang Seymour Design Studio

special sales

For general information on IDG Books Worldwide's books in the U.S., please call our Consumer Customer Service department at 1-800-762-2974. For reseller information, including discounts, bulk sales, customized editions, and premium sales, please call our Reseller Customer Service department at 1-800-424-3422.

Manufactured in the United States of America

what's so irreverent?

It's up to you.

You can buy a traditional guidebook with its fluff, its promotional hype, its let's-find-something-nice-to-say-about-everything point of view. Or you can buy an Irreverent guide.

What the Irreverents give you is the lowdown, the inside story. They have nothing to sell but the truth, which includes a balance of good and bad. They praise, they trash, they weigh, and leave the final decisions up to you. No tourist board, no chamber of commerce will ever recommend them.

Our writers are insiders, who feel passionate about the cities they live in, and have strong opinions they want to share with you. They take a special pleasure leading you where other guides fear to tread.

How irreverent are they? One of our authors insisted on writing under a pseudonym. "I couldn't show my face in town again if I used my own name," she told me. "My friends would never speak to me." Such is the price of honesty. She, like you, should know she'll always have a friend at Frommer's.

Warm regards,

Michael Spring

Michael Spring
Publisher

contents

introduction

It took a new millennium for the sight, but it was well worth it: the Queen of England holding hands with the Prime Minister and woodenly swaying to a mass singalong of *Auld Lang Syne*. Strange but true, there was Tony Blair at midnight, January 1, 2000, Greenwich Mean Time, with his wife on one side and the Queen to his right, Elizabeth II tight-lipped as ever and desperately trying to figure out the words to the traditional New Year's Day carol and overwhelmed by the majesty of something profoundly and identifiably English yet not crusted over with the trappings of monarchy. And in another turnabout, it was the Labor P.M. who came under fire for spending an extravagant amount of money on a millennial circus at the expense of bread. The biggest dome in the world, with a canopy covering 20 acres? *Obviously*. At a cost of £758 million, paid for with monies from the National Lottery? *Brilliant*. The Dome at Greenwich, which served as the centerpiece of the city's millennium fetes, is not even a permanent structure—it will be rather unceremoniously dismantled after a paltry 50 years. In a country with its fair share of social problems, such extravagance does leave a slightly bitter taste in the mouth, no matter who's responsible.

Say what you will about the Dome, and I've said a few things myself, it's not the only topic that can make a Londoner's blood boil. That is a task dutifully carried out by the royal family. The biggest news on that front, since Her death, is the marriage of Prince Edward, now Earl of Wessex, to Diana lookalike Sophie Rhys-Jones, now Countess of Wessex. Why has this marriage meant so much to Londoners? Because it hit home to us how little we care about the royal family these days. The new Earl is ridiculed in the press for his attempts at television programming—a string of lukewarm biographies of his relatives, for example. He retaliates by accusing his countrymen of being a nation that despises successful people. No worries for him there. Frankly, we are fed up with the royals because we know now what they are: a successful tourist attraction, a slice of Old World history, and not much else.

However blasé the Londoner may be about the royals, their continued existence raises a dilemma for the visitor. Do you do the royal thing, or act cool and ignore it? Do you, as you secretly are dying to, visit Buckingham Palace, Kensington Palace, Kew Palace, Hampton Court Palace, the Crown Jewels, the Queen's Mews, St. James's Palace, and take day trips to Windsor Castle? Oh, the hell with it; you do the royals, knowing that the pomp and circumstance of royal London today is as hollow as St. Paul's dome. Still, the history is fascinating (if you choose, say, Hampton Court when it's not busy, over boring old Buck House) and the riches are impressive (if you don't think too hard about how they were amassed or to whom they should belong). And what of Diana? No one expected that more than two years after her untimely death, London would have no official memorial. At the moment, when the committee is not bickering and sulking, decisions are being made as to what, where, and how the Princess of Hearts should be remembered. The likely outcome of all this wrangling looks to be a flower garden at Kensington Palace, complete with extra-smelly blooms for the blind.

Releasing preconceptions before you get to London is a good idea all 'round. If you arrive hyped up with a headful of Big Ben in the mist and jolly, rollicking pub singalongs, or gritty all-night illegal warehouse raves, or of whatever your ideal London consists, you'll be disappointed. If you took seriously the recent spate of "London Rocks!" articles that spackled the glossy magazines, you are also in for a mild shock. Although there is a fabulous restaurant scene (read on), certain privations are still operational that will always impede the ultimate good time: namely, taxis that still disappear when you're desperate, and public pay phones that still act weird, despite being brand new (you won't see those pretty red booths anymore). The only good news on this front is that hopefully, by the time you read this, London's famously prohibitive licensing laws (pubs closing at 11 p.m.) will have been relaxed. Fingers crossed.

To avoid further disappointment, you should also release another common misconception: that London is a beautiful city. Of course, there are many parts that are, but great chunks of England's capital are quite hideous. Tottenham Court Road—where Londoners buy electronic, hi-fi, and computer goods, and you'll almost certainly exit the tube there at some stage—is one of the ugliest streets in Europe. Oxford Street is no great shakes either, and all over the place, including most of the city, there is plenty of uninspired architecture that got hurled up after the World War II Blitz, plus acres of projects (called council housing here), awful Sixties blocks, and just tatty, shabby mush. There's a certain urban *jolie-laide* style about this real London, however, unlike the charmless reality of another misconception that should be corrected early on—that all the theater here is great. If you believe that, you may as well just tear up a dozen ten-pound notes now for practice.

Guidebooks—and many of the first-time visitors who are their consumers—would prefer it if London would stick to its old image, the one that left after the Fifties, when the "Great" in Great Britain still seemed an appropriate qualifier, and ladies wore white gloves to tea. That city of polite rituals, colonial hauteur, and gracious monuments was demolished once and for all by the Swinging Sixties. That—plus the punky Seventies, and the money-mad Eighties—rendered London a much more complicated place, harder to grasp and still harder to penetrate. Neither has the much-vaunted Nineties re-swinging of London made the place more accessible. Its latest title, The New Capital of Europe, has just made the city more smug, while failing to increase the number of taxis.

For a signifier of the complexity of modern London—a palimpsest of four decades' changes—look at the Royal Festival Hall. This South Bank concert hall was built in the Fifties for the Festival of Britain—a public-relations scheme to swell the native breast with postwar hope and pride. It retains its original function as home of the London Philharmonic, but it also stages, say, the environmental flick *Koyaanisqatsi*, with Philip Glass conducting his score to it, while installed in the foyer are exhibitions like *After Auschwitz* and *Homeworks*, in which soon-to-be-lost crafts of the British Isles (blacksmithery, thatching, etc.) were demonstrated by their final practitioners. Upstairs, the masses are fed in the People's Palace, whose first chef was buzz-cut, Cockney Gary Rhodes, well known for extolling on TV the virtues of almost-lost British dishes like faggots and spotted dick. The entire building, along with its South Bank Centre neighbors, is meanwhile due to be enshrined in a post-post-Postmodern, National Lottery–funded crystal canopy, designed by Sir Richard Rogers, who is most famous for the Centre Georges Pompidou in Paris. It's easy to relate to the visitor's bewilderment at this spaghetti of cultural crossed wires—especially when you've been expecting Beefeaters and roast beef.

Another preconception is ready to bite the dust—the local cuisine, the dried-up meat, leathery Yorkshire pudding and sad, colorless vegetables of lore. Neophytes are astonished to find London in its gastronomic late twenties, with teenage rebellions long past, and a glorious culinary confidence set in, influenced by every cuisine of the world. England is, of course, officially part of Europe now, and boundary-free work permits mean more cross-fertilization with neighbors. The concrete link with France via the Channel tunnel has underlined that connection. London is also every bit as much a melting pot as New York, with West Indian, Bangladeshi, and Pakistani culture particularly firmly integrated. Look at Soho. Quite unlike its New York namesake, this square mile or so of the deepest West End, having hosted successive immigrant waves, and gone through a protracted sleaze period, never lost its cosmopolitan, bohemian spiciness, and has settled in as London's playground of clubs and restaurants and hot gay scene.

Of course, it's not wrong to seek auld London towne, but that is not the focus of this guide. The London that can't be packaged is harder to find, but more rewarding because it's personal. How to get personal with people who stay inside by the fire, throw dinner parties for each other, and belong to exclusive clubs is a challenge, especially now that the chattering classes have *en masse* fallen in love with The Restaurant. To begin a relationship with London, it's best to dilute, or eschew, the tourist trail. See all the big sights on one visit, and you'll come away with your stiff-upper-lipped British bulldog prejudices reinforced—because it's relentless, hard work. And you won't meet a soul who isn't a fellow tourist.

If you'd rather befriend the Londoner, there's no foolproof method. For every American who visits twice a year with their adopted London family whom they met in the line at the National Theatre, there's a sad story of a lonely week being snubbed in the pub and dining in Siberia. Since knowing people is the best route to some version of the real London, though, you should reach out, regardless of the British reputation. It's only habit that keeps us from talking to strangers, and the worst you'll have to deal with is a withering glance or a muttered reply. Pubs—those communal sitting rooms with large drinks cabinets—sometimes offer the perfect environment to get chatting, though they do revolve around alcohol, and still tend not to be the most comfortable environments for lone women, even when they look like coffee lounges or farmhouse kitchens. But alcohol sure does loosen the British tongue. Failing that, ask questions—we love trying to explain our culture. Ask about the rules of cricket; the class system; the difference between a *Guardian* and a *Telegraph* reader; whether anyone has heard of John Grisham and who's Jeffrey Archer anyway; what's with Brits and toilet humor; and, by all means, ask about the weather, which remains a popular and safe topic.

Where to go to meet the candidates for your friendly overtures depends on where you're coming from. Suburbanites and professionals won't bond with youth-culture-oriented neighborhoods, like Notting Hill, Camden Town, and Shoreditch. Perhaps only New Yorkers, San Franciscans, Angelenos, and other big-city babes, who speak the language of street style, will. On the other hand, Chelsea—the swinging King's Road of the Sixties—is now full of the scenes made by models and trust-funders, Eurotrash and bankers, and is (along with neighboring Knightsbridge) quite the place to which Elvis Costello didn't want to go. For Chelsea's diametric opposite, try Brixton, a 'hood far more West Indian than white-guys-with-dreadlocks Notting Hill, and also home to dyke chic, bike messengers, and young families restoring Georgian houses. It also has a reputation for being unsafe, and all of that makes it a draw for the hip and intrepid city anthropologist. Professors and freelance creatives may find soul mates in Islington, where Camden kids go when they grow up. Islingtonians work in TV or the print media, or act, and never leave their borough of restaurants, pubs, bookshops, and the Almeida—London's best Off–West End theater.

But since you're not moving here, and time is limited, even the Almeida may be further off the West End than you have time to wander. Perhaps, like the priciest hotels on the British Monopoly board, you'll just keep landing on Mayfair and St. James's, following the royal path from Kensington to Belgravia, and merely grazing the green and pleasant surface of the city. That's OK. Whatever you do in London, you'll be left to get on with it. Let's hope you feel at home here too.

London Neighborhoods

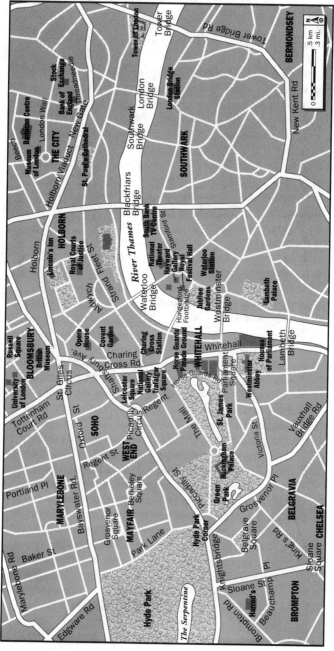

you
probably
didn't know

How to get London smarts... You can't. Or at least it's not that easy. London's reputation for impenetrability is no myth. As a "bloody foreigner," you'll probably have to live here for at least two years just to qualify for your provisional Londoner license, and that's just for tourist rights. Still, many "Londoners" are imported from the British provinces—so they may understand your desperation to fit in, though they will be loath to admit it. Tip for the top on this front is to think of London as a series of small towns. If you want to fit in, pick an area that appeals and stick to it— almost no one in London maintains rep in more than one area. Swallow your pride and be persistent.

Where to get a drink after hours... British licensing laws are bizarre. As things stand, alcohol cannot be sold after 11 p.m., when pubs are legally bound to give punters 20 minutes drinking-up time before ejecting them unceremoniously into the night. Since everyone, including those responsible for them, considers these laws daft, there has been an increasing laxity in their enforcement, and many bars are already open until 12 or 1. As you will hear in the Nightlife section, rumors are abounding that licensing laws are going to be officially relaxed in the new millennium. Other rumors suggest, however, that the laws may be tightened even further in some residential areas. To locate late-drinking spots, avoid overly residential areas (check out Soho and the largely commercial districts of Clerkenwell/Farringdon and Shoreditch). West London is also getting laxer—but, frankly, the best way to find out what's hot and what's not is to ask in the bar you're in for local recommendations. If all else fails, remember that most hotels are able to bypass the licensing laws regarding guests and can keep you tanked up into the wee small hours. Also, restaurants can serve booze until 12 if you're eating, and nightclubs often have late licensing, although rarely beyond 3 a.m. Late bars are a lottery; many have rude doormen and an irritating entry policy (if you know/have slept with/will sleep with/might consider sleeping with me/my friend). Lastly, be prepared for cover charges and crowds in late-night bars.

Where are the insomniacs?... **Bar Italia,** on **Frith Street** in Soho. The tiny, echt-Italian, stand-up espresso bar with a Rocky Marciano altar and stale panettone contains London's only life after 4 a.m.

Where the hot neighborhoods are... There are four. For an evening out, **Soho** is still the place, as it has been since the '50s. It has a thriving and friendly gay and mixed scene and an atmosphere that is seriously relaxed. Soho is also restaurant land and home to London's small but worthwhile Chinatown. Many, however, have come to feel that Soho is too anonymous and too full of tourists and therefore not the place to experience London. In the '80s **Camden Town** took over the mantle, or at least helped to share the burden of it. Here is still the center for live music, struggling bands, and scruffy, booted youth. Here also are street markets, vintage clothes, and even a smattering of goths and punks, those symbols of London's street-style roots (even though most of them these days are not even British, let alone Londoners). **Notting Hill** is an altogether more modern arbiter of what's hot in London town. Home to many of the artistes who have put London on the style map, Notting Hill is another restaurant land, but it also offers bars, galleries, markets (such as Portobello, arguably London's finest), West Indian culture, the biggest street carnival in the northern hemisphere, and antiques galore. Native Notting Hillbillies look cool and deconstructed, so you can't tell if they're slackers or trustafarians with a best-seller under their belts. Lastly, **Shoreditch**, the newest kid on the block, is East London's capital of cool. The artists of Shoreditch are thought to be more "genuine, man" than their West London counterparts. A sparsity of residential space means later drinking, but some may be put off by the post-apocalyptic landscape. Shoreditchers seem to believe that trees are passé, so bizarre sculptures serve the streets instead. Each to his own.

Where to park... Nowhere, because you didn't rent a car, did you? What's that? You did? Well, more fool you. Try to avoid broken meters, red lines, double yellow lines, single yellow lines before 6:30 p.m. and after 8:30 a.m. and residents' zones. You may be able to ignore a ticket but not one of the surly, massive clamping units that roam the city, ruining lives. The big yellow immobilizing wheel clamps will take a day to have removed and cost £120. Towing also happens, and results in the same loss of time/cash, with the added bonus of trying to figure out exactly where they might have taken little Herbie. Unclaimed cars are crushed, so do not stall tracking down your errant roadster. If you're looking for safe and easy parking, find an NCP park; the rates are exorbitant but you can find these places all over London—and I can assure you that you will never, ever, find a legal space to park on the street in this city.

Children's Hour

Some of our favorite characters in children's literature are Londoners. Mr. and Mrs. Dearly, who owned Pongo, Perdita and the 99 other dalmations, lived on the Outer Circle of Regent's Park while Wendy and Michael Darling left their Victorian house on the north side of Kensington Gardens for NeverNeverLand. As for bears, Paddington had a station named after him from which British Rail trains still depart for the West Country, and a certain bear named Winnie had residence for a time in the Polar Bear pit at the London Zoo.

When to avoid London... Christmas. Everything shuts down for interminable turkey and the Queen's oh-so-relevant speech about which members of the Commonwealth are next to attempt independence.

Where the top chefs are... Oh please, where aren't they? Example: Once upon a time, 192, the Notting Hill restaurant, had a kitchen run by a fellow named Alastair Little. His protégés included Rowley Leigh, Dan Evans, Adam

Robinson, and Angela Dwyer. Each of these people now has at least one establishment of their own, and many have nurtured other chefs who have gone on to run their own places. Other eateries can be traced to the Roux Brothers or Anton Mosimann or Prue Leith and Ruthie Rogers. Even the kitchen in my apartment has a celebrity chef who keeps turning up and garnishing my beans on toast with fresh coriander and sundried tomatoes. But, hey, that's London. To find the cuisine of your dreams, simply scan the million newspaper gastroporn sections.

How to afford that grand dinner... Lunch, prix fixe. The three-hour lunch never did die here, so you'll be in good company. Also, each February, the *Financial Times* does a promotion where top tables go for a ridiculously cheap 5 or 10 pounds; entrance ticket is a copy of *FT,* printed on its distinctive pink paper, and booking is essential.

What's that ringing sound?... A mobile, darling. Cell phones are to London as cockroaches are to New York.

How to save buckets of cash on museums... Obviously, you can go to the free ones, like the **British Museum**, and you could even be cheap and ignore the suggested voluntary donation at some others. But once you've exhausted those possibilities, you'll have to buy a White Card, the cultural discount card that, having not been heavily promoted, has passed most Londoners by. This is a three- or seven-day passport ticket to 16 museums and galleries, including the **V&A** (which is apparently confused about how voluntary its voluntary donation is), its South Kensington neighbors the **Natural History** and **Science Museums**, the **Courtauld Institute Galleries**, and the **Hayward** and **Barbican Galleries**. See Diversions for full details.

How to stay with London friends when you haven't any... Upscale B&Bs are a new thing in a country where a B&B sign normally heralds a depressing room with no matching furniture. Unlike American B&Bs, which are often small inns, these London digs are truly private homes with rooms to let to an exclusive few. The **Bulldog Club** agency (tel 0207/371–3202, fax 0207/371–2015 or www.bulldogclub.com) is top drawer—Maggie Jackson practically runs a credit check on you before you're allowed into her friends' tiny houses—and **Gail O'Farrell**'s got some gorgeous cottagey places in Hampstead and Highgate (phone her at 0207/722–6869). The **English Speaking Union** has a hosting scheme (tel 212/879–6800), though the standard of decor is not guaranteed, and there's always home-swapping. This works like it sounds: trading places with your counterparts in London. Although nearly all participants describe their abode accurately in the home-swap catalogs, Americans often experience a degree of culture shock when staying in an English home, running into privations like snowed-up iceboxes, lack of central heat, doormanless walk-ups (a normal London flat), and stick-shift cars with the wheel on the wrong side. If you're persnickety, or if you're Martha Stewart and believe God is in the details, don't swap your home. Otherwise, register with Intervac (tel 01225/892208); Homelink International (tel 01344/842642, Linfield House, Corse Hill Rd., Virginia Water, Surrey GU2S 4AS); Home Base Holidays (tel 0208/886–8752, 7 Park Avenue, London N13 5PG); or the Worldwide Home Exchange Club (tel 0189/261-9300).

Where the queen gets her groceries... Fortnum & Mason.

How to order Indian food... With 1,500-odd Indian restaurants in London alone, curry is England's national cuisine. Everyone orders the following: onion *bhajia* (onion fritters), *murgh tikka masala* (yogurt-spice-marinated chicken breast, baked in the tandoor oven and served with thick sauce), *sag ghosh* (lamb with spinach), *mattar paneer* (peas with cubes of Indian curd cheese), *tarka dahl* (garlic lentil sauce), and *pulau* rice (cooked in ghee and stock). If you want heat, order *vindaloo*; for extra mild and creamy, have *korma*. Beware of young men in packs on Saturday nights ordering chicken *biriani* and buckets of lager.

How to get designer labels cheap... The best sources are "warehouse sales," where a single designer or a group offload samples and surplus to the cognoscenti. Look in the *Evening Standard*'s Tuesday fashion section, and in *Time Out*'s "Buys and Bargains" section for notices. Or call the office of your favorite London designer (Katharine Hamnett, Jasper Conran, Nicole Farhi) and ask about the next sample sale. See the Shopping chapter for more.

How to hear Queen Victoria... The **National Sound Archive** (tel 0207/412-7440, The British Library, 96 Euston Rd., NW1 2DB, London) has a recording of Her Majesty made around 1880. Hear it (and about a million more historic sound bites) by appointment.

How to get theater tickets when they're sold out... From the theater. Every theater holds at least one row of "house seats" that the management keeps for their own use. If no one fabulously important wants to see the show that night, or the theater didn't overbook, the tickets are sold at the last possible moment, along with the "returns"—unpicked-up bookings. Some theaters want you to queue up that morning, others an hour or two before curtain. Call ahead to each theater for the policy. The better hotel concierges—usually the ones at posh hotels—are good at getting ahold of these in their special way.

What to do on Sunday... Sunday used to be a really dead day in London, before the Sunday trading laws, based on the Christian Sabbath notion, got eroded. Now Sunday is the busiest shopping day of the lot, with accompanying lines and traffic jams. If that doesn't put you off, beware of the hours, since large stores are currently allowed only a six-hour window, and *which* six hours they pick varies. But what most bona fide Londoners really do on Sunday is wade through a huge stack of Sunday papers—look on the newsagent's shelf that day and you'll see what we mean. What else could you do? Go to market (especially the East End ones—Brick Lane, Petticoat Lane, Spitalfields); have an old-fashioned lunch; stroll in the park; see a movie. Some theaters are experimenting with performances on this traditionally "dark" day, too.

What not to do on Sunday... Don't go to the South Ken museums, or see the show at the Tate or the Royal Academy, unless you like crowds.

What the weather's like... This wouldn't be the number-one topic of conversation in London if anyone understood the British climate. Guidebooks tell you stories about 40-degree winters and 70-degree summers, but literally anything could happen. There was a hurricane in 1987, a 97-degree heat wave in 1989, the hottest August and the wettest June on record in 1997, and nearly always a fortnight in April when temperatures hit the upper 80s—which sometimes gives way to frost in May. Sometimes the rain sets in for a week, but not in dramatic downpours or picturesque thunderstorms—just relentless soaking drizzle. The local light is flat and diffuse, which is sheer misery on those endless wet days, but absolute perfection on a sunny day in a park.

Do we need a gun?... No, the recent spate of high-profile muggings and purse snatchings notwithstanding. The police increasingly carry firearms, it's true, but London is still a relatively safe city, a result of the fact that personal firearms are not yet an issue in the UK. Still, the usual commonsense city precautions for taking care of your property and your person apply. More distressing is the rise in the number of homeless people you'll see wherever you go.

How to tell where you are... Look at a map of London. See how big it is? London, which grew out of a pack of once-separate villages, is still divided into 32 boroughs—plus the City of London—each separately governed by its own council. Every corner street sign (big white rectangles, mounted on walls at about knee level) tells you which borough you're in, in smaller letters above the street name. But the borough system doesn't really tell you where you are; postcodes are marginally better, once you've deciphered them. The letters simply refer to compass points, with the C of EC1 and WC2 and so on denoting "central." The numbers seem helpful at first: West Central One is indeed sandwiched between West One, West Central Two, and East Central One, with North One and North West One to the (that's right) north. Travel a bit farther, however, and you find that W2 segues into W11, that W8 is next to SW7, and W9 is NW6's neighbor.

Why the Londoner crossed the river... To get back to the other side. South Londoners hate the snobbish attitude of the majority that lives on the north side and thinks it needs a passport to cross a bridge. South London highlights include the National Theatre and South Bank Centre (on every visitor's list); Shakespeare's Globe, (which should be); the "Gastrodrome" and the Design Museum by Tower Bridge; the OXO Tower; Battersea Park and Clapham Common in which to escape other tourists; and neighborhoods to explore, such as Brixton.

How to enjoy Heathrow... Invest in a Virgin Atlantic business-class ticket—or Upper Class, as they cheekily call it. Virgin is the airline belonging to Richard Branson, that gently ridiculed, yet nationally beloved tycoon/visionary. The flight itself is groovy, with its masseuse/manicurist, wine-tastings, seat-back gambling and way better than average grub, but you want to spend an actual vacation in the Upper Class Lounge at Heathrow. Go early for a haircut, massage, and shoeshine; practice your putting; nap in the rooftop conservatory; listen to CDs in the soundproof lounge; play state-of-the-art computer games. The decor's funky and the Virgin staff friendly—it's an airport lounge fantasy.

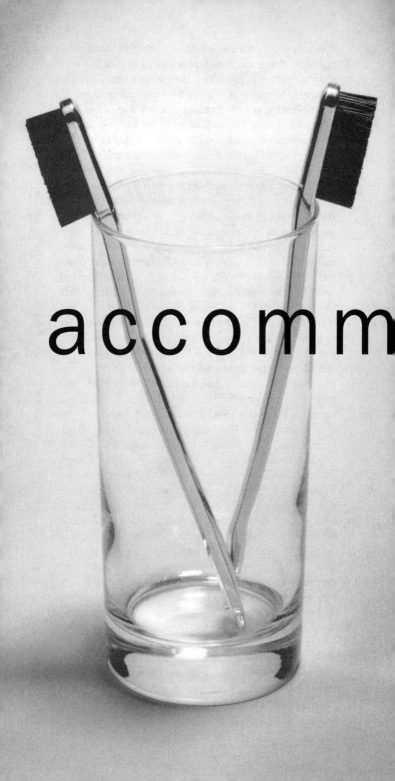

accomm

1

odations

Face it: This city
makes you pay
through the nose
for a place to lay
your head. You'll
have to capitulate
and consign half

your vacation funds to the hotel bed. Still, it pays to think ahead and spend those pounds wisely. London is blossoming with smaller, independent hotels, which often labor under the term "boutique hotel." We list several, and they're very good bets, offering so much deeper a London experience than those cookie-cutter chains or even some of the swankiest grand hotels. Of course, the best (and cheapest) way of all to get under London's skin is to stay with friends. If you don't have any, you can buy the next best thing—the hospitality of strangers in upscale B&Bs, still a relatively new concept in town.

Winning the Reservations Game

Try not to arrive roofless. Booking ahead not only gives you peace of mind, it also yields any special, weekend, or corporate rates that might be offered. Typically, though, it's the more expensive and bigger places that offer discounts, while the smaller hotels, guest houses, and B&Bs don't reduce their already lower rates. If you book a packaged holiday, you may be given a hotel's most boring, most boxy, smallest room, but the rates are probably the lowest you could get for that property. Check into half-price programs—they're worth it if they include the hotel you like, which you can find out by calling ahead. Usually, you register, join, or buy a directory, which then accesses savings of up to 50 percent on the hotels in that program. Some to try are **Privilege Card International** (3391 Peachtree Rd. NE, Suite 110, Atlanta GA 30326, tel 800/236–9732), **Europe Hotel Directory** (Entertainment Publications, 40 Oakview St., Trumbull CT 06611, tel 800/445–4137), and **Great American Traveler** (Access, Box 27965, Salt Lake City UT 84127, tel 800/331–8867). You can also book hotels—more than one at a time, if you like—with a call to the London Tourist Board's Credit Card Hotline, which takes Access or Visa (tel 0207/604–2890). You will normally be asked for a deposit when you make a reservation, which will be deducted from the final bill. If you haven't made reservations in advance or are only booking a short stay, you may be asked to pay for the room on arrival. If so, check out the room before money changes hands.

Is There a Right Address?

To a certain sort of Londoner (they're usually called Sloane Rangers, after their Sloane Square stomping grounds), **Knightsbridge** is the center not only of London, but of the world. For tourists, too, it's hard to beat, well served with tube, restaurants, and shopping—and Hyde Park on the doorstep. Just south of Knightsbridge, Belgravia is embassy territory, and some of the priciest real estate in town. As a tourist base it sure is peaceful, but there's not much more, except for pleasant strolls and Hyde Park.

Famously swinging in the Sixties, **Chelsea**, a onetime artists' ghetto west of Belgravia, is expensive to live in and lovely to walk in. Its main drawback for visitors is inaccessibility, since there's a weird dearth of tube stops. There are buses galore, though, and attractions enough in the borough itself. Also west of the West End, green, peaceful, and expensive residential **Holland Park** is 10 minutes by tube from practically anywhere, yet has a distinctive out-of-the-maelstrom ambience, and one of London's loveliest small parks. **Kensington** is busier and more urban than neighboring Holland Park, while sharing some of its green and pleasant peaceful feel. South Kensington, with its high-ceilinged houses, contains those giant Victorian cultural palaces—the museums. Streets are quieter and prices higher than farther north—except on the main roads (Brompton, Gloucester, Cromwell), where the opposite is the case. North of Holland Park, **Notting Hill** is the hippest district, centering on Portobello Road with its market. Antiques shops, a Caribbean-style carnival in August, and exciting young restaurants and galleries give Notting Hill a multicultural buzz. (With the arrival of the film *Notting Hill,* however, some say the area has lost it hip credibility, and have fled east to **Shoreditch** and **Clerkenwell.** While thin on accommodations, these districts see plenty of other action; see Dining, Shopping, and Nightlife.) East of Notting Hill is **Bayswater,** between Oxford Street and Queensway, between residential and midtown, and between swanky and seedy. It's full of cheapo hostelries in huge white wedding-cake Victorians. Those we list are on the upper end of this spectrum, though still bargains, easy to get around from, and bang on Hyde Park.

Mayfair is London's true center, and you'll feel most urbane and sophisticated staying here. Bond Street shopping, Cork Street art galleries, tree-filled squares, restaurants—it's all here. Less expensive and less tony are Oxford Street and the streets to its north. Just across Piccadilly from Mayfair, **St. James's** has been known as "Gentleman's London" on account of its anachronistic clubs and its legions of shops selling hats, canes, shaving sets, ties, shirts, and handmade shoes. It retains an old-fashioned and courtly air, has two beautiful parks, its own palace, good restaurants, and top hotel rates. East of Regent Street, **Soho** on weekend nights is the nightclubbers' theme park, with hordes of youths and a thriving gay scene.

Other times, the confusing grid of streets is restaurant paradise. Great fun; only one hotel.

On the east side of Charing Cross Road, **Covent Garden** is another center of London, not packed with hotel beds but rife with shopping, strolling, eating places. It's as near as you can get to theaterland. North of Covent Garden lies **Bloomsbury**, made famous by Virginia Woolf and her circle. Convenient to the British Museum and lined with moderate small hotels, it's somewhat dusty and noisy but nevertheless a central place to stay. We list one hotel in the **Docklands**, a decidedly offbeat location way downstream on the Thames. This is London's new business district that never quite took off—part ghost town, part riverside theme park, it's a part of town that some people will love.

The Lowdown

Old faithfuls... The "Old Lady of Park Lane" is first in line. She is **Grosvenor House**, Forte's flagship, built on the grounds of the Earl of Grosvenor's late-18th-century estate. She's bulky, none too glamorous, and, like many an old friend, reassuringly homey and undemanding. The more glitzy **Savoy** never changes either, and we're glad of that, while the nearby **Fielding** is like the frumpy friend, dressed in sweats but seen in the right places. Some surprisingly wealthy people savor the continuity of the little Fielding.

Grand duchesses... Masquerading as an old friend, but more of a snob than she cares to admit, is **The Connaught**, where you practically need a letter of introduction to get a room. It's considered very crass to ask for prices here. The **Dorchester** is the place to unpack your ball gown, or boogie in the nightclub if you lack an invitation to the ball. **Claridges** is the epitome of understated elegance—royalty feels at home on the sweeping marble stairs here, as do ancient dowagers lunching on smoked fish in its restaurant, the Causerie.

Favorite uncles... Slightly racy, a little unpredictable, these are relatively new guys in town. In brazen Soho, **Hazlitt's**, with its nooks and crannies, Victorian bathtubs, and many thousands of etchings, is popular with antiques dealers and literary lions. Its younger but bigger brother, **The Gore**, shares its style. The **Stafford** has an interesting side—the carriage house rooms, which have the names of racehorses on their stable doors, are fun. **The Landmark** is full of surprises—it's a fully fledged grande dame with no dress code in an unstarchy part of town, with an outrageous atrium behind its unremarkable façade. More of a collection of pied-à-terres than a hotel, the slightly down-at-heel **Dolphin Square** is redolent of clandestine encounters, especially in the brasserie and in the bar overlooking the swimming pool with its Fifties-era murals, while the library at the **Covent Garden** is the very place for avuncular advice sessions over a glass of bubbly.

Where to misbehave... The **Savoy** has always had a louche air about it, perhaps because it has its own theater, or maybe it's the handmade beds or the breezes rolling in off the Thames. Many Londoners who had a rock 'n' roll phase misspent part of their youth in the bar of the **Columbia**, which never closes to the bands in residence; the bedrooms, meanwhile, host photo shoots for sleazy fashion articles in famous glossy magazines. Completely the opposite form of chic has its home base at **The Hempel**, which is so pristine, hushed, and downright Amish, you can't help wanting to besmirch its surfaces. At **The Portobello**, the round-bed suite with a fully functioning Edwardian brass bathing machine is practically perverted. If your age is still in the single figures, then **Pippa Pop-Ins**—a hotel that caters exclusively to children—is the place to be naughty.

Britishest... Every other hotel in London has a faux-Brit chintzy decor, a couple of four-poster beds, and afternoon tea, but no hotel is more genuinely English than **The Connaught**, where oils hang in oak-paneled hallways and you get the feeling that your nanny may be lurking around the corner to scold you for making too much noise. **Basil Street** is the cut-price version—it's like a dowager Knightsbridge aunt's house. The B&B agency the **Bulldog Club**, mind you, books you into actual dowager aunts' houses in Knightsbridge, Kensington, and all the best addresses; while taking an apartment at **Dolphin Square** will make you the temporary neighbor of many Members of Parliament, not to mention Princess Anne.

ACCOMMODATIONS | THE LOWDOWN

Worst simulated English... The clear winner of the Lionel Bart "London!" award is the **Lanesborough**. Great Britain was never as British as this—all with drawing rooms, frills, and furbelows, and a genuine Jeeves on duty in every room (though the management is forever having to train new butlers, as American guests poach them). Honorable mention: **Browns**, especially for the venerable afternoon tea service, heavy on scones with lashings of clotted cream. Tea is better elsewhere (see For Afternoon Tea, in Dining), but the tourists don't seem to know this.

Eurotrashiest... What with the Channel Tunnel and all, London now seems like Europe's latest capital. The question these days is more to ask what neighborhood is not Eurotrashy. The style kids with cash would be seen dead in only a few hotels, and, frankly, darling, they'd rather stay with friends, but if they have to buy a bed, they get it at **Sydney House**. Those who don't sneer at hostelries flock—*flock*—to **The Metropolitan**, which was shamelessly designed expressly for them, though the **Halcyon** and **Claridges** are still OK, and while **Blakes** is a bit too music-biz, **The Hempel** continues to be a safe bet from the plebs—at least for the moment.

Was that RuPaul in the elevator?... Again, the **Halcyon** wins hands down (everyone from RuPaul to Snoop Doggy Dogg stays here), with locals such as Sting or the members of Pink Floyd joining them there for dinner. The truly hip, however, slum it at the always so-out-it's-in **Columbia**. Madonna and Michael Jackson have been known to choose fittingly ungroovy hotels: Ms. Ciccone has queened it at the **Lanesborough**, while the Weird One went to the **Montcalm** (which has London's only nonallergenic bedrooms. Surely no coincidence?). **The Metropolitan**'s Met Bar has young Hollywood, half the music biz, and all the fashion crowd in a holding pattern (with Momo and the Soho House taking the overflow).

Suite deals... A person could move into the penthouse at **Dukes**—though not overopulent, it's deeply carpeted, with plenty of space and a balcony, and you wake up looking at distant Westminster Abbey. **Hazlitt's** sole suite—a black oak Tudor fantasia with its own "Great Bed of Ware"—is fun for playing Lancelot and

Guinevere, while Hazlitt's sister hotel, **The Gore**, has a suite with a bed Judy Garland once owned, and outrageous Grecian tiles in the bathroom. The **Stafford's** carriage rooms have fireplaces and Jacuzzis (downstairs), and entrances off their own cobbled mews. Two bargains in accidental suites (they don't claim to be, but they are virtual suites): the none-too-handsome basement (#77) at **Bryanston Court** and the **Commodore's** wonderfully quiet, lemon yellow duplex (#11).

Silent nights... Yes, the **Commodore** is quiet, as is the above-mentioned **Stafford** and its neighbor, the even quieter—since it's set in its own gaslit alley—**Dukes**. The huge **Forte Posthouse Kensington** is also secreted in its own streetlet. Another group of neighbors with peaceful postcodes are the **Beaufort**, the **Franklin**, and the **Claverley**, tucked on a residential South Kensington side street just off the Brompton Road. Nearby, in Chelsea, the **Sloane** and **Sydney House** won't keep you up late—neither will ambient noise at **Blakes** and **The Portobello**, though your fellow guests' partying might. While at Blakes' sister, **The Hempel**, the peaceful garden square (which Anouska Hempel failed to have renamed Hempel Square) brings peace as deafeningly Zen as the decor. High rooms at the **London Hilton** don't even need their sound insulation. The most peacefully positioned hostelry of all is **Holland House Youth Hostel**—too bad its dorm-style sleeping arrangements take away your privacy.

Best park view... **Holland House Youth Hostel**, being inside Holland Park, has to lead this category. If you like to look upon green, though, this is a fine city. All the Park Lane grands (**Grosvenor House**, the **London Hilton**, the **Dorchester**), as well as the **Lanesborough** and **The Metropolitan**, overlook Hyde Park—if you get a room on the park side, of course—and at the latter, if you snag a corner suite, you are practically floating on top of the trees, so many windows do they boast. From the **Hilton**'s highest floors, you can also see a corner of the queen's private gardens at Buckingham Palace. A different side of Hyde Park is available for half the rates at the **Columbia** and the **London Elizabeth**. Peep into private squares from **Dorset Square**, **Egerton House**, the **Franklin**, **The Hempel**, and **The Portobello**. Stay in rooms 201–205 at the **Athenaeum** to get an eyeful of gorgeous Green Park.

May I get that for you, sir?... Service is a difficult commodity to pin down, since star individuals move on, but Donald and Alex, the pair of lovely concierges at the **Athenaeum**, have been there for a long time and show no sign of leaving. In general, this hotel apparently attracts kind people. The **Beaufort**, similarly, has an all-female staff that goes out of its way to make you happy, as does the neighboring crew at the **Claverley**. The ferociously modern **Halkin** looks like the kind of place where you'd get snubbed for no reason, but the Armani-uniformed Euro types who work there are especially nice, as are the informal staff at the very central **Covent Garden**. The small **London Elizabeth** has a loyal team of Irishly smiling staff, while the tiny **Sloane** retains gorgeous and conscientious young Spaniards and Swedes until their wanderlust moves them onward.

Bargain beds... Top-value prize goes to the high-end B&B agency the **Bulldog Club** for the ultimate in homey luxury. You get to live in the kind of house you'd want to own if you lived in London, and will probably be given the insights of the family that actually does live there. **London Homestead Services** is the less tony version of the same thing, with truly inexpensive, very variable, but inspected and shipshape homes in all neighborhoods, including outlying boroughs and 'burbs. It goes without saying that the **Holland House Youth Hostel** is cheap; those allergic to communal living should note that there are a couple of rooms (as opposed to dormitories) here.

The millionaire look, at Scrooge rates... All the hotels of David Naylor-Leyland and of Tim and Kit Kemp's Firmdale Hotels are beautiful to behold. **Egerton House** was Mr. N-L's first, and the one on which he lavished his best pieces and spared no expense. He takes the furniture home when it's too threadbare for his hotel. The penthouse suite at his **Dukes** hotel looks pricier than it is, and his **Franklin** hotel also gives a good deal of swank for the money. The Firmdale hotels we list are the **Covent Garden**, **Pelham**, and **Dorset Square**, the latter having slightly lower rates, the first being the priciest. All three have probably been in the British decor-porn magazine, *World of Interiors*. (We must have missed that issue.) The two tiny independents that run away with the honors in this category, however, are the **Sloane** and **Sydney**

House. Each is the love child of its doting owner; each owner possesses such an eye! And at the Sloane, if you really love what Sue Rogers has done, you can take it home. Yes, every antique and gewgaw, along with the TV/VCRs, is for sale, and not at millionaire prices, either.

Family values... If your family wants to stay together in a family room, here are the best deals in town. The **Edward Lear** has three enormous rooms with very little in them but beds and thin carpets. Close by, but nearer Madame Tussaud's and Regent's Park (the zoo!), **Hotel La Place'**s five family rooms are a great value. Both properties are child-friendly, as is **Basil Street**. Some of the many family rooms at the **Columbia** are big enough to play hide-and-seek in on a rainy afternoon; you can fit a family of five (one being a baby) in here for a hundred quid a night, English breakfast included. The **Commodore**, down the block, has better-looking multiple rooms, but they aren't the best rooms in the place—those are the two-level almost-duplexes, in which you could easily fit a family if you request a cot. For older kids who demand their own room, **Dolphin Square'**s larger apartments are the business. Or, if younger kids are demanding their own room, give them their own hotel: Send them to **Pippa Pop-Ins**, a unique lodging where parents can drop off their youngsters for the night, almost as if at a baby-sitter's house, and where security is only slightly less stringent than that at Fort Knox. At the **Stafford**, there are some triples, or you could fit an extra bed in a carriage-house room without feeling cramped. The way-out (of town) **Holiday Inn** also has large rooms for an offbeat family vacation.

For history buffs and Anglophiles... It was founded by Lord Byron's butler, honeymooned in by FDR, and was the place where Alexander Graham Bell made his first experimental telephone call. No wonder **Browns** is the number-one pick for amateur historians, especially when you consider the fame of its afternoon tea (you'd do better, actually, to take tea elsewhere). **Grosvenor House** has quite a history, or at least the land it stands on does. See the oils in and around the fake library—they depict the former Earl of Grosvenor's estate on this site. And above the fireplace in the main lobby (the other end from Park Lane), see the painting of Victorian ice-skaters on a rink that is now the Ballroom. **The Savoy** celebrated its centenary during the past few years, and has certainly had its share of rollicking parties and happenings. For a re-creation of the lifestyle of the late cousin-to-the-queen Lord Mountbatten, check in at, yes, **The Mountbatten**. (You'd have thought London's so rich in history, it wouldn't need to package it thus.) **Dorset Square**, conversely, has only cricket-bat motifs and memorabilia to remind guests that the first lord's cricket ground was in the very square they're overlooking. The oldest house of all? The surviving Jacobean parts of the **Holland House Youth Hostel**.

For enemies of chintz and Regency... You're in trouble. Cabbage roses, brocade, and Regency stripes are de rigueur, with the English-country-house look beating all others hands down. Relief is possible in places where low budgets forbid decor, like the youth hostel **Holland House**, and also at the **Edward Lear**, the **Columbia**, and certain floors of **Dolphin Square**. **The Portobello** has a faded Victorian look filtered through the owners' Sixties heyday, all very reminiscent of sets from the Mick Jagger/James Fox cult movie *Performance*. But the standouts for different decor are Anouska Hempel's also-slightly-Sixties (and seventies) **Blakes**, and the stunning, Milano-modern **Halkin**, both of which have been overtaken by miles by their own younger siblings, **The Hempel** and **The Metropolitan,** respectively.

Best health club... Among the swanky grands is a surprise winner, the **Forte Posthouse Kensington**, which has a bi-i-ig pool, two squash courts, and sauna/steam rooms, all at rock-bottom rates. **Dolphin Square** has an even bigger pool, squash courts, and weight machines, but the public's allowed in, so it's busy. The **Grosvenor House** health club has a big pool, plus a good gym that also gets busy with nonresidents. **The Landmark** has a pool that's on the small side, but chlorine-free and pretty. Fitness on Five at the **London Hilton** is the flashiest and newest facility. It has personal trainers, plus sessions of acupuncture or hypnotherapy, but no pool. Best for sybaritic spas, with the only sweat that generated by the sauna, are the **Athenaeum**'s little basement salon and the Elizabeth Arden–run pampering joint at the **Dorchester**. **The Metropolitan**'s reflexology, aromatherapy, and shiatsu rooms are the best for alternative care.

Taking care of business... The Savoy wins surprisingly many accolades from the corporate world; it's handily located, too, in a part of the West End that's as near to the City as the West End gets (10 minutes in a cab). The **Halkin** is a fantastic business base—rooms have two phone lines, with conference-call capability, a fax (request it), and the Reuters news service—and the very look seems so efficient, with none of the flounces and curlicues that are endemic to London hotels. The **London Hilton,** like most Hiltons, is OK for business stays, and there'll probably be a convention group around to prove it; ditto at **Grosvenor House**, where there's a huge business center. The **Athenaeum**'s apartments are great for anyone who needs to entertain in a homey atmosphere, while the **Commodore**, which also has a business center, is a good pick for small businesses that don't splurge on expenses. Many hotels are upgrading their computer-friendly aspects, with ISDN lines and the like. Most hotels listed have web sites (see Index), and it is worth checking facilities in advance, as this is an area that is in constant flux.

The twilight zone... There's eccentric on purpose and then there's plain weird. In the first category, **The Portobello** wins the "individual piece of furniture" award for the Edwardian bathing machine in its suite—a perverted though functional contraption of brass rods and faucets. The **Sloane** easily takes the conceptual prize for its bright idea of selling not only time in a room, but the furnishings of the room itself, should you be interested; **Pippa Pop-Ins** gets a special mention for providing rooms to people incapable of booking them or paying for them—namely, children. Since the noncomformist is highly prized in England, it's not necessarily an insult to succeed in the "plain weird" category. **Basil Street** isn't weird, but it is deeply anachronistic, with its Parrot Club, counterpanes, and slightly threadbare Persian rugs. **Dolphin Square** is a time warp of a different stripe, with a mini-mall of shops that seems still stuck in the 1950s, and an atmosphere to match. The **Fielding** has the charm of a warmhearted person who dresses appallingly; meanwhile, **The Metropolitan** has the *froideur* of a coldhearted person who dresses like a fashion plate—yes, London's swankiest new hotel belongs in the twilight zone for the quantity of complaints we've heard about its haughty staff.

Try these when there's no room... You won't have a hope at the grands during sold-out times, but **The Landmark**, being a little off center, has been known to have a spare bed at the eleventh hour. So has the very expensive **Lanesborough**. The **London Hilton** and the **Grosvenor House**, being huge, might have rooms, too. Paradoxically, some of the less-known tiniest places are worth calling at the last minute—specifically the **Sloane**, **Sydney House**, and **Hotel La Place**. Three Bayswater addresses that might yield a late-booking success are (in descending order of cost) **Whites**, the **London Elizabeth**, and the **Columbia**. Among more central properties, try the Radisson Edwardian Hotels: **The Mountbatten** and **The Marlborough**.

The Index

£££££	over $400	over £260
££££	$300–$400	£200–£260
£££	$190–$300	£130–£200
££	$110–$190	£80–£130
£	under $110	under £80

Athenaeum. This Regency-meets-Art-Deco-at-Laura-Ashley-style independent is the nonobvious Mayfair choice, scoring for low-attitude service, cute little health club, and attention to detail (just check out the minibar); the Athenaeum is also good to remember for its 34 apartments. Its restaurant, Bullochs, is Mediterranean-esque, semicasual, and inexpensive.... *Tel 0207/499–3464 or 0800/335–3300, fax 0207/493–1860; www.athenaeumhotel.com. 116 Piccadilly W1V 0BJ, Green Park tube stop. 133 rms. £££–££££*
(see pp. 21, 22, 24, 25)

Basil Street. Staying at this venerable hotel, you can breakfast at Harrods, yet it's peacefully set back from the Knightsbridge maelstrom. Antiques are strewn about, though it's not remotely designed. Guests—American academics and English country ladies (who get use of the private ladies' club)—come back and back and back, until they're "Basilites," and thus eligible for frequent-stayer miles.... *Tel 0207/581–3311, fax 0207/581–3693; www.absite.com/basil. Basil St. SW3 1AH, Knightsbridge tube stop. 92 rms. £££* **(see pp. 19, 23, 25)**

Beaufort. One of the first of the swelling genre of boutique hotels, where you have a latchkey instead of a reception desk and a sitting room instead of a lounge, this one includes all drinks and room service. Run by a female team of fiendish efficiency, the Beaufort's even nearer to Harrods than Basil Street is. It gets top marks for friendliness, squashy-couch designer decor, and not charging premium phone rates.... *Tel 0207/584–5252, fax 0207/589–2834; www.thebeaufort.co.uk. 33 Beaufort Gardens SW3 1PP, Knightsbridge/South Kensington tube stops. 28 rms. ££££*
(see pp. 21, 22)

Blakes. Anouska Hempel, once synonymous with swinging Beatles London, became Lady Weinberg and opened this glamorous stage-set hotel. Her eclectic visual vocabulary (Biedermeier and black lacquer; moiré walls and halogen spotlights; oatmeal raw silk) has since been imitated to cliché, but despite some very tiny rooms, the Blakes style still stuns. So do the ridiculous prices in Blakes the restaurant.... *Tel 0207/370–6701, fax 0207/373–0442. 33 Roland Gardens SW7 3PF, South Kensington tube stop. 52 rms. ££££–£££££*
(see pp. 20, 21, 24)

Browns. Ever-popular with Connecticut Yankees, Browns does the ersatz Victorian country house fairly well, though its soulless afternoon tea is overrated. Labyrinthine corridors and dark-stained wooden staircases connect the various town houses that comprise this hotel begun in 1837 by Lord Byron's butler. There's no health club.... *Tel 0207/493–6020, fax 0207/493–9381; www.brownshotel.com. 30 Albermarle St. W1X 4BP, Green Park tube stop. 118 rms. £££££*
(see pp. 20, 23)

Bryanston Court. Best Western affiliation brings Americans to this functional, better since recent refurbishment, independent hotel. Most rooms are small, with postage-stamp-size bathrooms, but rates are great for this area behind Marble

Arch. There's a rather elegant lounge with leather chesterfield sofa, oils, and a fireplace, plus a restaurant and a bar.... *Tel 0207/262–3141, fax 0207/262–7248; www.bryanston-hotel.com. 56–60 Great Cumberland Place W1H 8DD, Marble Arch tube stop. 54 rms. ££* **(see p. 21)**

Bulldog Club. For a £25 three-year membership, you can book a room in one of Maggie Jackson's 20 gorgeous houses in good neighborhoods. Accommodations will be similar to the best U.S. B&Bs, but most unusual in London. You'll get bargain-deluxe treatment—full British breakfast, tea/coffee makers, mineral water, flowers, fruit, newspaper, and robe in your room, plus use of the family phone.... *Tel 0207/ 371–3202, fax 0207/371–2015; www.bulldog.com. 14 Dewhurst Rd. W14. ££* **(see pp. 19, 22)**

Claridges. Palatial, peaceful, and nearly perfect, this Savoy Group classic hosts the royal, political, and business worlds in spacious rooms, some of which feel like 1930s ocean-liner staterooms, others like the setting for a fox-hunting week-end. Take tea in the foyer, dine in the salmon-pink restaurant, or—best—do the smorgasbord in the cozy Causerie.... *Tel 0207/629–8860, 0800/637–2869, fax 0207/499–2210; www.savoy-group.co.uk. Brook St. W1A 2JQ, Bond St. tube stop. 200 rms. £££££* **(see pp. 18, 20)**

Claverley. The Beaufort's neighbor, the quaint and friendly little Claverley has decor of rampant color and occasional four-poster beds. An enormous English breakfast is included, plus tea, coffee, and hot chocolate anytime in the wood-paneled reading room or lounge. A very few single rooms without bath are inexpensive.... *Tel 0207/589–8541, fax 0207/584–3410. 13–14 Beaufort Gardens SW3 1PS, Knightsbridge tube stop. 36 rms. £–£££***(see pp. 21, 22)**

Columbia. An anomaly—half rock 'n' roll hangout, half family tourist bargain—this vast Victorian opposite Hyde Park (which many rooms overlook) is clean and bright, if no great shakes in the decor department. Acres of first-floor lounges, a 24-hour bar, a breakfast room that serves din-ner, too, and an echoing peach lobby. The bedrooms are not very big.... *Tel 0207/402–0021, fax 0207/706–4691; www.columbiahotel.co.uk. 95–99 Lancaster Gate W2 3NS, Lancaster Gate tube stop. 100 rms. DC not accepted. £* **(see pp. 19, 20, 21, 23, 24, 26)**

Commodore. Another bargain, down the block from the Columbia, this well-run, quiet hotel has some special duplex rooms in subdued colors. Rates include continental buffet breakfast in the separately owned Spanish restaurant in the basement.... *Tel 0207/402–5291, fax 0207/262–1088; www.commodore-hotel.com. 50 Lancaster Gate W2 3NA, Lancaster Gate tube stop. 90 rms. ££***(see pp. 21, 23, 25)**

The Connaught. The honorary consul would feel at home here among the spacious corridors, the invisible staff of old retainers, and the sizable rooms. Beneath the air of picturesque aristocratic decay, all is shipshape, spotless, and silent as Sunday. The eponymous Anglo-French restaurant and its Grill are among the best in town.... *Tel 0207/ 499–7070, 0800/223–6800, fax 0207/495–3262; www.info.theconnaught.co.uk. Carlos Place W1Y 6AL, Bond St. tube stop. 90 rms. £££££* **(see pp. 18, 19)**

Covent Garden. The latest in Tim and Kit Kemp's line of couture baby grands. This one outdoes its sisters in theatrical ambience, achieved through layer upon layer of calorific drapes and antiques, and an adorable library, with an open fire, where the tea—or champagne—is always flowing.... *Tel 0207/806–1000, fax 0207/806–1100; www.firmdale.com. 10 Monmouth St. WC2H 9HB, Covent Garden tube stop. 50 rms. ££££* **(see pp. 19, 22)**

Dolphin Square. This '30s-era quadrangle, a 5-minute cab ride from the Houses of Parliament (many MPs keep a pied à terre here), has functional rather than beautiful apartments. What it lacks in hotel services it makes up for in the health club, with its famous pool mural, squash courts, and gym; its brasserie, with jazz brunches; its shops and a laundromat.... *Tel 0207/834–3800, fax 0207/798–8735; www.dolphin-squarehotel.co.uk. Dolphin Square SW1V 3LX, Pimlico tube stop. 151 rms. ££–£££* **(see pp. 19, 23, 24, 25)**

Dorchester. A legend among hotels, there is no faulting the opulent Dorchester, with its miles of gold leaf, marble, and antiques, plus climate control, marble bathrooms, cable TV, etc. There's not only a beauty spa and gym, but also a nightclub, lounges, shops, ballrooms, and three restaurants.... *Tel 0207/629–8888, 0800/727–9820, fax 0207/409–0114. Park Lane W1A 2HJ, Hyde Park Corner tube stop. 244 rms. £££££* **(see pp. 18, 21, 24)**

Dorset Square. A designer/architect couple, Tim and Kit Kemp have a clutch of hotels around town (the **Covent Garden** is the newest), all distinctively English-countrified with loads of swagged drapes, lace antimacassars, antique cushions, and candlesticks, in the best possible taste. The Dorset Square is in a pair of Regency houses behind Oxford Street, overlooking the garden square where cricket was born.... *Tel 0207/ 723–7874, 0800/553–6674, fax 0207/724–3328; www.firmdale.com. 39–40 Dorset Square NW1 6QN, Baker St. tube stop. 38 rms. DC not accepted. ££–£££*

(see pp. 21, 22, 24)

Dukes. In the heart of St. James's, this flagship of small-hotel maven David Naylor-Leyland has its own gaslit driveway; oil portraits of assorted dukes in the foyer justify its name. Rooms have great detail (heated towel rack, real hair dryer, portable mirror, many outlets), and the staff is young, friendly, efficient. Green Park is steps away.... *Tel 0207/ 491–4840, 0800/381–4702, fax 0207/493–1264; www.dukeshotel.co.uk. 35 St. James's Place SW1A 1NY, Green Park tube stop. 64 rms. £££* **(see pp. 20, 21, 22)**

Edward Lear. The former residence of Lear, a 19th-century artist and author of nonsense verse, lies behind Oxford Street at the Marble Arch end. There's nothing luxurious about the place, but it's survived for many years on friendliness and low rates, and continues to pull in a high percentage of repeat guests.... *Tel 0207/402–5401, fax 0207/706–3766; www.edlear.com. 30 Seymour St. W1H 5WD, Marble Arch tube stop. 31 rms. AE, DC not accepted. £***(see pp. 23, 24)**

Egerton House. The first Naylor-Leyland property (also see Dukes) is still strong, liked by bankers in particular, for some reason. Credit good antiques, a lovely garden view in back (but no access), and a charming staff. Trademarks of these hotels are intimate size, no restaurant (but 24-hour room service), good-value rates, and a greater tendency toward vivid colors than your average English-country-style place.... *Tel 0207/589–2412, 0800/473–9492, fax 0207/584– 6540; www.egertonhouse.co.uk. Egerton Terrace SW3 2BX, Knightsbridge tube stop. 30 rms. £££*   **(see pp. 21, 22)**

Fielding. This eccentric guest house occupies an alleyway in the dead center of Covent Garden, where shopping and theater—and opera—collide. Expect rickety stairs instead

of an elevator, showers instead of tubs in the tiny bathrooms, and no room service or restaurant, although there is
a breakfast room.... *Tel 0207/836–8305, fax
0207/497–0064. 4 Broad Court, Bow St. WC2B 5QZ,
Covent Garden tube stop. 24 rms. ££* **(see pp. 18, 25)**

Forte Posthouse Kensington. The two best things about
this large and utilitarian hotel are the location—set well
back from the traffic, but steps away from Kensington High
Street—and the fabulous health club, with squash courts,
gym, and large pool. Boxy rooms are perfectly adequate;
investing in an "executive" may be worthwhile, since
they're twice the size.... *Tel 0207/937–8170, fax 0207/
937–8289; www.posthouse.com. Wrights Lane W8 5SP,
Kensington High Street tube stop. 544 rms. ££–£££*
(see pp. 21, 24)

Franklin. Yet another Naylor-Leyland lodging, you can spit on this
one from its sister Egerton House, with which it shares most
of its characteristics. There's a handsome double parlor for a
lounge, with stairs leading down to a long private garden....
*Tel 0207/584–5533, fax 0207/584–5449; www.franklinho-
tel.co.uk. 28 Egerton Gardens SW3 2DB, Knightsbridge tube
stop. 47 rms. ££–££££* **(see pp. 21, 22)**

The Gore. Very near the Albert Hall and Kensington Gardens is
this big Victorian house hung with trillions of prints and
strewn with antiques. Some rooms are funny follies—one
with Judy Garland's former bed, another all leopard skins,
another with a Tudor minstrels' gallery and oaken four-
poster. Bistrot 190 serves as restaurant.... *Tel 0207/
584–6601, fax 0207/589–8127. 189 Queen's Gate SW7
5EX, Gloucester Rd. tube stop. 54 rms. ££–£££*
(see pp. 19, 21)

Grosvenor House. A Forte flagship, with a snob chef (Nico
Ladenis), the "old lady of Park Lane" has been translated into
the current London hotel idiom of English country—heavy
color, marble floors and fireplaces, velvet couches, and flowers. Best of all: one of the city's most impressive hotel health
clubs, complete with pool. There's also a lounge for tea, and
two more restaurants aside from Nico's domain.... *Tel
0207/499–6363, fax 0207/493–3341; www.forte-
hotels.com. Park Lane W1A 3AA, Marble Arch tube stop. 454
rms. ££££* **(see pp. 18, 21, 23, 24, 25, 26)**

THE INDEX · **ACCOMMODATIONS**

Halcyon. In lovely, leafy, residential Holland Park, the Halcyon quietly attracts celebrities. Light-filled, high-ceilinged rooms are dressed in swags of drapery, delicious colors (like mulberry and black, or lemon custard, apple green, and white), and occasional themes, like the Egyptian Room (desert tent effect), the Blue Room (moon and stars in cobalt skies), and the Halcyon Suite with its heavenly conservatory. The Room at the Halcyon has an excellent kitchen.... *Tel 0207/727–7288, 0800/457–4000, fax 0207/229–8516; www.halcyon-hotel.co.uk. 81 Holland Park W11 3RZ, Holland Park tube stop. 44 rms. £££–£££££* **(see p. 20)**

Halkin. The Halkin stands out by a mile, with its exotic wood trim and paneling and many-hued marble, its nonfogging mirrors and keypad lighting controls. Totally Milanese, from the friendly Armani-wearing staff to the Italian restaurant (expensive), it's away from the traffic, behind the Lanesborough (see below) in tiny Belgravia. In-room VCRs, faxes, and two-line phones please image-conscious Wall Street types. See also its brash sister, the Metropolitan.... *Tel 0207/ 333–1000, fax 0207/333–1100; www.halkin.co.uk. 5 Halkin Street SW1X 7DJ, Hyde Park Corner tube stop. 41 rms. ££££–£££££* **(see pp. 22, 24, 25)**

Hazlitt's. The only hotel in Soho has kept its fans, though its funky antiquey style has been appropriated by others. Visual trademarks include Victorian clawfoot tubs in the bathrooms and multitudes of prints on all walls; it has no elevator, no room service (except for breakfast), no lounge, and no restaurant (but that's the last thing you need on this street of restaurants).... *Tel 0207/434–1771, fax 0207/ 439–1524. 6 Frith Street W1V 5TZ, Leicester Sq. tube stop. 23 rms. £££* **(see pp. 18, 20)**

The Hempel. Seen Blakes? This, Anouska Hempel's other place, is its diametric opposite. In its smooth white lobby, you lounge on a padded dip in the floor by a single blue flame of a fireplace, having entered via a room of single orchids upstanding in serried ranks. Remember your room number for next time; "I'd like the beige one," would lead to confusion.... *Tel 0207/298–9000, fax 0207/ 402–4666; www.hempelhotel.com. 31–35 Craven Hill Gardens. W2 3EA, Lancaster Gate tube stop. 43 rms. ££££* **(see pp. 19, 20, 21)**

Holiday Inn. Fellow guests at this Docklands hotel are guaranteed to be conventioneers. Rooms in the old wing, a converted warehouse, are brick-walled and charming, and they boast the river views you came all this way out here for. Don't accept a room in the other wing. There's a health club, a courtesy bus (though it stops running too early), a riverboat taxi service to Canary Wharf and London Bridge at peak times, and three not-very-good restaurants.... *Tel 0207/231–1001, fax 0207/231–0599; www.holidayinnnd.co.uk. 265 Rotherhithe St. SE16 1EJ, Rotherhithe tube stop. 386 rms. ££–£££* **(see p. 23)**

Holland House Youth Hostel. Possibly the world's best city youth hostel setting, though the accommodations themselves are as basic as dormitories get. It's housed partly in the remains of a Jacobean mansion and partly in a modern block, set in the middle of gorgeous little Holland Park.... *Tel 0207/937–0748, fax 0207/376–0667. Holland Walk W8 7QU, Kensington High St. tube stop. 201 beds. AE, DC not accepted. £* **(see pp. 21, 22, 24)**

Hotel La Place. Just-off-center, not far from Regent's Park—and the Regent (see below)—this small, sweet hotel has good facilities for the price.... *Tel 0207/486–2323, fax 0207/486–4335; www.hotellaplace.com. 17 Nottingham Place W1M 3FF, Baker St. tube stop. 20 rms. ££* **(see pp. 23, 26)**

The Landmark. The extraordinary feature of this relative newcomer—once the Great Central Hotel, then British Rail offices—is the soaring, palm-filled, skylit eight-story Winter Garden atrium, which about half the bedrooms overlook. Rooms are very spacious and there's a pretty pool in the basement health club. There's a good Italian restaurant, but many prefer the small menu served right in the Winter Garden itself.... *Tel 0207/631–8000, fax 0207/631–8080; www.landmarklondon.co.uk. 222 Marylebone Rd. NW1 6JQ, Baker St. tube stop. 309 rms. ££££–£££££*
(see pp. 19, 24, 26)

Lanesborough. A Disneyesque version of Regency London, converted from the former St. George's Hospital. The bar is lined with random leather-bound books; check-in is achieved by signing the visitor's book; bedrooms contain fax machines, personalized stationery, an umbrella, big jars of bath unguents, a disturbing infrared security system that knows where you are—and (no joke) a butler of your own. The hotel's Conservatory restaurant is somewhat twee.... *Tel 0207/259–5599, fax 0207/259–5606; www.lanesborough.com. Hyde Park Corner SW1X 7TA, Hyde Park Corner tube stop. 95 rms. £££££* **(see pp. 20, 21, 26)**

London Elizabeth. Set near the depressing guest houses of Sussex Gardens, this likable and friendly family-run hotel was redesigned by the owner's American wife. Rooms are fresh and English-chintzy in pale blues and yellows; some have tiny balconies, deluxe rooms have Hyde Park views. There's an old-fashioned Continental restaurant, the Rose Garden, and 24-hour room service.... *Tel 0207/402–6641, fax 0207/224–8900; www.londonelizabethhotel.co.uk. Lancaster Terrace W2 3PF, Lancaster Gate tube stop. 51 rms. ££* **(see pp. 21, 22, 26)**

London Hilton on Park Lane. It's not the only grand hotel on the block, but it is the tallest, with great high-floor views for which you pay a premium. The boring room decor has Regency stripe brocade and repro Chippendale. The fabulous feature here is the Fitness on Five health club, with personal trainers, three studios, a gym, and a spa. There's a brasserie/cafe and a bar; on floor 28 is the restaurant Windows; in the basement, Trader Vic's hokey Polynesian.... *Tel 0207/493–8000, 0800/445–8667, fax 0207/208–4142; www.hilton.com. 22 Park Lane W1Y 4BE, Hyde Park Corner tube stop. 446 rms. ££££–£££££* **(see pp. 21, 24, 25, 26)**

London Homestead Services. A B&B agency, with fewer swanky uptown addresses than the Bulldog Club (see above), but far more in outer boroughs and residential neighborhoods. All homes have been inspected; the minimum stay is three nights; not all rooms have private bathrooms, in which cases rates are superlow. See London as she is lived.... *Tel 0208/949–4455, fax 0208/549–5492. Coombe Wood Rd. Kingston-Upon-Thames, Surrey KT2 7JY (mailing address). 200+ rms. Londonwide. £* **(see p. 22)**

The Marlborough. From here you can spit on the British Museum, shop Covent Garden, and take in a few plays. It's a Radisson Edwardian, a reliable if unexciting chain, with decor that nods to that era. It has an unnecessary brasserie; rooms are fairly large and well insulated from traffic-heavy Gower Street.... *Tel 0207/636–5601, fax 0207/636–0532; www.radissonedwardian.com. Bloomsbury St. WC1B 3QD, Tottenham Court Rd. tube stop. 173 rms.* £££–££££ **(see p. 26)**

The Metropolitan. London's latest louche pocket grand, from the owner of the Halkin, is to its neighbors—the Dorchester, Four Seasons, Grosvenor House—as Kate Moss is to Liz Taylor. The Met Bar is the hangout du jour—or was for about a year—and Nobu (compare and contrast Nobu NYC, and Matsuhisa LA) does service as dining room. The best rooms have many windows overlooking Hyde Park; all are beige and cream, with pearwood fittings, minibars stocked with Budvar beer and Red Bull natural stimulation beverage, and Kiehl's products in cool bathrooms. Cool all 'round. Beware, though; reports of snottiness from DKNY-clad doormen are rife....*Tel 0207/447–1000, fax 0207/447–1100; www.metropolitan.co.uk. Old Park Lane W1Y 4LB, Hyde Park Corner tube stop. 155 rms.* ££££ **(see pp. 20, 21, 24, 25)**

Montcalm. Once the hippest deluxe lodging, with a Studio 54–style club in the basement, this Japanese-run (Nikko) establishment is now a haven of peace, complete with Japanese breakfast and London's first low-allergen room.... *Tel 0207/402–4288, fax 0207/724–9180; www.nikkohotels.com. Great Cumberland Place W1A 2LF, Marble Arch tube stop.*£££–£££££ **(see p. 20)**

The Mountbatten. Sister to the Marlborough (see above), this hotel has a gimmicky theme—everything pays homage to Lord Mountbatten. It's in an absolutely central Covent Garden location, secreted in one of the winding lanes. There are so many restaurants nearby, you won't need the French brasserie, but the bar's handy.... *Tel 0207/836–4300, fax 0207/240–3540; www.radissonedwardian.com. Seven Dials WC2H 9HD, Covent Garden tube stop. 127 rms.* ££££ **(see pp. 24, 26)**

Pelham. Another, earlier number from Tim and Kit Kemp (see Dorset Square), this one is slightly grander, being in a high-ceilinged South Kensington town house, though the abundant antiques and drapery are familiar. Kemps restaurant is up to the neighborhood competition, and it offers 24-hour room service.... *Tel 0207/589–8288, or 0800/553–6674, fax 0207/584–8444; www.firmdale.com. 15 Cromwell*

Place SW7 2LA, South Kensington tube stop. 41 rms. DC not accepted. £££ **(see p. 22)**

Pippa Pop-Ins. Over 12? You can't stay here, then. It's an extremely security-conscious kids-only hotel, where parents can drop off the children for the time of their little lives, and go out on the town knowing the kids are in safe and loving hands. Prices include meals, toys, and TLC.... *Tel 0207/385–2458, fax 0207/385–5706. 430 Fulham Rd. SW6 1DU, Fulham Broadway tube stop. 5 rms. DC not accepted. £* **(see pp. 19, 23, 25)**

The Portobello. Once the haunt of major rock stars and other celebs, the peaceful and still hip Portobello has seen better days. A beautiful lounge leads to huge private gardens (no access for hotel guests, but many rooms enjoy a view over it). Decor features such follies as freestanding canopied Victorian tubs, a four-poster bed with its own stairs, and wood-paneled cabin rooms which make a virtue out of being small. The place has style all right—plus breakfasts included in the rate and a 24-hour basement bar that serves food.... *Tel 0207/727–2777, fax 0207/792–9641. 22 Stanley Gardens W11 2NG, Notting Hill Gate tube stop. 22 rms. ££–£££* **(see pp. 19, 21, 24, 25)**

The Savoy. There's something especially glamorous about this over-a-century-old Thames-side Victorian/Art Deco palace, the only London hotel with its own theater. As with all the Savoy Group hotels, it has handmade beds, most staff are from its world-renowned training school, and the showerheads are the size of hubcaps. The Savoy Grill is one of London's power-lunch places; the Restaurant and more casual Upstairs aren't at all bad, and the American Bar brought the martini to town.... *Tel 0207/836–4343, 0800/223–6800, fax 0207/240–6040; www.savo group.co.uk. Strand WC2R 0EU, Aldwych tube stop. 202 rms. £££££* **(see pp. 18, 19, 23, 25)**

Sloane. Though you won't see price tags, everything here, from the 18th-century oaken teapot or the Edwardian silver-backed hairbrushes to the canopied, carved four-poster bed is for sale; you can even buy the TV. This gimmick is saved from being tacky by the incredibly good taste of owner and antiques-auction-addict Sue Rogers. The decoris stunning, the young European staff disarming, the rooftop terrace charming, and the Chelsea location central. No restaurant, but there's 24-hour room service.... *Tel 0207/581–5757, 0800/324–9960, fax 0207/584–1348; www.premierhotels.com. 29 Draycott Place SW3 2SH, Sloane Sq. tube stop. 12 rms. ££* **(see pp. 21, 22, 25, 26)**

Stafford. Sandwiched between the Ritz and Dukes is this little place in an 18th-century town house. It's remarkable for its barrel-vaulted wine-cellar private dining salon, and for the dozen secluded Carriage House rooms in back, converted from stables and overlooking a cobbled mews. Decor here and in the main hotel tries a little too hard to be British, with displays of firearms and silverware and some overbearing color schemes, but everyone means well and there is air-conditioning. The American Bar, its ceiling strung with toys, is a useful martini hideaway, and there's an English restaurant.... *Tel 0207/493–0111, 0800/525–4800, fax 0207/ 493–7121; www.thestaffordhotel.co.uk. St. James's Place SW1A 1NJ, Green Park tube stop. 80 rms. ££££–£££££* **(see pp. 19, 21, 23)**

Sydney House. Superchic but without pretensions, this Chelsea boutique hotel was designed and is run by young Jean-Luc Aeby, who has an eye for the witty antique—more of a flea-market than a Sotheby's sensibility. There's 24-hour room service rather than a restaurant, and satellite TV in the rooms, some of which are pretty small.... *Tel 0207/376–7711, fax 0207/376–4233; www.sydneyhousehotel.com. 9–11 Sydney Street SW3 6PU, South Kensington tube stop. 21 rms. £££* **(see pp. 20, 21, 22, 26)**

Whites. One of the white palaces that line Bayswater Road, this is the only one with any glitz. The hybrid Victorian–Louis XV decor leans heavily to the rococo, in lemon and rose and powder blue colors. The best rooms have high ceilings and balconies overlooking Hyde Park. There's a little-known restaurant/bar with a pretty conservatory facing the park—great for breakfast, tea, or aperitifs.... *Tel 0207/262–2711, fax 0207/262–2147. Lancaster Gate W2 3NR, Lancaster Gate tube stop. 54 rms. £££–££££* **(see p. 26)**

THE INDEX

ACCOMMODATIONS

Central London Accommodations

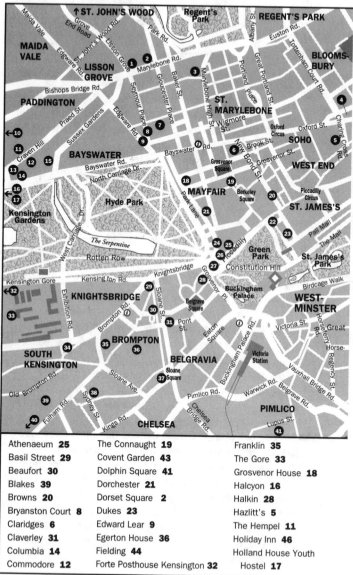

Athenaeum **25**	The Connaught **19**	Franklin **35**
Basil Street **29**	Covent Garden **43**	The Gore **33**
Beaufort **30**	Dolphin Square **41**	Grosvenor House **18**
Blakes **39**	Dorchester **21**	Halcyon **16**
Browns **20**	Dorset Square **2**	Halkin **28**
Bryanston Court **8**	Dukes **23**	Hazlitt's **5**
Claridges **6**	Edward Lear **9**	The Hempel **11**
Claverley **31**	Egerton House **36**	Holiday Inn **46**
Columbia **14**	Fielding **44**	Holland House Youth
Commodore **12**	Forte Posthouse Kensington **32**	Hostel **17**

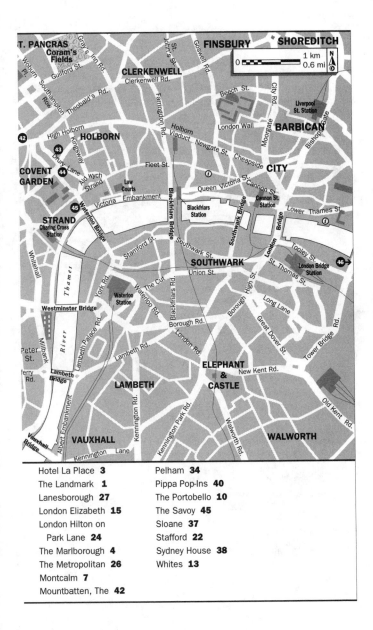

Hotel La Place **3**	Pelham **34**
The Landmark **1**	Pippa Pop-Ins **40**
Lanesborough **27**	The Portobello **10**
London Elizabeth **15**	The Savoy **45**
London Hilton on	Sloane **37**
Park Lane **24**	Stafford **22**
The Marlborough **4**	Sydney House **38**
The Metropolitan **26**	Whites **13**
Montcalm **7**	
Mountbatten, The **42**	

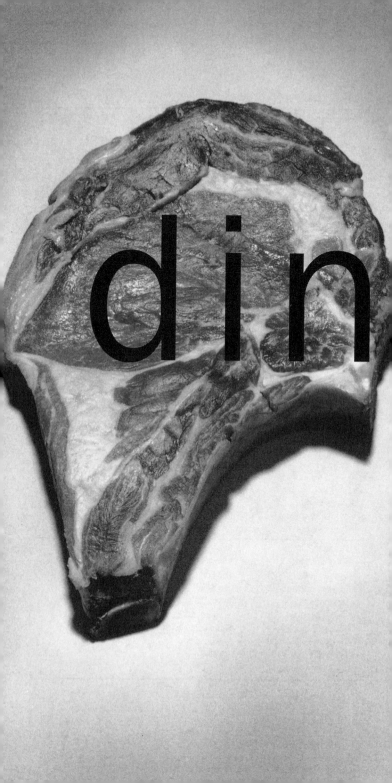

ing ²

The true London
cuisine is jellied
eels, mashed
potato, and an
emerald green
gravy known as
liquor. If that

doesn't whet your appetite, the better known great British dish is fish and chips—white, flaky fish battered and deep-fried, served with big, fat fries shaken with vinegar. Even more common is curry. A fixture on every high street in the British Isles, Indian tandoori houses serve marinated, spiced dishes cooked in the clay *tandoor* oven, as well as other bastardized dishes mostly of Bangladeshi origin. South Indian vegetarian food can be found in London, too, along with the latest craze—*balti*, a gloppy curry named after the Pakistani word for the iron wok-like *karahi* in which it is cooked.

Only in London

So, has there really been a restaurant explosion here? Yes. Not only is there a new place opening every day, but everyone is now a foodie. Newspapers have become mere excuses for pages and pages of gastroporn. *Ready Steady Cook*, a kitsch kitchen show, is the hit of TVland, closely followed by the venerable *Masterchef*, which stages cook-offs between real people, and it's a rare chef who lacks a media outlet for his (and they're usually male) once strictly culinary ambitions.

The '90s restaurant was an aircraft hangar—a huge, echoey, hard-edged, dress-up stage, where an Asian (mostly Thai) tinge to menus based around French bistro, or Italian, or pan-Mediterranean dishes began to yield to North African and Middle Eastern influence. Now, small, artisanal, chef-owners' gaffs are more the chic thing, Mittel Europa is usurping the Middle East, and sushi is the fast food du choix, with a peculiar proliferation of cafes where you pick your own nigiri and maki off a conveyor belt—which is not recommended.

As for beverages, you'll certainly find French wines, but every restaurant that isn't making a point of its Gallic roots also has New World wines, as well as German, Italian, and other European (Spanish, Bulgarian, Portuguese) bottles on its list. English wine exists, but barely; beer is the British drink. Among the types of beer, bitter is less aerated, more hoppy, deeper, and, yes, more bitter than most American beers. Local brews include Fuller's, Young's, beers called things like Dogbolter and Rail Ale, from the Firkin division of Allied Breweries, and the ever-increasing numbers of microbrewed beers.

How to Dress

Unless otherwise noted in the Index below, dress however you like. Only the swankiest dining rooms, and a few French throwbacks, bother with a dress code, although lunch can be a business-dressy affair, and there is less of a penchant for dressing down on all possible occasions than of old. The weather rules out shorts and tank tops nearly all the time, but if it ever gets hot enough to wear them to dinner, go ahead— London's heat waves are so rare, when they do occur the city loses its collective mind, taste, and sense of decorum.

When to Eat
Conservative mealtimes are the rule: breakfast, 7:30 to 9:30; lunch, 12:30 to 2:30 (1 p.m. is prime); dinner, 7 to 9:30. Afternoon tea is from 3:30 to 5:30, though hardly anyone takes it. It is *not* "high tea": High tea is a nursery meal (what Mary Poppins would have served the Barks children at Cherry Tree Lane), a cross between tea and dinner that's eaten around 6 p.m., or else it's the northern English term for dinner (you may hear a Yorkshireman asking for his tea way after 5:30). Lunch is often called dinner, and dinner is frequently known as supper. The upstart meal of brunch is always called brunch, and where it exists (mostly in Covent Garden and South Kensington), it's served oneish to four-thirtyish on weekends.

Getting the Right Table
Unless a restaurant doesn't accept reservations (noted below in the Index), it's always a good idea to book a table in advance. In fact, it's often essential, especially in this week's dozen or so hot spots. A few places must be reserved weeks (River Café), or even months (Aubergine) ahead, unless you have an "in". The trick to this is knowing someone, and/or being someone. A few hotel concierges (e.g., the Metropolitan's) have table-conjuring ability in the trendy places; others get preferential treatment in local haunts (e.g., the Covent Garden—the Ivy; the Stafford or Dukes—Le Caprice; the Portobello—the Sugar Club).

Where the Chefs Are
As you've gathered by now, where the chefs aren't is more of a mystery. But here are a few of the grander names as an appetizer. One chef who so reveres himself that there is little space left for anyone else's superlatives is **Marco Pierre White,** who has a suitably grand home in the Meridien's Oak Room, and has also bought half the restaurants in London to convert into MPW-style Frenchie upscale joints. He was the protégé of superfamous (from TV) **Michel Roux**, whose son of the same name now handles the two-Michelin-star cuisine at Le Gavroche. Another hotel with a superchef is Grosvenor House, where the self-taught **Nico Ladenis** holds court at

DINING | INTRODUCTION

Chez Nico at Ninety Park Lane. And one of the very rare three-Michelin-starred establishments in town is Chelsea's La Tante Claire, where gifted Gascon **Pierre Koffman** has been making foodies faint for years now.

Chefs of less exalted price are no less revered by the cognoscenti; in fact, they're more so. Among the adored are: New Zealander **Peter Gordon** at the Sugar Club; **Fergus Henderson**, who comes to food via architecture, as his restaurant St. John shows; and former soccer player (and Marco Pierre White sous-chef) **Gordon Ramsay** at Aubergine. Also notable, though not this year's models, are the still innovative and exciting **Alastair Little**, with his eponymous restaurant; the Square's **Philip Howard**; and the duo at the River Café who put modern Italian food on the map, **Ruth Rogers** and **Rose Gray**. **Sally Clark** of Clarke's is another woman chef who's doing great things. Her near neighbor at Kensington Place, **Rowley Leigh**, is patchy, but still worth watching.

The Lowdown

Book before you fly... London has become quite New York in this respect. Newspapers run op-eds about how irritating it is that you can't just show up without a res any more. Of course, you still can in many a neighborhood dive, but these days—read my lips—you should always call ahead. The most popular places need advance planning-and-a-half. Top of the list now, as ever, are **Aubergine** and the **River Café**, and the little sister of the former, **L'Oranger**, has joined the several-weeks-ahead-club too. Those other gorgeous sister restaurants **Le Caprice** and **The Ivy** are perennial sellouts, with The Ivy taking the lead by a furlong. If you want a weekend, either call *now*, forget it, or be famous. Beyond the West End, **Moro** is small and a constant sellout, while two south of the river that require forethought are **OXO Restaurant & Brasserie**, especially during summer, and **Livebait**. Both are generally deemed *vaut le detour,* while **Putney Bridge** also gets mobbed, but by local luminaries. In West London, always reserve for the **Sugar Club**, **Assaggi**, and **192**, and forget about **Wódka** on a weekend, unless you made that call. Weekends also find **Belgo Noord** and **Casale Franco** mobbed by north London locals, while weekday lunches are impossible at the **Savoy Grill** and **Orso**—same reason, different clientele.

Celebrate here... The hokey choice is the **OXO Restaurant & Brasserie**, but you'll have to splash out in the restaurant, because the weird, cadaverous lighting in the brasserie will ruin the mood. The ceiling, for some reason, is made out of slats that rotate at whim, displaying either navy, or turquoise, and letting in a blueish glare from above. **Quaglino's** was the watchword for a big night on the town in the '20s, then was resurrected by Sir Terence Conran in the early '90s, when all London talked about it again. Now, though still nominally glamorous due to its size and its movie-star staircase, it's nothing but a feeding trough for herds. Drop in for a preprandial, though. The good Conran option is that terrace overlooking Tower Bridge, at **Le Pont de la Tour**. If you're pulling out all the stops, **The Oak Room** is so pretty, Marco Pierre White is widely thought a genius, especially by Marco Pierre White, and the waiters are properly pampering. For something completely different, **Belgo Zuid** has stark concrete (carved with quotes from Rabelais) and is cheap and suitably raucous. For the daytime, **Belvedere**, in Holland Park, is heavenly; or you could eat there early on a summer's evening before a performance at the park's open-air theater nearby. Champagne and oysters at **Green's** is especially and seriously British, followed by tea and cake at **The Fountain**. For a precious lunch, perch on a love seat at **The Causerie** and have the waiters refresh your smorgasbord plate frequently. And from the sublime to the ridiculous, the Chinese restaurant **Gracelands Palace** is forever full of hen nights and birthdays, come to worship at the court of the King, a.k.a. owner and Elvis impersonator Paul Chan.

Suddenly starving in Covent Garden... There *seem* to be so many places to eat in this neighborhood, yet few are worthy. **Joe Allen** is good for any time, but impossible to locate: Walk down Exeter Street and when you think you're close, look for a small brass plaque and follow the staircase down. Right by the tube station is **Maxwell's**, also simple and cheap, but stick to the burgers and fries. Bigger, French food is fine at the brasserie **Le Palais du Jardin**, where the crowd is a good sign (not always the case around here); small or big food is excellent, and very healthy, at the casual vegetarian spots, **Neal's Yard Dining Room** and **Food For Thought**, and there's always the **Prêt à Manger** at 77 St. Martin's Lane (head toward Trafalgar Square).

Caught in Portobello with low blood sugar... The **Brasserie du Marché aux Puces** was made for this purpose. It's way up in the Golborne Road regions, past the Westway flea market, and a long, long way from the antiques market you came for, but it's a worthy destination, serving food with a French accent. Closer to the antiques stalls, if you want a cocktail for unwinding, crowded **Beach Blanket Babylon** is the place; its restaurant— fantastical-looking, in its Antonio Gaudí-meets-the- Addams-Family style—serves good grilled meats and fish, salads, and pasta. The absolute, all-purpose, favorite dive of the area, however, is **192**. Whatever the time of day, there'll be hangers-out at this wine bar to the stars (or people who think they are). On the cheaper side, the **Sausage and Mash Cafe** serves lots of different sausages with a variety of flavored mash and gravies. Finger-licking good. Cheapest of all is the **Lisboa Patisserie** on Golborne Road. Sample the deep-fried fish and prawn balls—delicious.

Most comforting... At the **Gay Hussar**, a long-lived Hungarian restaurant in Soho, bouncy banquettes envelop people wearing tweed jackets with leather elbow patches, who consume vast portions of cold cherry soup, goulash, and *paprikás töltött palacsinta* (chicken-veal- paprika pancakes). Knightsbridge's **St. Quentin** is pure Paris, elegant yet unstuffy, handsome yet undesigned, serving wonderful unfashionable food without attitude. Lovely, friendly **Costas Grill**, on the other side of town in Notting Hill, is a comforting Greek taverna, with a matching garden. A high class of nursery tea can be relived (or discovered) at **The Fountain**, in Fortnum & Mason, where auntly waitresses serve Elegant Rarebit (cheese on toast with bacon and tomato), ice cream with tiny jugs of hot butterscotch sauce, and pots of Earl Grey tea. Back west, this time in Shepherd's Bush, we find **Patio,** an excellent, inexpensive Polish place whose set meal includes vodka. Can't be bad.

For grown-ups... When your parents dressed up and left you with the baby-sitter, such are the places you imagined they went. A sophisticated place, sober, but not stuffy, is **L'Oranger,** where spectacular food stands in for the pizzazz of London's louder restaurants. At **The Square**, diners dress expensively to partake of Philip Howard's inspired prix-fixe menus. You'd better be mature enough at **Clarke's** not to mind eating what you're given, because Sally C. sets the menus herself, based on what's best available fresh today. Her well-heeled patrons are rarely disappointed. At **Alastair Little**, the minimal decor leaves you free to concentrate totally on your plate, where the excellent hybrid Modern Brit/Med/Pacific Rim cuisine features a lot of fish. The high-priced blue-and-yellow Chelsea salon that is **La Tante Claire** attracts grown-up and wealthy palates to the inventive cooking of chef Pierre Koffman. Pizza is tailored to restrained and genteel tastes at Mayfair's **Condotti**, with its walls full of Paolozzi paintings; likewise the burgers at Covent Garden's **Christopher's**. The **Savoy Grill** exists for captains of industry, newspaper editors, and parliamentarians who eat only the most British foods—beef Wellington, liver and bacon, fish pie.

For kids... Actual kids are happy with the burgers at **Tootsies, Maxwell's,** and **Ed's Easy Diner,** and particularly like the '50s styling, on-table jukeboxes, and extrovert waitstaff of the latter. If it's pizza they're longing for, the noisy American-style **Chicago Pizza Pie Factory** is ideal. **Marine Ices**, an ice-cream parlor near Camden Lock, and **Lauderdale House**, a park cafe next to Highgate Cemetery, seem to have been simply made for kids. Somewhat higher on the culinary scale, **Wok Wok's** bright colors and fun bowlfuls of noodles are pretty kid-friendly, and the exalted **River Café** extends a surprisingly warm welcome to small people, though they'd better be budding gourmets. **The Fountain** at Fortnum & Mason is a useful good-behavior bribe—a dress-up and sit-tall place for ice-cream-sundae special occasions.

Party hearties... The *patron* of **Wódka** brews his own stickily wicked cherry vodka, which—along with *ziborowa* and *krupnik*, and wines from everywhere but Poland—fuels many a private-room party. See the bach-

DINING | THE LOWDOWN

elors stagger upstairs around midnight. An insidery but jolly atmosphere goes down in the restaurant itself, too. **Belgo Zuid** is the opposite of a serious salon, what with waiters dressed as medieval monks, and vast quantities of *moules-frites* and Belgian *kriek* beer around. The noise level is high, as it is at **St. John**, which looks like a supercool school refectory with a buzz that invites good times. Strangers have been known to get very interactive around the grand piano in the frescoed upstairs room at South Kensington's tony, yet louche, **Star of India**, especially when owner Reza Mohammed is in an ebullient mood.

Pre- and post-theater... For West End theaterland, Japanese-y **Wagamama** is perfect for fast-fueling before curtain up, though it closes too early for after. The **Savoy Grill** shifts gears and ceases to be the power players' canteen in the evenings, when it offers a two-part before-and-after-theater supper. *The* place for late-night after-the-curtain-calls dining is where the actors themselves go (in London as in New York), **Joe Allen**.... Unless you're the star, in which case you take your entourage only to **The Ivy**. You may not know what time the curtain falls on the play you're seeing, but they do, and will take your reservation accordingly. A bargain, speed-delivered pre-theater deal is offered from 6 to 7 p.m. at that toniest of American transplants, **Christopher's**. On the other side of Charing Cross Road, in Soho, are several options that will feed you late at night. Get French-ish bistro food at **Café Bohème**, if you can squeeze in past the crowds of drinkers. **Melati** serves good Malaysian food, and lacks any bar scene at all. One place to drink, eat, people-watch, and extend your evening almost as long as you like is the **Atlantic Bar and Grill**, with its eclectic menu and late-night weekend crowds. Less frenetic than that, the beautiful **Criterion**, across the street, serves until midnight, and is easy to reach fast from any of the West End houses. So is Mezzo, but do you really want to pay the £5 per person cover charge for music (in the restaurant after 10:30)? Up in Islington, the "Off–West End" Almeida Theatre has the divine, upscale pizzas of **Casale Franco**, in a hidden courtyard nearby, though be warned that you're not allowed to order only the pizza, and there are no reservations, so come very early to make the play on time. If curry is your thing, **Soho Spice** (no relation to the girls) is spacious and convenient for West End shows.

Stargazing... It helps to watch a little British TV before attempting to celebrity-spot in this town—this ain't no L.A. Movie folk and rock people do visit, though, and seem to feel at home among the leafier parts of town, generally toward the west—so much so these days, they buy places here. **The Room at the Halcyon** in Holland Park harbors many a local celeb, some of whom have fame that spread farther than Dover: John Cleese, for instance, and Sting, Mick Jagger, and Elton John. Nearby, in groovy Notting Hill, the wine bar **192** hosts fashion designers, writers, and anyone with the last name Freud (author Esther and sister, designer Bella) or Conran (Jasper the designer, Shirley the sometime superwoman, not Terence the patriarch), although many split their time between here and Tom Conran's **The Cow** around the corner. **Daphne's** hosts glitzy ladies of the Ivana Trump ilk, and **Le Caprice** (it was one of Diana's favorites) and **The Ivy** attract movers and shakers in the worlds of architecture, business, art dealing, publishing—you name it. The latter is also very much a thespian haunt, being in theaterland, a tonier choice than the perennial actor's hangout **Joe Allen**, another West End option. If you know their faces, you can spot homegrown politicians and big-time reporters and columnists at power lunches at the **Savoy Grill**, while Labour left-wingers favor the **Gay Hussar** in Soho; architects and anyone writing for the *Guardian* go to **St. John**, in the City. **Wódka** is the secret Kensington hangout of people from all strata—Jerry Hall and Charles Saatchi to name two utterly unrelated sometime regulars. Magazine mavens like Joe Allen's sister restaurant, **Orso**, for lunch—go there to spot future New York editors.

Beautiful people... London, since it got swinging again, is a model's favorite city. You also get what you always got here—incredibly cool and interestingly dressed people posing for all they're worth. Apologies for the unavoidable past-the-"sell-by"-date on this list of their hangouts: **Nobu**, the London version of Matsuhisa's New York and L.A. supersushi joints, is in the Metropolitan hotel, and is good for posing. Open all night, though fueled by caffeine instead of alcohol, is **Bar Italia**. All around it, Soho attracts youth and the best-looking gay men in town. Proper restaurants with tables full of pulchritude include **Aubergine**, **OXO**, **Le Caprice**, and **The Ivy**; **Daphne's** has the moneyed crowd whose clothes, at least, are good-looking. Both **Kensington Place** and **Wódka** attract professionally groomed fashion-biz characters.

Most romantique... Any place whose name translates into "the love apple" is probably conducive to amorous encounters, and so it is at **La Pomme d'Amour**, with its conservatory garden and classic but light French cuisine—even its Holland Park location, reminiscent of a Paris boulevard, is kinda cute. Near neighbor the **Belvedere** outdoes it for setting, however, since it has one of the most gorgeous London locations, in Holland Park itself. In town, **Le Caprice** feels delicious and decadent, with its modern black-and-silver color scheme and its well-spaced, white-dressed tables. The service here tends to pamper diners, too. Ditto at **L'Oranger**, which has the sweetest courtyard tables in summer, as well as exquisite food. There's something illicit about Soho's **French House Dining Room**, hidden above the ever-crammed pub of the same name, with its photos of French boxers; it's lined with mirrors, and upholstered in vermilion. It's the earlier success of Fergus Henderson and Margot Clayton, the pair responsible for St. John, so the food's great, too, in a hearty, naked way. Way north, **Lemonia** is a breath of the Aegean, lighter and leafier of decor than most London Greek places, and so authentic you'll imagine you're getting a suntan.

Britburgers... Oh yes, there is such a thing, and there are a few good examples of the art of short-order cooking around town, most of them in Covent Garden, burger capital of London. Conveniently close to that tube stop is **Maxwell's**, the (relocated) place that brought the trendy-burger to London in the '70s. Between here and the Strand is tiny **Christopher's**—decidedly not a burger joint, but the downstairs cafe serves good burgers for less money, with less swank and swagger. Just around the corner, **Joe Allen**, as you'd expect from the twin brother of Joe's New York original, also turns out a near-perfect patty. The West London chain **Tootsies** is well worth remembering, too, and it has crinkle-cut fries to die for. That other great American culinary import, Tex-Mex, is also popular. Two of the best are **Cactus,** with a South American spin, and **Exquisite,** which also serves pasta. Both are very reasonably priced and friendly.

Really old but still alive... This is usually a recommendation in the world of restaurants—they have to be doing *something* right to stay in business so long. London has fewer very venerable eating houses than you might expect in such a historic city, but the oldest of all, **Rules,** is *very* old. Founded in 1798, it's probably serving the same game-laden menu, give or take the odd fruit sauce and sprig of lemongrass. Younger by far, but showing tenacity, is the beautifully preserved Victorian **Manze's** by Tower Bridge, for the traditional dishes of jellied eels and pie and mash. **Clark & Sons** is another one; it's been here in Exmouth Market since 1930, but the interior's been tragically redone (See "Cockneys and East Enders," below, for more about London eels.) Some of London's loveliest places are those that persisted through decades of low profile, only to attain a sort of hipness again by accident. The **Gay Hussar,** in Soho, is one such—never in fashion and never out of it. **Bahn Thai,** nearby, was one of the pioneers of a cuisine that now challenges Indian as London's native nosh. **St. Quentin**'s exact simulation of a Paris brasserie only improves with the patina of age.

Overrated... **Quaglino's** is glamorous and fun and very big, but it's not the culinary heaven the out-of-towners that pack it every night seem to think it is, and the service can be decidedly offhand. Something similar could be said for a couple of the other Conran juggernauts, although they continue to succeed mightily. **Mezzo** was the biggest until **The Bluebird** came along in 1997. The characteristic shared by all three is that their menus read deliciously, but their meals are curiously disappointing. People find them soulless—hardly surprising given the scale. Opinion is divided over **St. John.** Some hate Fergus Henderson's style—scorn has been heaped on his appetizer of a bunch of carrots and a boiled egg on a plate—but many dishes are stunningly original without gimmick, like his signature salad of bone marrow and parsley. The food at the clamorous, table-hopping **Kensington Place** isn't what it used to be either. Sometimes boring foodwise, you might say. As for **The Oak Room,** does it really deserve its three Michelin stars? The reverence accorded to chef Marco by his elderly lady groupies (there's always a table of them in) would attest to its success, but only they and professional restaurant critics can judge the place with any consistency—the prices, among the highest in the land, prohibit frequent visits by anyone else, so who can know? Sadly, Marco's newer place, the restaurant at **Pharmacy,** is also overrated. The same is true at the equally overstyled **Mash** restaurant, run by previously Midas-like Oliver Peyton.

Auld London towne... **Rules** (see above) is the auldest of all, serving deer and grouse to the gentry and the hoi polloi for two centuries. A handful of other places, often in the grand old hotels, serve once-reviled English food and serve it right. The **Savoy Grill** has two sides to its menu—literally: There's a French side and a British one, both good, but you're safe with the steak-and-kidney here. **Simpsons-in-the-Strand** is the master carver, where great trolleys bearing joints of roasted meat are wheeled to your table and served with spuds, gravy, and the correct accompaniments (Yorkshire pudding and horseradish for beef, mint sauce for lamb, applesauce for pork). This 1828 wood-paneled Edwardian also offers "pig's nose with parsley and onion sauce" for breakfast. The seafood soul of Britain is expressed beautifully at **Green's Restaurant and Oyster Bar**, another wood-paneled establishment, where native oysters (small and strong) or "big" ones precede Devon crab salad or, if you insist, something with meat. Finally, if your credit cards can take some pounding, don't forgo **The Connaught**. There's the (again) wood-paneled restaurant and the smaller green-and-gold grill, both serving perfect English food from a kitchen presided over by French-man Michel Bourdin for over 20 years.

Cockneys and East Enders... It's easily argued that this stuff is the real London cuisine: fish and chips, pie and mash, breakfast fry-ups, and mixed grills. When it's good, it's very, very good, and mostly very, very bad for you. Fish and chips—cod, plaice, or haddock deep-fried in batter and served with thick, slightly flabby french fries, golden tan outside, fluffy white inside—has been appropriated by trendy restaurateurs not just in England, but on the other side of the pond, too. London's best are found at **Geales** and the **Sea-Shell**, and—if you like the dish—are worth a special trip. In Covent Garden, you could do worse than the **Rock & Sole Plaice**. Even if you're squeamish about grease, you'll probably like the sound of fish 'n' chips better than the other London dish: eels, stewed or jellied, and served with emerald green "liquor"—a kind of parsley broth. Pie and mash is more easily envisaged: ground beef with a pastry lid, and mashed potato—not creamed, not whipped, but mashed, and sliced like cake. **Manze's** is worth visiting for the beauty of the functional decor alone—the wooden high-backed benches, ornate green, brown, and white ceramic tiles, sawdust-covered floor, and marble-topped wrought-iron tables haven't changed a bit since the Victorian era. Also little changed is the way business is conducted at Smithfield, the main meat market; after 8 a.m., when the selling's over, the porters repair to the **Fox and Anchor** for the biggest British breakfast in town, black pudding (sausage made from boiled blood) and pints of bitter (there's a unique licensing situation here).

Vegging out... No city restaurant completely ignores the increasing ranks of people who don't eat things with faces, but some cater more than others. Among totally vegetarian restaurants, not too many enjoy gourmet ambience, however good the food. One unlikely exception is **The Place Below**—below, that is, a Wren church, in the crypt. Two nights a week, this wonderful cafe becomes a candlelit real restaurant, serving a divine set dinner. For lunch or tea, the spring blossom–canopied church courtyard of **The Wren at St. James's** is also a veggie haven. For a most haute meal, try the **Room at the Halcyon**, where up-and-coming chef Martin Hadden thoughtfully provides an entirely separate menu for veggies. In Covent Garden are two places which, though the food is fresh and delicious, close early, presumably following the weird *idée fixe* that vegetarians don't eat out at night. **Food For Thought** has horrible chunky yellow pine decor and 1,000-watt lighting, whereas at least **Neal's Yard Dining Room** makes an attempt at ambience, with an on-view kitchen and natural light. A great way for vegetarians to feed is on the cuisine of South India, at **Diwana Bhel Poori** and other places along Drummond Street, not far from the British Museum.

Something fishy... Alastair Little has a special affinity for fish, always doing something interesting and pan-Pacific with it. Those Conran places **Quaglino's** and **The Bluebird** serve *plateaux de fruits de mer* that approximate the ur-plateaux of La Coupole and its ilk. So does that better Sir Terence palace, **Le Pont de la Tour.** Oysters are best at **Green's**; at yet another Conran shop, the **Bibendum Oyster Bar**; and at **Daphne's**, where shellfish are still on the diets of the ladies who lunch. **Belgo Zuid**, living up to its Belgian provenance, has the most fun with mussels. Near Piccadilly Circus is a useful, relatively budget piscine emporium, **Cafe Fish**. It's no great gourmet shakes, but the fish is fresh, the execution reliable. Broiled fish is wonderful at the good, Greek **Lemonia**. **Costas Grill** on a fine summer's night in the small garden is evocative of Greek island vacations, if you drink enough retsina with your *psari*. The *pulpo* (octopus) tapa and the *zarzuela* (seafood stew) at **Rebato's** are memorable, as was the carp in aspic at **Wódka**, which may or may not be back on the menu. Sushi is still not worth bothering with in London on the whole, except for expense-account-only **Nobu**. Actually, just about every good restaurant is friends with fish these days, but perhaps none more so than **Livebait**.

For oenophiles... Wine lists in London used to be all French, and mostly Bordeaux and Burgundy at that, but this is far from true now. New World wines—from Australia, Chile, and, yes, even California—are ubiquitous, and you'll see Italian, German, and some Spanish wines, plus various Eastern European bottles on many a list. All the grand dining salons fulfill the Important Wines requirement, of course, with only French on the list at **Le Gavroche** and **Chez Nico**; mostly French, with a little German and Italian, at **The Connaught**. The requisite Places with Interesting Lists include **192**, which picks out seasonal selections on your behalf. If you're homesick for Californian wines, go straight to **Clarke's**, because Sally Clarke and her Cali cuisine share a special affinity for them. If wine's your thing but the budget is tight, you could do a lot worse than **The Wine Factory.** It offers simple but good pasta and pizza with wines sold at shop—rather than restaurant—prices (£10 in a restaurant; £6 here).

But is it pizza?... There is, contrary to the opinion of any Yankee expat you may encounter, good pizza in London. It's not necessarily the New York style—thin, crisp-crusted, oregano-laden pie—nor Chicago's thick, chewy, doughy variety, though both are available. Instead, what you get here is a hybrid that owes its provenance directly to Sicily. **Casale Franco**, in far-off Islington, serves amazing, irregularly shaped pies with bubbles and charred bits on the crust; piled on top are whole basil leaves and roasted tomatoes and slices of prosciutto and artichoke hearts and other good stuff. The trouble is the restaurant's absurd and greedy policy of not allowing these to be your entrée at peak hours. They don't take reservations, either. So forget that, and head to the reliable **Pizza Express** chain. Ordering anything but pizza here is a grave error, but the thin, crisp, Italian pies are fine. Get the Veneziana (onions, raisins) and have 15p donated to the Venice in Peril fund. **Condotti**, in the heart of Mayfair, is the Rolls-Royce of pizza joints, serving the usual suspects, plus a potato-crusted four-cheese pie, between art-encrusted walls. There are other pizzerias of note, but they're too outlying to appear in a city guide.

Neighborhood places where Londoners go... The **Brackenbury** is hidden in a backstreet in Hammersmith, yet is packed every night. Not only is its "new British" food always interesting, the atmosphere is warm and homey, the service sweet, even since the original owners sold up and moved on. Every neighborhood these days has at least one restaurant loved by the locals, and worth a look by you, especally if you want a deeper view into this city's life. Putney, a families' and affluent media folks' village of big Edwardian houses upstream on the Thames, lacked a locus until the stunning, spaceship-like, glass-walled **Putney Bridge** opened. Now *le tout* southwest London hangs at the bar, gazing at the tide. The food—by an ex-St. John man—is better than acceptable, if not worth the trek alone. On the other hand, the food at these two West London places certainly is worth crossing town for; and many people do just that, making reservations essential—especially at the **Sugar Club**. Once a humble above-the-pub dining room, **Assaggi** has become almost as much of a draw. Further west, upstairs at the **Star of India** has long been the open secret of Fulham dwellers and Chelseaites, plus a coterie of movie actors who know they can dine without gawpers when back in town. The totally unposh bit of West London by Olympia (exhibition center) has a tiny Persian restaurant row, on which **Yas** takes the lavash for the most friendly, reliable, late-opening (till 5 a.m.!) and bargain-rate restaurant for miles. Back across the river, in the former wasteland between the Bridges Waterloo and Blackfriars, the fish place **Livebait** was such a hit, it sold itself and doubled its size, but is still selling every table every night. Another plainly decorated place, the Spanish/Moorish cuisine-serving **Moro**, in the recently trendified Exmouth Market (in totally trendy Clerkenwell/Farringdon), has probably had to expand by now too, judging by the two-week wait for a reservation. Also in this neck of the woods is the all-new **Las Brasas** tapas bar. Cheap tapas of the highest quality in a bustling and casual setting is the game, although service can be a bit stretched at busier times.

Is this a pub or a restaurant?... The disappearance of the grungy British boozer from the streets of London has its bright side: namely, the emergence of the gastropub. In these, you can still imbibe only liquid sustenance, but hungrier, healthier people can eat really well at about a third of the price of a restaurant. The exception to the lower check part is **Assaggi**, which is really a separate restaurant, despite being above the Chepstow. Notting Hill has so many examples of this genre, the challenge is finding a pub that doesn't do food. **The Cow** is darling—for its oysters-and-Guinness suppers in the bar downstairs, and for its cozy dining room upstairs, where a River Café alumna cooks. At Camden's **The Engineer**, there's a separate restaurant, too, serving Euro-Brit comfort food. Mercifully, this means you can reserve a table for bigger groups, though not in the garden—a summertime mob scene, especially Sunday evenings when the softball teams descend from nearby Regent's Park. The original gastropub, **The Eagle**, is still going strong—stronger than ever, actually, since its Farringdon nabe is now quite the hot spot, and its rustic southern European food has overtaken fish 'n' chips and curry as the basic local cuisine. An entirely residential corner of Hammersmith, near Ravenscourt Park, lacks any of Farringdon's gallery/shop/design studio buzz, but boasts the incredibly successful food pub the **Anglesea Arms**—so successful that Dan Evans's hearty stews, risottos, salads, and fish take hours traveling from his kitchen to your mouth. By contrast to the pub-with-restaurant, some restaurants keep bars that have independent personalities: for instance, the vast **Atlantic Bar and Grill**, the Piccadilly Circus of late-night bars, located just off Piccadilly Circus itself. The food ranges from acceptable to good, but the reason to eat here is to secure a good table during rush hour. **192** is Notting Hill's social club, mobbed with barflies—although the food is good, the wine list (it's officially a wine bar) is even better. **Bar Italia**, in Soho, is a coffee bar, period—no alcohol, little food, much posing. Nearby, in Covent Garden, **Joe Allen** has a New York–style proper bar with bar stools, as this true Manhattan transfer should, and **Maxwell's** does those sugary blender cocktails for office workers. Riverside restaurants that give good bar are: **OXO**, **Le Pont de la Tour**, and **Putney Bridge**—all, obviously, best on a summer's night. Special mention in this category must go to the three **Belgo** restaurants (three and counting, that is). Belgian beer is the thing here, and the list includes more than a hundred. Beware the hangover.

Tapas: the craze that stayed... Somewhere around the end of the '80s, somebody wheeled those Spanish tidbits called *tapas* into London, until every restaurant had a little dish of *boquerones* (marinated fresh anchovies) and a slice of *tortilla* (potato omelet) on the table. Iberian was in. **Rebato's**, just south of the river, and **Galicia**, in the nether regions of Portobello, are both long-long-standing Spanish restaurants that do tapas (as opposed to tapas bars), both *muy autentico* and—especially Rebato's—hopping on weekends. The food at Rebato's is much better than at Galicia, but Galicia has a sweet, homey ambience. Camden Town's **Bar Gansa** is another keeper, serving a bigger range of little food than most, with great giant fries, of the "big chips" sort you can get in every pub-resto these days. Other spots worth mentioning are **Laxeiro,** in the heart of Columbia Road's flower market (see Diversions), and **Las Brasas** (see above). Next, watch tapas devolve into pan-global versions: Asian wonton tapas; Central European blini tapas; Middle Eastern meze tapas; Moroccan bastilla tapas....No, wait, that's already happened.

Cheap 'n' cheerful... Fish and chips, pie and mash, these are always bargains, but there are other things to eat when belts are tight. Indian food, as we've noted, is the real

British cuisine, and virtually any high street tandoori house will be good. For English diner–equivalent food, the **Chelsea Kitchen** has been there since Chelsea was the swinging center of the world, and it's still likeable. There's good French diner food, and a lovely, casual ambience at the wine bar in picturesque Shepherd's Market, **L'Artiste Musclé**, while Thai bargains are offered at **Ben's Thai**, above a big pub in untouristy Maida Vale. There's always a line for the noodles and "health dishes" and communal fun food of the frighteningly popular **Wagamama**, and **Belgo Zuid** is a bargain if you stick to mussels and fries (which is what they do best). In Piccadilly, as central as can be, the spring blossom–canopied church courtyard of **The Wren at St. James's** is perfect for lunch or tea. All around town you'll see Paris-style brasseries, which can be useful, with their baguette sandwiches and goat's-cheese salads and Toulouse sausages. Out of the (disappearing) Dôme, Café Rouge, and **Café Flo** chains, the last is marginally the best, useful for its "Idée Flo" two-course simple meal—useful, but dull. Better is the Asian version of the functional brasserie, **Wok Wok**, where a refueling of stir-fried noodles, vegetables, chicken, seafood, spices, in or out of broth is guaranteed fast, inexpensive, and surprisingly fresh and good. Lastly, and mostly, you'll get sick of the sight of sandwich monarch **Prêt à Manger** branches, but they're ubiquitous because they provide what we need—speedily, deliciously, prettily (those industrial metal floors, that funky recycled paper packaging…).

Indian institutions… There are so many good neighborhood curry houses that they alone could fill this book, but we single out this pair as examples of their genre: On a Notting Hill strip of several Indian eateries, find the frenetic institution **Khan's**. It retains its popularity because of its soaring skylike ceilings, palms, and low prices, but mostly because of its popularity. (Nothing succeeds like success.) **Star of India** is the grown-up Khan's, with superb—they call it evolved—cuisine, controlled hubbub, and fancy murals. Nearby, **The Bombay Brasserie** offers perhaps the best Raj atmosphere in the western world at its Sunday lunchtime buffet. Pith helmet strictly optional. Over in the East End Bangladeshi community around Brick Lane, the same role is fulfilled by the

Nazrul, whose waiters' jackets say on the pocket "Naz Rules," and which is almost embarrassingly inexpensive. Near Euston Station, **Diwana Bhel Poori** isn't much on ambience, but does great South Indian meals. Nearby, rock-bottom cost and complete immersion in another culture is available at the **Indian YMCA**. Also central, albeit not as dirt-cheap as the last three spots, is **Soho Spice,** a modern, well-designed restaurant with vibrantly colored walls, furniture, waiters' uniforms, and even food; the tandoori salmon is highly recommended.

Best Asian... London has ambassadors from most Asian kitchens, and has had for decades. First to arrive were the Cantonese; then Hong Kong chefs who wanted to remain part Brit; and the Chinese food scene is changing again. Dim sum here have a good reputation and the biggest, most ornate, and best known place to partake of those unrecognizable steamed things on trolleys is **New World**. Among Chinatown Cantonese, **Fung Shing** is not only reliable, but prettier than most, in restful pale green. Malaysian food is not available everywhere, but its satays and noodle dishes are easy to eat, as Londoners have been doing for years at **Melati**. The *Tom yam koong* (very spicy shrimp soup), *pad Thai* (noodles with every-thing), green and red curries, and so on of Thailand have been thoroughly adopted in this town. Try Thai in Soho at **Sri Siam** and **Bahn Thai**, or make an outing to far-flung Maida Vale and the nongourmet but pleasing **Ben's Thai**. Japanese is proliferating, but rarely well, except at **Nobu**, where the interpretation is personal to that inter-national Matsuhisa man, but extremely pricey. Cheaper Japanese that is still highly edible can be found at **Misato,** in Soho. Pan-Asian is butting in everywhere, mostly as accents on menus (like at Sugar Club and Putney Bridge), but at **Wok Wok**, it's the entire idea.

The rest of the world... The melting pot that is London offers many other ethnic culinary experiences. Moroccan and North African food is everywhere. **Pasha,** the brain-child of posh restaurateur Mogens Tholstrup, is cleaning up at the pricier end of the market. For those without a platinum card, the brand-new **Yima Cafe,** in Camden, is a good choice. The food of Eritrea is admirably re-created at a low, low cost in Brixton at **Asmara.** West African food in the East End is best represented by the Nigerian **Obalende Suya,** whose chicken kirikiri is reputedly "imprisoned for hours in notorious herbs and spices." Crossing the Atlantic, and moving northward to Archway, we start in Brazil, in a friendly little restaurant filled with locals. **Sabor do Brasil** offers national specialties, and the English owner, whose Brazilian wife runs the kitchen, will happily guide you through the menu. If Caribbean-style cuisine is what you crave, try **Bamboula,** a new place in Brixton. The menu is a little more experimental than in the more traditional local spots, but its staples—curried goat and the like—are still grade A. Unfortunately, while friendly, the service is as authentic as the food—come prepared for a West Indian wait. Just chill out with a couple of rum punches and take it all as it comes.

The French connection... Time was, going to a London restaurant was a big night out, and the restaurant was Escoffier-French, with great batteries of flatware and waiters who said "*Et pour madame?*" and served the vegetables from the left. Now, of course, we understand that French is not the only cuisine, even if France is still the most food-obsessed nation of Europe, and we understand this partly because there aren't so very many French restaurants left. **L'Artiste Musclé** may be the least pretentious, most basic (in a good way) French place in town. The check is also reasonable at Covent Garden's **Le Palais du Jardin**, a creditable simulated French brasserie. Going up the scale, the *comme il faut* award for all-around French authenticity, lovability, and understated charm goes to the Knightsbridge **St. Quentin**, with its beauteous, summery setting and reliable, slightly old-school cuisine. If you're going to lavish many pounds on the French meal-fairly-near-France of your life, do it at **La Tante Claire**. It never misses. Those who crave extra waiterly flourishes, a surfeit of very rich people, and even richer ingredients, favor **Le Gavroche**, where Michel Roux, Jr.'s cuisine is as classical as you'll find. Then there are those who worship **Chez Nico**, a serious Park Lane salon that impresses without being much fun.

Old Italian... Soho was originally the home of London's Italian community, and a few red-sauce survivors of the rent wars remain in this groovy, schmoozy neighborhood. Some we don't recommend, but you've gotta love **Pollo** for

its grungy plastic-ivy, pine-paneled decor, and hordes of art-student club kids feeding on chicken cacciatore, ravioli in brodo, and cassata. London's biggest bargain in old-fashioned pasta is still served at **Centrale**, which is lesser known, better, and hipper than Pollo. While in Soho, don't forget to drop in at **Bar Italia**, which functioned for years as the Soho Italian community's center before being adopted forever by clubbers. It got an architect's redesign recently, but much to the relief of old and new fans alike, it looks exactly the same. One venerable Italian place that has kept up with the times is **Bertorelli's**, where some of the kind waitresses have remained loyal through redecorations and chef changes and everything. They still offer the fabulous olive bread with big smiles.

Noov Italian... Actually, **Bertorelli's** has kept up so well, it belongs in this category, too, for the inventive but not over-challenging food of Maddalena Bonino. Queen of the sturdy southern style that replaced the creamy-ragù-giant-pepper-mill Italians is the **River Café**. Anyone who went there before 1994 will be surprised at the new lighter, bigger room, with its long mirrored bar; anyone who's never been there before will be surprised at the lack of any river view. Its prices, which used to seem outrageous, haven't risen much and now appear more reasonable in the big picture, especially for food of this quality. More central, and close to Bertorelli's, is Joe Allen's Italian cousin, **Orso**, also a carbon copy of the New York version. Astonishingly, it manages to attract a similar crowd to its NYC model, though London's has fewer thespians and more magazine editors. An edge of Portobello-land harbors **Assaggi**, which serves food of the River Café school, which is to say, the ingredients are the best available, and not much mucked about with. **Mediterraneo** is another, newer Portobello resident with simple, uncluttered food. **The Eagle** does rather play with its food, but then you should come here feeling downright greedy, to partake of the latest versions of Italian gypsy cuisine.

Best prix-fixe... The places presenting the most shocking checks are the hotel dining rooms, the big star chefs, the haute French places, and permutations of same. But at any of these, big savings can be harvested over lunch—a lunch that could run for hours. **Chez Nico**, **The Connaught**, **The Oak Room**, **Bibendum**, and **La Tante Claire** all offer

DINING | THE LOWDOWN

a three-course lunch for around £30. Some of those include coffee, but none the half bottle of wine that **Le Gavroche** throws in for £39. **The Ivy**'s weekend set lunch is a steal, as is **L'Oranger**'s every day (except Sunday) mid-day meal—£18 for two courses, £22 for three courses—not to mention its just-under-30-quid dinner. At **Kensington Place**, fill in the missing weekday lunches for £14.50 for three courses. **Aubergine**—if you can get in at all—isn't so frighteningly priced if you go the £24 lunch route; there's also the seven-course £55 dinner to consider. **Alastair Little**'s three courses for £25 is looking more like a bargain as the prices edge up everywhere. All the Conran places do set meal deals. If you must do **Quaglino's**, do it pretheater, with the 5:30 to 6:30 £14.50 three-course menu; in Soho, **Mezzo** has a similar 6 to 7 p.m. sitting on the Mezzanine floor (which is better anyway), for a bargain £7.95 for two courses. **The Bluebird**'s early-bird £11.50/£14.50 menu is pointless without anywhere to go nearby (OK, there's the Royal Court), but the best of these prix fixes is at **Bibendum**—the only truly good place in the pantheon—where there's a £28 three-course lunch. **OXO**'s set lunch, at £23.85, for some reason, is the only way to afford the restaurant.

The great British breakfast... If your hotel only does Continental, repair for morning sustenance to any greasy-spoon caff you happen upon. Good luck—they're a dying breed. For under a fiver, you can order: bacon, egg (fried), sausage, black pudding, a slice (fried bread), beans (baked), mushrooms (fried or poached), tomatoes (griddled), and toast. If that's not enough, add kippers, liver, kidneys, or porridge (oatmeal). If you can't find a caff, head to **Simpsons-in-the-Strand**, which offers the works in Edwardian splendor from £11.50, actually anointing it "The Great British Breakfast," which is off-putting. The quality is not as high as it looks like it's going to be, but it does come with coffee, OJ, newspaper, and pastries. In St. James's is the best genteel purveyor of the traditional breakfast: **The Fountain**. Early risers (or night people) can try the **Fox and Anchor** pub, at its best very early when the meat porters from nearby Smithfield market are still there. The best bet for a delicious fry-up, though, is at the **Organic Café**. It may be a bit of a trek to Queen's Park, but the meat (all organically reared) of the sausages is truly exquisite.

aren't remotely publike, but neither is the southern Italian food. Try the pasta "loaf" of eggplant, radicchio, fontina, and gruyère.... *Tel 0207/792–5501. 39 Chepstow Place W2. Notting Hill Gate tube stop. Reservations essential. DC not accepted. £££* **(see pp. 44, 55, 56, 61)**

Atlantic Bar and Grill. This late-night spot looks like a jazzed-up, parquet-floored ocean liner. Despite being the size of a small village, it gets packed most nights, and weekends are a zoo. Some food's good.... *Tel 0207/734–4888. 20 Glasshouse St. W1, Piccadilly Circus tube stop. Reservations weekends. DC not accepted. £££* **(see pp. 48, 57)**

Aubergine. London's hottest reservation is a table at former soccer star (honestly) Gordon Ramsay's place. Apparently, his supermodern, audacious Frenchy style can't miss.... *Tel 0207/352–3449. 11 Park Walk SW10, Sloane Sq. tube stop. Reserve months ahead. ££££–£££££* **(see pp. 44, 50, 62)**

Bahn Thai. A longstanding Soho Thai often called the best in town, with a menu several pages long. Softshell crab, duck with honey dipping sauce—and a decor of bamboo chairs and halogen spotlights.... *Tel 0207/437–8504. 21A Frith St. W1, Leicester Sq. tube stop. Reservations for dinner. £££*
(see pp. 51, 59)

Bamboula. New and unassuming Brixton Caribbean place with a slightly quirky menu. Try old faves like curried goat or "sudden-fried chicken".... *Tel 0207/737–6633. 12 Acre Lane. SW2, Brixton tube stop. ££* **(see p. 60)**

Bar Gansa. Plainly decked out in lemony hues and some Iberian gewgaws, this successful tapas bar in Camden Town is not for quiet conversation on weekends. Try *Albondigas* (meatballs), *boquerones* (fresh anchovies), tortilla, and chorizo.... *Tel 0207/267–8909. 2 Inverness St. NW1, Camden Town tube stop. No reservations. £* **(see p. 57)**

Bar Italia. This Soho institution is the ur-espresso bar, always open, nearly always full of life, and lined with Rocky Marciano-abilia. Sandwiches, panettone, and unmemorable gelati are the meager food choices, but the espresso and cappuccino are the business.... *Tel 0207/437–4520. 22 Frith St. W1, Leicester Sq. tube stop. No reservations. No credit cards. £* **(see pp. 49, 57, 61)**

Beach Blanket Babylon. This outrageous-looking dungeon-like fantasy is the nearest thing to a singles bar you'll find in Notting Hill. Cross the drawbridge to the restaurant to pick up a meal here, too—Mediterreanean is the style.... *Tel 0207/229–2907. 45 Ledbury Rd. W11, Notting Hill Gate tube stop. Reservations for dinner. AE, DC not accepted. ££–£££* **(see p. 46)**

Belgo Zuid. New third restaurant in the Belgo chain. Giant pine, concrete, and steel-lined refectory-style dining hall with waiters dressed as monks (!). Order mussels and fries, *waterzooi* (fish stew), or wild boar sausages. Also check out Covent Garden's Belgo Centraal (tel 0207/813–2233. 50 Earlham St.) and Chalk Farm's Belgo Noord (Tel 0208/267–0718. 72 Chalk Farm Rd.).... *Tel 0208/982–8400. 124 Ladbroke Grove, W10, Ladbroke Grove tube stop. ££–£££* **(see pp. 45, 48, 54, 58)**

Belvedere. A beautiful midpark setting for this serene room of huge windows and white linens far outstrips the Med-Brit menu (blackened tuna; confit of duck, garlic mash; welsh rarebit; chocolate marquise).... *Tel 0207/602–1238. Holland Park, Abbotsbury Rd. W8, Holland Park tube stop. Reservations advised weekends. ££££* **(see pp. 45, 50)**

Ben's Thai. A big off-the-beaten-track Art Nouveau pub harbors this wood-paneled dining room upstairs. There's better Thai food in town, but value and casual ambience this has got.... *Tel 0207/266–3134. The Warrington Hotel, 93 Warrington Crescent W9, Warwick Ave. tube stop. Reservations for dinner. AE, DC not accepted. ££* **(see pp. 58, 59)**

Bertorelli's. Been around forever, but you'd never know it from the fabulous modern decor (a '97 refit), the great service, the friendly buzz, and the modish (but not *too*) menu—garganelli with green beans and cobb nuts; monkfish ragout; panna cotta.... *Tel 0207/836–3969. 44A Floral St. WC2, Covent Garden tube stop. £££* **(see p. 61)**

Bibendum. This cherished French treat, beneath the stained-glass windows of the Michelin tire man (this was that company's HQ), is still on the money, with Matthew Harris at the stove.... *Tel 0207/581–5817. Michelin House, 81 Fulham Rd. SW3, South Kensington tube stop. DC not accepted. Reservations advised. £££££* **(see pp. 60, 61)**

Bibendum Oyster Bar. In the same exquisite, exuberantly tiled Art Nouveau building as the Bibendum restaurant (and the Conran Shop), eat *plateaux de fruits de mer*, crab or Caesar salads, as well as oysters, in great style.... *Tel 0207/589–1480. Michelin House, 81 Fulham Rd. SW3, South Kensington tube stop. No reservations. DC not accepted. £££* **(see p. 54)**

The Bluebird. Here's a menu extract from the newest Conran: "14.00 Panfried rouget + risotto, fennel, bisque; 13.75 Veal scallopini + borlotti, sage, prosciutto." Is that irritating, or what? Especially because enough deliciousness is rarely achieved for those prices. But the formula works, and still they flock.... *Tel 0207/559–1000. 350 King's Rd. SW3, Sloane Sq. tube stop. ££££* **(see pp. 51, 54, 62)**

The Bombay Brasserie. Delightful slice of authentic Raj in the restaurant attached to Bailey's Hotel. The Sunday lunch buffet is unrivaled.... *Tel 0207/370–4040. Courtfield Rd. SW7, Gloucester Rd. tube stop. ££££* **(see p. 58)**

Brackenbury. Take a cab to reach this secret Hammersmith pocket, where market availability dictates the menu—saffron turbot and mussel stew, onion-thyme tart, blood-orange sorbet. Loud and friendly.... *Tel 0208/748–0107. 129 Brackenbury Rd. W6, Hammersmith tube stop. ££* **(see p. 55)**

Las Brasas. Excellent new tapas at Farringdon. Good value for lunch; the spicy potatoes and chorizo are wonderful.... *Tel 0207/250–3401. 63A Clerkenwell Rd. EC1, Farringdon tube stop. ££* **(see pp. 56, 57)**

Brasserie du Marché aux Puces. This big-windowed, wood-floored eatery does laid-back French-ish food, like salmon tartare, duck magret, *saucisses de Toulouse*.... *Tel 0208/968–5828. 349 Portobello Rd. W10, Ladbroke Grove tube stop. No credit cards. £££* **(see p. 46)**

Cactus. Chalk Farm Tex-Mex with South American chefs. An all-you-can-eat buffet (£4.88) has been the same price for years.... *Tel 0207/722–4112. 85A Haverstock Hill, NW3, Belsize Park or Chalk Farm tube stop. £* **(see p. 51)**

Café Bohème. Most useful as a Soho rendezvous and after-hours drinking den, this Continental brasserie nevertheless has okay food, along the ciabatta-roast-veg-goat's-cheese-sandwich axis.... *Tel 0207/734–0623. 13 Old Compton St. W1, Leicester Sq. tube stop. Reservations for dinner. DC not accepted. ££* **(see p. 48)**

Cafe Fish. A handy stop in midtown, with a menu divided into cooking methods (steamed, *mennière*, fried, grilled), this bustling spot does fish standards and has a fast, cheap, busy basement wine bar.... *Tel 0207/930–3999. 39 Panton St. SW1, Piccadilly Circus tube stop. ££ (wine bar), £££ (restaurant)* **(see p. 54)**

Café Flo. The best of the nearly identical Parisian wannabes, this cafe—and its branches—does a good, fast, cheap soup-or-salad, steak-or-fish-with-fries deal.... *Tel 0207/836–8289. 51 St. Martin's Lane WC2, Charing Cross tube stop. DC not accepted. £–££* **(see p. 58)**

Le Caprice. Old London fave reopened by the classy Corbin-King duo is wonderful. Shiny '80s black furnishings, sparkly lighting, and Japanese-y flowers set the scene for a round-the-world menu. Service is perfect.... *Tel 0207/629–2239. Arlington House, Arlington St. SW1, Green Park tube stop. Reservations essential. ££££* **(see pp. 44, 49, 50)**

Casale Franco. Ask, or you'll never find the cobbled courtyard entrance to this Islington staple. Famous for great pizza, it has an arrogant no-pizza-only policy, no reservations, and a sometimes surly staff, but the brick-walled warehouse chic and the compulsory other food (calves' liver, polenta, salads) are fine.... *Tel 0207/226–8994. Behind 134 Upper St. N1, Highbury and Islington tube stop. No reservations. AE, DC not accepted. ££–£££* **(see pp. 44, 48, 54)**

The Causerie. How sweet it is to perch on delicate couches at low oval tables and be cosseted by charming French waiters as you load up at this 30-dish smorgasbord. An unexpected bargain.... *Tel 0207/629–8860. Claridge's Hotel, Brook St. W1, Bond St. tube stop. Jacket and tie required for men. £££* **(see p. 45)**

Centrale. Basic as it gets—there's not even a bathroom—this Italian Soho diner nevertheless serves great pasta and minestrone; the risotti you can live without, though.... *Tel 0207/437–5513. 16 Moor St. W1, Leicester Sq. tube stop. No reservations. No credit cards. £* **(see p. 61)**

Chelsea Kitchen. They do not lie: Since Chelsea swung in the sixties, this has been its kitchen, filling up folks with wholesome fodder—from egg and chips to beef stew with veggies, moussaka, chicken curry, and apple crumble and custard.... *Tel 0207/589–1330. 98 King's Rd. SW3, Sloane Sq. tube stop. No reservations. No credit cards. £* **(see p. 58)**

Chez Nico at Ninety Park Lane. Nico Ladenis, self-taught superstar of London cuisine, keeps a lower profile than he used to, maybe because he's finally settled down in the patrician salon he deserves. Here you'll find well-padded seats and patrons, obsequious service, and complicated perfection on the plate, replete with foie gras. Dress smart.... *Tel 0207/409–1290. Grosvenor House, 90 Park Lane W1, Marble Arch tube stop. £££££* **(see pp. 54, 60, 61)**

Chicago Pizza Pie Factory. Where deep-dish lives in London. Chicago pop radio blares and it's pretty authentically American, down to the eager service.... *Tel 0207/629–2669. 17 Hanover Sq. W1, Oxford Circus tube stop. Reservations for kids' Sunday lunch. DC not accepted. ££* **(see p. 47)**

Christopher's. Upscale East Coast dining transplanted, uncut, to Covent Garden. Up the stone stair is a soaring mirrored space, where opera music fills the air and you can dine on plain broiled steak, chicken, and fish; creamed spinach, or nutmeggy mashed potatoes; and salsas and salads. Brunch is best.... *Tel 0207/240–4222. 18 Wellington St. WC2, Covent Garden tube stop. ££££ (restaurant)* **(see pp. 47, 48, 50)**

Clark & Sons. Get the full monty jellied eels, or pie with mash served from an ice-cream scoop, like school dinners. The character was renovated out of this shop, just as it was renovated into its groovy 'hood.... *Tel 0207/837–1974. 46 Exmouth Market EC1, Farringdon tube stop. No credit cards. Closed evenings. £.* **(see p. 51)**

Clarke's. Chef-owner Sally C. trained in Paris and California, and duly displays both influences in food that's classically treated and tastes fresh. Ingredients are respected so much that each night's menu is dictated by the best available—one set menu, whatever Sally has chosen, period.... *Tel 0207/221–9225. 124 Kensington Church St. W8, Notting Hill Gate tube stop. No AE, DC. ££££–£££££* **(see pp. 47, 54)**

THE INDEX

DINING

Condotti. This is Mayfair pizza, meaning art on the walls, an extra few quid on the check, and a most unusual potato-crusted four-cheese pie on the list of usuals.... *Tel 0207/499–1308. 4 Mill St. W1, Oxford Circus tube stop. Reservations for lunch. ££* **(see pp. 47, 55)**

The Connaught. This correct dining room is the ultimate purveyor of one sort of English experience—the aristocratic one (not even a fantasy for many regulars here). The restaurant is bigger and clubbier, the grill lighter, more intimate, but both serve the French master chef's British dishes—pickled tongue and boiled silverside (brisket), game, roasts—plus some classic French (tournedos Rossini, for example).... *Tel 0207/ 499–7070. Carlos Place W1, Green Park tube stop. Jacket and tie required for men. ££££* **(see pp. 52, 54, 61)**

Costas Grill. A welcoming Greek taverna-diner that serves good Hellenic staples (homemade hummus with hot pita, moussaka). Garden's a polite word for the yard in back, but it's most useful on a warm night.... *Tel 0207/229–3794. 14 Hillgate St. W8, Notting Hill Gate tube stop. Reservations for dinner. No credit cards. £* **(see pp. 46, 54)**

The Cow. Tom Conran's Dublin pub in Notting Hill, a strong contender for London's pub of the millennium, with oysters and soda bread as bar snacks, and a good, cozy dining room upstairs (a separate business), serving fresh sardines stuffed with lemon and pine nuts; chargrilled lamb with merguez; posh pizzas; gooseberry fool with shortbread.... *Tel 0207/221–0021. 89 Westbourne Park Rd. W2, Westbourne Park tube stop. AE, DC not accepted. ££* **(see pp. 49, 56)**

The Criterion. Byzantine splendor in Piccadilly Circus, another domain of Marco Pierre White. A grown-up atmosphere, a good percentage of beautiful people, and classical French dishes with interesting bits, like Gravadlax and beignets of oyster with citrus butter, or ballottine of wild salmon. The hangar-size place has a golden mosaic ceiling and cerulean drapes.... *Tel 0207/930–0488. 224 Piccadilly W1, Piccadilly Circus tube stop. ££££* **(see p. 48)**

Daphne's. Where the lady lunches: Big hair and gilt buttons are de rigueur after dark, when your baubles should be real. Food is from the Mediterranean hit parade (fritto misto, sea bass baked with fennel, an unctuous Caesar salad, and

risotti); what really matters is which flagstone-floored conservatory you're seated in.... *Tel 0207/589–4257. 112 Draycott Ave. SW3, South Kensington tube stop. ££££*
(see pp. 49, 50, 54)

Diwana Bhel Poori. Staples of the South Indian menu include the *masala dosa* (a paper-thin rice/lentil flour pancake encircling spiced potato and green coconut chutney) and *bhel poori* mixtures (tortilla chiplike bits mixed with tamarind and coconut chutneys and spiced yogurt). It's delicious, enlivening food, served in a basic pine-table cafe.... *Tel 0207/387–5556. 121 Drummond St. NW1, Euston tube stop. No reservations. £* **(see pp. 53, 59)**

The Eagle. The first of the foodie pubs, still serving excellent rustic Mediterrean dishes, such as its famous marinated rump steak sandwich called Bife Ana. Beware crowds at peak times.... *Tel 0207/837–1353. 159 Farringdon Rd. EC1, Farringdon tube stop. No credit cards. ££***(see pp. 56, 61)**

Ed's Easy Diner. Some say this is a great burger, others accuse Ed of grease-mongering, but you also get a '50s decor with jukebox, cheese fries, kosher dogs, and peanut butter shakes.... *Tel 0207/439–1955. 12 Moor St. W1, Leicester Sq. tube stop. AE, DC not accepted. £* **(see p. 47)**

The Engineer. Sir Larry's daughter, Tamsin Olivier, is one of the hip young owners of this sitting room of a pub-resto, with its gorgeous garden and easy menus—roast chicken with scallion mash; wild mushroom and chestnut risotto; chocolate rum cake.... *Tel 0207/722–0950. 65 Gloucester Ave. NW1. Chalk Farm tube stop. AE, DC not accepted. ££***(see p. 56)**

Exquisite. A wide selection of Tex-Mex at this new, if not exactly inspirational, restaurant. Good-sized portions.... *Tel 0207/359–9529. 167 Blackstock Rd. N4, Finsbury Park tube stop. £–££* **(see p. 51)**

Food For Thought. Here is meatless, microwaveless, nearly guiltless vegetarian happy food—happy because it's good, cheap, generous, and fresh. Thick slices of whole-meal bread, stir-fries, and maybe spinach-ricotta filo, followed by cakes and cookies.... *Tel 0207/836–0239. 31 Neal St. WC2, Covent Garden tube stop. No reservations. No credit cards. £* **(see pp. 46, 53)**

The Fountain. It's even more English than Mary Poppins, who would feel at home on the comfy chairs here. Order quaint food (things on toast, pies, and poached Dover sole) and/or Vesuvian sundaes oozing sauces and cream and fruit.... *Tel 0207/734–8040. Back of Fortnum & Mason, 181 Piccadilly W1 (entrance on Duke/Jermyn St.), Green Park tube stop. £–££* **(see pp. 45, 46, 47, 62)**

Fox and Anchor. This pub by Smithfield, the meat market, serves big plates of meat. It opens at 7 a.m., and has a unique license to serve alcohol with breakfast.... *Tel 0207/ 253–4838. 115 Charterhouse St. EC1M, Farringdon tube stop. No reservations. DC not accepted. £*(**see pp. 53, 62**)

French House Dining Room. Above the Soho pub of the same name is a tiny, cozy dining salon, all red banquettes and mirror. It serves Scottish–French nursery food—crab and mayonnaise, giant lamb shanks, homemade cake, and ice cream.... *Tel 0207/437–2477. 49 Dean St. W1, Leicester Sq. tube stop. ££–£££* **(see p. 50)**

Fung Shing. London's Chinatown, though improving, is not a patch on New York's or San Francisco's, but this cool green place has authentic dishes like salt-baked chicken, fried intestines, and stewed duck with yam.... *Tel 0207/437– 1539. 15 Lisle St. WC2, Leicester Sq. tube stop. Reservations for dinner. £££* **(see p. 59)**

Galicia. In the Notting Hill netherlands is this easygoing family-run Spanish restaurant, with a tapas bar in front. The food is hit-or-miss—the more Iberian the dish, the better it is.... *Tel 0208/969–3539. 323 Portobello Rd. W10, Ladbroke Grove tube stop. AE not accepted. £–££* **(see p. 57)**

Le Gavroche. A center of gastroporn, run by the Roux brothers. Son of Albert, Michel Roux, Jr., wears the toque in this dark green subterranean *boîte*, applying the highest classical traditions to family recipes, in a menu littered with foie gras, truffles, and lobster.... *Tel 0207/408–0881. 43 Upper Brook St. W1, Marble Arch tube stop. Jacket and tie required for men. £££££* **(see pp. 54, 60, 62)**

Gay Hussar. Rub elbows with old Labour politicians and other lefty intelligentsia at this beloved old Soho Hungarian—

literally, since the enveloping banquettes are shared. Eat big: "heroic goose" is one dish, appropriately. Cream is a favored ingredient.... *Tel 0207/437–0973. 2 Greek St. W1, Leicester Sq. tube stop. £££* **(see pp. 46, 49, 51)**

Geales. One of the best places to get ye famous British fish 'n' chips, it even has a restaurant attached—they're usually takeout only. Ordering anything else would defeat the object, but you could try a side of mushy peas.... *Tel 0207/727–7969. 2 Farmer St. W8, Notting Hill Gate tube stop. AE, DC not accepted. No reservations. £* **(see p. 52)**

Gracelands Palace. Paul Chan is the only Chinese restaurateur to perform Elvis impersonations. It's not famous for food, so make sure you book on a show night.... *Tel 0207/639–3961. 881 Old Kent Rd. SE15, Elephant and Castle tube stop, then 53, 172, or 173 bus. AE not accepted. £–££* **(see p. 45)**

Green's Restaurant and Oyster Bar. A manly set of wood-paneled rooms provides a surprisingly sybaritic time among nobs and establishmentarians. Quaff champagne from London's best list and feast on oysters, grilled halibut, or calves' liver..... *Tel 0207/930–4566. 36 Duke St. SW1, Green Park tube stop. Jacket and tie for men. ££££*
(see pp. 45, 52, 54)

Indian YMCA. Imagine the dining hall at Delhi University—that's what you have here, only less humid. Get thoroughly, spicily fed for very little; stand in line for a meal ticket first.... *Tel 0207/387–0411. 41 Fitzroy Sq. W1, Warren St. tube stop. No reservations. No credit cards. £* **(see p. 59)**

The Ivy. There is nothing wrong with The Ivy: no nastiness toward nobodies, lots of eclectic dishes (blinis and caviar to shepherd's pie; irresistible Desserts R Us); and nearly every night, a glamorous feeling that you're in the place where things happen. You are.... *Tel 0207/836–4751. 1 West St. WC2, Leicester Sq. tube stop. Reserve several days ahead.* *££££* **(see pp. 44, 48, 49, 50, 62)**

Joe Allen. You could be at the original on Manhattan's 46th Street Restaurant Row, from the brick walls to the corn muffin with broiled chicken breast and salsa; from the cobb salad and warm banana bread with caramel sauce to the

THE INDEX

DINING

theatrical flock after curtain.... *Tel 0207/836–0651. 13 Exeter St. WC2, Covent Garden tube stop. No credit cards.* £££ **(see pp. 45, 48, 49, 50, 57)**

Kensington Place. Chef and newspaper columnist Rowley Leigh has had his turn as flavor of the month, but now he's settled into being just hugely liked by the legion of table-hopping regulars, who call this glass-walled echo chamber "KP." Grilled foie gras on sweet-corn pancakes is his signature appetizer.... *Tel 0207/727–3184. 201 Kensington Church St. W8, Notting Hill Gate tube stop. AE, DC not accepted.* £££ **(see pp. 50, 51, 62)**

Khan's. Most agree that this institution—a downmarket Indian version of Kensington Place—fails to deserve its popularity, what with barely civil waiters and only so-so curry. But it's still fun, huge, cheap, and good-looking, and curry nonexperts will be happy.... *Tel 0207/727–5420. Westbourne Grove W2, Bayswater tube stop.* £ **(see p. 58)**

Lauderdale House. An exquisitely situated park cafe, with crafts stalls, an aviary, and Highgate Cemetery next door. There's more big food here than is usual in such places— lasagna, homemade quiches, and so on.... *Tel 0208/ 341–4807. Waterlow Park, Highgate Hill N6, Archway tube stop. No credit cards.* £ **(see p. 47)**

Laxeiro. Well-established tapas bar, perfect for a bite during Sunday's Flower Market. The filet of beef with mustard dressing is a winner.... *Tel 0207/729–1147. 93 Columbia Rd. E2, Old St. tube stop. No credit cards. No bookings.* £–££ **(see p. 57)**

Lemonia. A big, beautiful, plant-filled, friendly pseudo-taverna on the street where the well-heeled locals go to get well fed. London Greeks are usually from Cyprus, and the personnel here are no exception.... *Tel 0207/586–7454. 89 Regent's Park Rd. NW1, Chalk Farm tube stop. AE, DC not accepted.* ££ **(see pp. 50, 54)**

Lisboa Patisserie. One-shop pit stop for Portobello shopping. Located on the hugely colorful Golborne Road. Try the *petiscos* (fried tidbits of prawn and fish). There are bakeries and delis next door.... *Tel 0208/968–5242. 57 Golborne*

Rd. W10, Ladbroke Grove tube stop. No credit cards. No bookings. £ **(see p. 46)**

Livebait. Adored by most, always packed, this tiled cafe-like place serves plain grilled fish, he- or she-crabs, cockles and mussels, and fanciful inventions like pork, cod, and fennel pie in brioche crust. House-baked breads and some prawns arrive unbidden.... *Tel 0207/928–7211. 43 The Cut SE1, Waterloo tube stop. Reserve several days ahead. AE, DC not accepted. £££* **(see pp. 44, 54, 56)**

Louis Patisserie. Hampstead's traditional Sunday pastime is standing on line for the Hungarian pastries Louis Gat's been baking for 35 years. Poppy-seed cake, baked cheesecake, and lousy coffee.... *Tel 0207/435–9908. 32 Heath St. NW3, Hampstead tube stop. No credit cards. £* **(see p. 63)**

Maison Bertaux. A little old Soho salon where you pick your pastry and have it brought to the plain upstairs room. It's in friendly rivalry with Patisserie Valerie (see below).... *Tel 0207/437–6007. 28 Greek St. W1, Leicester Sq. tube stop. No credit cards. £* **(see p. 63)**

Manze's. The most unspoiled pie and mash shop belongs to this eel dynasty.... *Tel 0207/407–2985. 87 Tower Bridge Rd. SE1, London Bridge tube stop. No credit cards. £.***(see pp. 51, 53)**

Marine Ices. Many flavors of ice cream and gelato are dispensed, along with sundaes and bombes, but you can also get a proper meal in this tiled and mirrored clean-cut parlor close by Camden Lock market.... *Tel 0207/485–3132. 8 Haverstock Hill NW3, Chalk Farm tube stop. No credit cards. £* **(see p. 47)**

Mash. Disappointing, overstyled restaurant/bar. Food is good, but portions are small.... *Tel 0207/637–5555. 19 Gt. Portland St. W1, Oxford Circus tube stop. ££££* **(see p. 52)**

Maxwell's. This place practically introduced the all-beef patty with correct fixings to London nearly a quarter-century ago. Avoid the Reuben sandwich.... *Tel 0207/836–0303. 8–9 James St. WC2, Covent Garden tube stop. DC not accepted. ££* **(see pp. 45, 47, 50, 57)**

THE INDEX

DINING

Mediterraneo. Good, simple Italian cooking is what's on offer, with seafood a specialty. Grilled scallops and king prawns with rosemary oil is highly recommended.... *Tel 0207/ 792–3131. 37 Kensington Park Rd. Ladbroke Grove tube stop. ££££* **(see p. 61)**

Melati. Pine-lined and brightly lit, this Indonesian is always full, as everyone in London returns to try to reach the bottom of the endless menu. *Tahu-telor* (bean curd omelet) is juicy, savory, chewy; the bizarre desserts of avocado, colored syrup, fruit, beans, and ice are an acquired taste.... *Tel 0207/734–6964. 21 Great Windmill St. W1, Piccadilly Circus tube stop. ££* **(see pp. 48, 59)**

Mezzo. Conran's Soho giant is best for the first-floor Mezzanine's bowls of Asian-ish, noodly, soupy food. Don't descend. The restaurant's overpriced, nonrelaxing, loud, and mediocre, and there's a music charge if you're still there after 10:30.... *Tel 0207/314–4000. 100 Wardour St. W1, Leicester Sq. tube stop. ££ (Mezzanine) ££££ (restaurant)* **(see pp. 51, 62)**

Misato. The best cheap Japanese in Soho. Bento and teriyaki are large, cheap, and reliable. Not much on atmosphere.... *Tel 0207/734–0808. 11 Wardour St. W1, Leicester Sq. tube stop. DC, AE not accepted. £–££* **(see p. 59)**

Moro. River Café/Eagle husband-and-wife chefs Sam and Sam Clark opened this instant hit in 1997. It's small, loud, casual, and serves Moorish-ish food—crab *brik à l'oeuf* (a Tunisian deep-fried pastry); casseroles of rabbit; spiced lamb brochettes.... *Tel 0207/833–8336. 34–36 Exmouth Market EC1. Farringdon tube stop. Reserve several days ahead. AE, DC not accepted. ££–£££* **(see pp. 44, 56)**

Nazrul. This very cheap, very basic BYOB Indian caff in the Brick Lane Little Bangladesh is more a cross-cultural thrill than a gastronomic one. But generations of students have loved it—join them if you're game.... *Tel 0207/247–2505. 130 Brick Lane E1, Aldgate East tube stop. No credit cards. £* **(see p. 59)**

Neal's Yard Dining Room. A burgeoning enclave of herbalists, masseurs, whole-food shops, and witchcraft-accessory stores, Neal's Yard is a Covent Garden must-see. This veggie cafe is a highlight, serving sampling platters of different

THE INDEX

DINING

world cuisines—African stews, Turkish mezze, Indian Thali.... *Tel 0207/379–0298. 14 Neal's Yard WC2, Covent Garden tube stop. No credit cards. £* **(see pp. 46, 53)**

New World. Cantonese dim sum are best in this gigantic place where trolleys whizz by. At peak times, about 700 people may be at their tables, clamoring for various little dishes of steamed goodies.... *Tel 0207/734–0396. 1 Gerrard Place W1, Leicester Sq. tube stop. £* **(see p. 59)**

Nobu. Order *omakase* (chef's choice) or Matsuhisa's patented "new style sashimi" (barely seared by hot, flavored oil) and be confused as to which city you're in. The blond-wood-on-white room is more L.A. Matsuhisa than New York Nobu, but the crowd's the same.... *Tel 0207/447–4747. Metropolitan Hotel, 19 Old Park Lane, W1, Hyde Park Corner tube stop. Reservations essential. £££££* **(see pp. 49, 54, 59)**

The Oak Room/Marco Pierre White. To the critics, and to himself, Marco Pierre White is London's best chef in the classical French style. See for yourself in this Belle Epoque room, but take out a bank loan first.... *Tel 0207/734–8000. Le Meridien Piccadilly Hotel, 21 Piccadilly, W1, Piccadilly Circus tube stop. £££££* **(see pp. 43, 45, 51, 61)**

Obalende Suya. East London Nigerian. Simple, cheap, and different—and worth the trek.... *Tel 0207/249–4905. 523 Kingsland Rd. E2, Dalston Kingsland BR and then bus. AE and DC not accepted. ££* **(see p. 60)**

192. A never-ending trend in Notting Hillbilly circles, this color-washed wine bar/restaurant has a long and interesting wine list, fashionable salad ingredients (gremolata, Jerusalem artichokes), and a high-decibel crush of cuties.... *Tel 0207/229–0482. 192 Kensington Park Rd. W11, Ladbroke Grove tube stop. Reservations essential for dinner. £££–££££* **(see pp. 44, 46, 49, 54, 57)**

L'Oranger. This offshoot of Aubergine is swanky yet friendly, romantic yet urbane. Marcus Wareing's fiendishly good Asian/French food—ravioli of duck confit in a consommé of cèpes, for example—reads well, eats even better.... *Tel 0207/839–3774. 5 St. James's St. SW1, Green Park tube stop. Reserve up to a month ahead. ££££* **(see pp. 44, 47, 50, 62)**

Organic Café. Queen's Park establishment, best for breakfast and good for veggies. Bit off the beaten track—but then that may be a bonus.... *Tel 0207/372–1232. 25 Lonsdale Rd. NW6. AE, DC not accepted. £–££* **(see p. 62)**

Orso. Joe Allen duplicated his Italian joint, Orso, from Restaurant Row, NYC, to rave reviews—the glossy clientele love the salads, pastas, pizzas, and the basement, which looks like the Medici family dungeon.... *Tel 0207/ 240–5269. 27 Wellington St. WC2, Covent Garden tube stop. DC not accepted. £££* **(see pp. 45, 49, 61)**

OXO Restaurant & Brasserie. To partake of the glorious river view, do you 1) get a bank loan for the unnecessarily pricey restaurant, or 2) suffer the hideous blue light in the brasserie? Summer solves the dilemma, with terrace tables. Eat pretentiously and fairly well (acorn-fed black pig charcuterie, etc.) in either.... *Tel 0207/803–3888. Barge House St. SE1, Waterloo tube stop. Reserve at least a week ahead. £££ (brasserie), £££££ (restaurant)* **(see pp. 44, 45, 50, 57, 62)**

Le Palais du Jardin. Wood-floored, halogen spotlit, this big brasserie is forever full because it's priced a notch below what it's worth. Volume can mar the service, and bits of the likeably hokey menu don't work, but there's always the shellfish stand.... *Tel 0207/379–5353. 136 Long Acre WC2, Covent Garden tube stop. ££–£££* **(see pp. 45, 60)**

Pasha. High-class Moroccan nosh where the food quality does not match up to the price tag, and the service is snooty. Not recommended.... *Tel 0207/589–7969. 1 Gloucester Rd. SW7, Gloucester Rd. tube stop. ££££* **(see p. 59)**

Patio. Cheaper than Wódka, with similar if less swanky fare. The set meal comes with vodka. The borscht is superb; the entrées are all very tasty. Excellent value.... *Tel 0208/ 743–5194. 5 Goldhawk Rd. W12, Goldhawk Rd./Shepherd's Bush tube stop. ££* **(see p. 46)**

Patisserie Valerie. The other essential Soho pastry shop, Valerie is older than Maison Bertaux, and bigger. Choosing the better *pain au chocolat* of the two is a toss-up.... *Tel 0207/437–3466. 44 Old Compton St. W1, Leicester Sq. tube stop. No credit cards. £* **(see p. 63)**

Pharmacy. Marco Pierre White's new kitchen was eagerly antic-ipated—but frankly not so well received. The food is good, but the decor is so bleak and functional that all but the most trendy (and unimaginative) diners have fled.... *Tel 0207/ 221–2442. 150 Notting Hill Gate. Notting Hill Gate tube stop. ££££* **(see p. 52)**

Pizza Express. London's favorite chain serves thin-crusted, always-good pies, with no surprises on top. The 10 Dean Street branch becomes a major jazz venue most evenings; this one is a former Victorian dairy, with its ceramic tiles intact.... *Tel 0207/636–3232. 30 Coptic St. WC1, Holborn tube stop. DC not accepted. Branches. ££* **(see p. 55)**

The Place Below. Inventive vegetarian food and a useful lunching place in the city, in the pretty crypt below a Wren church.... *Tel 0207/329–0789. St. Mary-le-Bow, Cheapside EC5, St. Paul's tube stop. Reservations for dinner. No credit cards. £–££* **(see p. 53)**

Pollo. In central Soho, on the Compton strip, here's another hangout for every student and clubgoer, and one they may never outgrow. Good pasta, nothing fancy, long lines, shared formica tables, great hubbub—this is Pollo.... *Tel 0207/ 734–5917. 20 Old Compton St. W1, Leicester Sq. tube stop. No reservations, no credit cards. £* **(see p. 60)**

La Pomme d'Amour. As the name suggests, the ambience here is tooth-achingly romantic. The interior is Provençal; the French food is classical-lite and often sublime.... *Tel 0207/229–8532. 128 Holland Park Ave. W11, Holland Park tube stop. Reservations on weekends. £££* **(see p. 50)**

Le Pont de la Tour. In Sir Terence Conran's "Gastrodrome" of converted-warehouse food emporia, just downstream from Tower Bridge. Salade niçoise or scallops with pancetta in the less swanky bar/grill is a relative bargain, but the shell-fish is hard to resist. Kill for a terrace table in summer.... *Tel 0207/403–8403 (restaurant), 403–9403 (bar). 36D Shad Thames, Butlers Wharf SE1, Tower Hill tube stop. £££ (bar/grill), £££££ (restaurant)* **(see pp. 45, 54, 57)**

Prêt à Manger. If you avoid these ubiquitous, PC, fast-food cafes because you're sick of the sight of them, you become eligible for the London Tourist Board Stupid Visitor award.

Thai chicken breast on malted-grain bread, chocolate fudge cake, fresh OJ is lunch for a fiver.... *Everywhere. Any tube. No credit cards. £* **(see pp. 46, 58)**

Putney Bridge. A neighborhood alternative to OXO, this spectacular glass-walled ship of a riverside place is packed with well-heeled locals schmoozing at the bar or eating home-pickled herring with crispy bacon or roast mallard in red wine sauce. Work up an appetite with a Thames towpath stroll.... *Tel 0208/780–1811. Embankment SW15, Putney Bridge tube stop. AE, DC not accepted. £££***(see pp. 44, 55, 57)**

Quaglino's. You feel like you're being filmed when you sashay down the sweeping staircase into this ocean liner of a restaurant, with its pillars and "Crustacea Altar." The food's OK—saffron crab tart, rosemary-crusted rabbit—but it's overpriced and the atmosphere is chilly, as Conran restaurants tend to be.... *Tel 0207/930–6767. 16 Bury St. SW1, Green Park tube stop. £££* **(see pp. 45, 51, 54, 62)**

Rebato's. In Vauxhall, south of the river, where no tourist has ever been, is this long-running real Spanish tapas bar/restaurant. The bar rotates 20-odd dishes (the *pulpo*—octopus—is essential); the restaurant serves Catalan and other regional dishes. Music on Friday and Saturday.... *Tel 0207/735–6388. 169 S. Lambeth Rd. SW8, Vauxhall tube stop. Reservations on weekends. £–££* **(see pp. 54, 57)**

River Café. This exceptional über-Italian salon began life as the staff canteen for Richard Rogers' architectural firm, run by his wife, Ruth, and her pal Rose Gray. They still run it, but it's become the style-setting place to go for sublime pan-Italian cooking.... *Tel 0207/381–8824. Thames Wharf, Rainville Rd. W6, Hammersmith tube stop and 11 bus. DC not accepted. Reserve a month ahead. ££££* **(see pp. 44, 47, 61)**

Rock & Sole Plaice. The claim to fame of this punning place: It's the only true "chippy" in midtown—and it's got sit-down tables. Only order fish 'n' chips.... *Tel 0207/836–3785. 47 Endell St. WC2, Covent Garden tube stop. £* **(see p. 53)**

The Room at the Halcyon. An exquisite little hotel by pretty Holland Park has a sun-filled basement restaurant with an atmosphere half genteel, half louche. Martin Hadden's fashion-plate food has been widely praised—ballottine of

quail with leeks and asparagus, or grilled sea bass with cele-
riac and a red wine sauce are typical of his considerable
style.... *Tel 0207/221–5411. 129 Holland Park Ave. W11,
Holland Park tube stop. £££* **(see pp. 49, 53)**

Rules. London's oldest restaurant looks Edwardian, though it
was founded in the Georgian age and renovated a moment
ago. Most customers are, predictably, doing business, or are
tourists who count as must-see being served pretty good
deer from Rules' Scottish estate, by waiters in long white
aprons.... *Tel 0207/836–5314. 35 Maiden Lane WC2,
Covent Garden tube stop. ££££* **(see pp. 51, 52)**

Sabor do Brasil. Brazilian specialties of wholesome stews with
beans and juicy meats are on the menu, but do ask for help if
you need it.... *Tel 0207/263–9066. 36 Highgate Hill, N19,
Archway tube stop. ££* **(see p. 60)**

St. John. An amusingly spartan refectory of metal-shaded bulbs
suspended from a soaring ceiling, iron rails, WHITE. While
getting noisily pissed on French wine, *Guardian* journalists
and architects devour Fergus Henderson's in-your-face food:
salted duck breast and red cabbage; deep-fried lambs'
brains; treacle tart..... *Tel 0207/251–0848. 26 St. John St.
EC1, Farringdon tube stop. ££–£££* **(see pp. 48, 49, 51)**

St. Quentin. Knightsbridge's long-running informal, classy
French place is so Parisian you feel you should get your
passport stamped at the door. Prix fixes are a great deal....
*Tel 0207/589–8005. 243 Brompton Rd. SW3,
Knightsbridge tube stop. ££–£££* **(see pp. 46, 51, 60)**

Sausage and Mash Cafe. Wide variety of bangers, spuds, and
sauces; interesting fishie and veggie ones, too.... *Tel 0208/
968–8898. 268 Portobello Rd. W10, Ladbroke Grove tube
stop. £–££* **(see p. 46)**

Savoy Grill. Power lunch is staged weekdays. Service is avuncular, discreet; each tycoon or bigshot has his own ban-
quette on the paneled perimeter, with nobodies plunked in
the center, staring at them.... *Tel 0207/836–4343. Strand
WC2, Aldwych tube stop. Jacket and tie required for men.
£££££* **(see pp. 45, 47, 48, 49, 52)**

Sea-Shell. One of the best-known fish 'n' chips joints in town, and one traditionally favored by taxi drivers; find it a little ways off Marylebone Road.... *Tel 0207/723–8703. 49–51 Lisson Grove NW1, Marylebone tube stop. £* **(see p. 52)**

Simpsons-in-the-Strand. Like eating on the set of a Merchant-Ivory movie: from the heavy oak paneling and Edwardian glitz to roasted animals circulating on silver trolleys.... *Tel 0207/836–9112. 100 Strand WC2, Aldwych tube stop. Jacket and tie required for men. £££* **(see pp. 52, 62)**

Soho Spice. Imaginatively designed, upmarket curry house. Mains are served *thali* style, with pots of vegetable curry, rice, and *naan* bread.... *Tel 0207/434–0808. 124–126 Wardour St. W1, Tottenham Court Rd. tube stop. £££* **(see pp. 49, 59)**

The Square. Philip Howard's inspired food is enhanced by perfect service. High-but-fair prix fixes attract the suit-and-tie, pearls-and-heels set.... *Tel 0207/839–8787. 6–10 Bruton St. W1, Bond St. tube stop. Reservations required. DC not accepted. ££££* **(see p. 47)**

Sri Siam. An elegant dinner that happens to be Thai in central Soho.... *Tel 0207/434–3544. 16 Old Compton St. W1, Leicester Sq. tube stop. £££* **(see p. 59)**

Star of India. Dine grandly upstairs on *shitar murg* (what? Tandoori pheasant?) amid Romanesque frescoes and live opera arias, while flamboyant owner Reza Mohammad table-hops.... *Tel 0207/373–2901. 154 Old Brompton Rd. SW5, Gloucester Rd. tube stop. £££***(see pp. 48, 55, 58)**

Sugar Club. The nondecor is no distraction from Peter Gordon's clean Med–Asian cooking (seared salmon on soba noodles, etc.). Nine out of ten cosmo Londoners call this their fave restaurant.... *Tel 0207/221–3844. 33a All Saints Rd. W11, Ladbroke Grove tube stop. Reserve at least two weeks ahead. DC not accepted. £££* **(see pp. 44, 55)**

La Tante Claire. Of all London's famous chefs, Gascon native Pierre Koffman is probably the most dedicated to his art; he's nearly always at his stove. If you're serious about food, this is the place.... *Tel 0207/352–6045. 68 Royal Hospital Rd. SW3, Sloane Sq. tube stop. Jacket and tie required for men for dinner. £££££***(see pp. 47, 60, 61)**

Tootsies. Burgers in two sizes, served with crinkle-cut fries, big salads, and banoffi pie and ice cream. Cheerful service in a place with vintage ads on brick walls.... *Tel 0207/229–8567. 120 Holland Park Ave. W11, Holland Park tube stop. No reservations. AE, DC not accepted. £***(see pp. 47, 50)**

Wagamama. Japanese noodly-soupy dishes, along with "health dishes" and sake and beer, are dished out in vast quantity at high speed. Also try the Soho Wagamama (tel 0207/292–0990. 10A Lexington St. W1).... *Tel 0207/323–9223. 4 Streatham St. WC1, Tottenham Court Rd. tube stop. No reservations. AE, DC not accepted. £* **(see pp. 48, 58)**

The Wine Factory. Pizza, pasta, and salads are good. The wine is excellent and extremely cheap (£5 up). For the boozy types among you.... *Tel 0207/229–1877. 294 Westbourne Grove, W11, Notting Hill Gate tube stop. £££* **(see p. 54)**

Wódka. Frequented by beau monde types, this minimalist-looking but warm-feeling spot has founded a new genre: modern Polish. Blinis are daubed with eggplant-olive mousse; pierogi are stuffed with veal and wild mushrooms.... *Tel 0207/937–6513. 12 St. Alban's Grove W8, Gloucester Rd. tube stop. £££* **(see pp. 44, 47, 49, 50, 54)**

Wok Wok. Inexpensive pan-Asian soups and noodles (Nasi Goreng are precisely cooked) in a bright, clean cafe.... *Tel 0207/437–7080. 10 Frith St. W1, Leicester Sq. tube stop. ££* **(see pp. 47, 58, 59)**

The Wren at St. James's. Cafe with an early (7 p.m.) closing and pretty churchyard tables. Simple, vegetarian, and cheap dishes; great cakes and pastries.... *Tel 0207/437–9419. 35 Jermyn St. SW1, Piccadilly Circus tube stop. No reservations. No credit cards. £* **(see pp. 53, 58)**

Yas. Cute, friendly, red-walled Persian oasis.... *Tel 0207/603–9148. 7 Hammersmith Rd. W14, Olympia tube stop. AE not accepted. Open till 5 a.m. ££* **(see p. 56)**

Yima. Wacky design makes this cheap Moroccan joint a feast for the eyes as well as the stomach..... *Tel 0207/267–1097. 95 Parkway, NW1, Camden Town tube stop. No alcohol allowed. ££* **(see p. 59)**

THE INDEX

DINING

Central London Dining

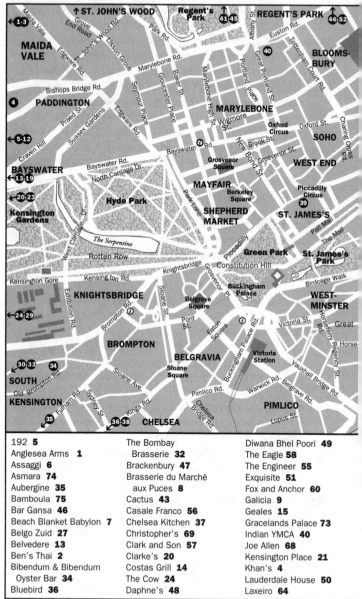

192 **5**
Anglesea Arms **1**
Assaggi **6**
Asmara **74**
Aubergine **35**
Bamboula **75**
Bar Gansa **46**
Beach Blanket Babylon **7**
Belgo Zuid **27**
Belvedere **13**
Ben's Thai **2**
Bibendum & Bibendum
  Oyster Bar **34**
Bluebird **36**

The Bombay
  Brasserie **32**
Brackenbury **47**
Brasserie du Marché
  aux Puces **8**
Cactus **43**
Casale Franco **56**
Chelsea Kitchen **37**
Christopher's **69**
Clark and Son **57**
Clarke's **20**
Costas Grill **14**
The Cow **24**
Daphne's **48**

Diwana Bhel Poori **49**
The Eagle **58**
The Engineer **55**
Exquisite **51**
Fox and Anchor **60**
Galicia **9**
Geales **15**
Gracelands Palace **73**
Indian YMCA **40**
Joe Allen **68**
Kensington Place **21**
Khan's **4**
Lauderdale House **50**
Laxeiro **64**

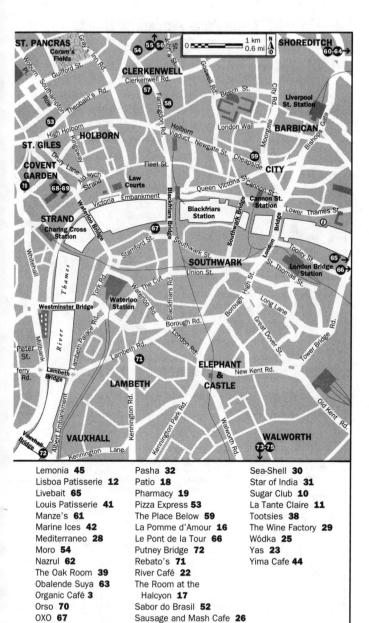

Lemonia **45**
Lisboa Patisserie **12**
Livebait **65**
Louis Patisserie **41**
Manze's **61**
Marine Ices **42**
Mediterraneo **28**
Moro **54**
Nazrul **62**
The Oak Room **39**
Obalende Suya **63**
Organic Café **3**
Orso **70**
OXO **67**

Pasha **32**
Patio **18**
Pharmacy **19**
Pizza Express **53**
The Place Below **59**
La Pomme d'Amour **16**
Le Pont de la Tour **66**
Putney Bridge **72**
Rebato's **71**
River Café **22**
The Room at the
  Halcyon **17**
Sabor do Brasil **52**
Sausage and Mash Cafe **26**

Sea-Shell **30**
Star of India **31**
Sugar Club **10**
La Tante Claire **11**
Tootsies **38**
The Wine Factory **29**
Wódka **25**
Yas **23**
Yima Cafe **44**

Mayfair, St. James's & Piccadilly Dining

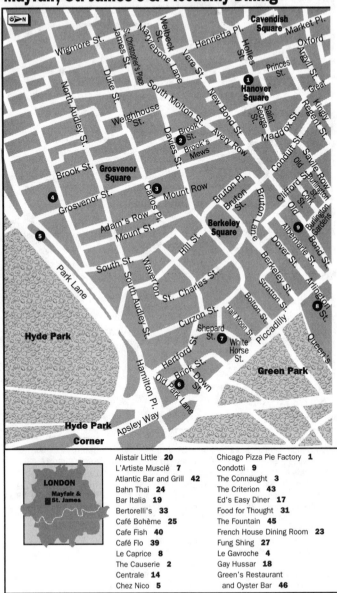

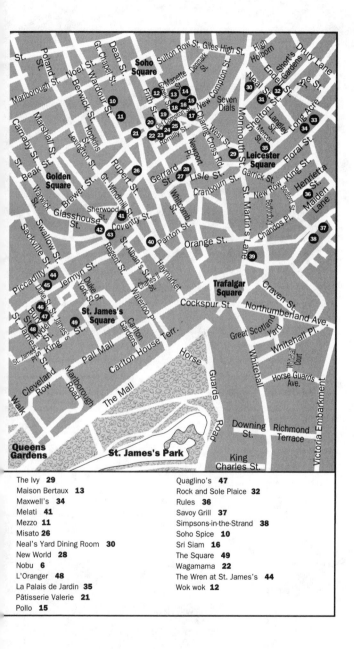

3

sions

As with any big-city vacation, a London visit demands a strategy—maybe more so than most, because this city's so big and sprawling, and there's so much to see. Decide what your priorities are. Does history turn you on? Is art your interest, or are you happiest just hanging? Time spent here is weather-dependent, too, since everything from the mood on the streets to the choice of activities changes in the rain. Fortunately, since rain can set in for three weeks without respite, there's plenty of scope for lousy weather.

Getting Your Bearings

The most important thing to do is to buy a copy of the pocket street atlas *London A to Z* (called simply "the A to Zed"— Londoners themselves always have one on hand). Buy one at the airport (every news agent in town sells it) and navigating the city will become much easier. What follows here is a potted geography of London, containing the only parts of the *A to Z* you need to know. **West End**: the center—you'd call this downtown. It's the younger of the two historic centers that London grew from, dating from 1050, when Edward the Confessor moved his court here and founded an abbey at… **Westminster** (SW1), where the Houses of Parliament are. **St. James's** (SW1), now a posh area of shops and hotels, is named after the (Tudor) Court of St. James's; dignitaries are still said to be ambassadors to St. James.

Mayfair (W1) includes Bond Street and Oxford Street and most of the grand hotels. **Soho** (W1), east of Mayfair, is a small quadrilateral packed with restaurants. **Covent Garden** (WC2) is the easternmost part of the West End, a target zone for shopping, museums, and restaurants. **The City** (EC2, EC4): The far older, Roman-founded center of town, dating from the first century A.D., it's still the financial center and still an autonomous entity. It is the City of London, with a capital *C*, a.k.a. "the Square Mile," although it isn't square. The Tower of London is here, also the Barbican and the Museum of London. In between Covent Garden and the City is the legal district, with…The **Inns of Court** (WC2), the historic barristers' quarters and courts. **Holborn** ("Hoe-bn") borders this, an in-between area; **Bloomsbury** (WC1) is also here, with the British Museum and the University of London.

West London: not West End. You'll spend a lot of time in neighborhoods like **Knightsbridge** (SW3), for Harrods, shopping, ladies lunching, and Hyde Park; adjacent **South Kensington** (SW5), for the big museums; residential **Kensington** (W8); and **Chelsea** (SW3, SW10), for King's Road shopping, riverside walks, and residential streetscapes.

Notting Hill (W11) is the hip place for restaurants and

Portobello Market; it's bordered by residential **Holland Park** (W11), which has a park and restaurants. **Hammersmith** (W6) offers pleasant Thames-side walks and some restaurants.

The East End: where Cockneys come from (which makes it the true center, some say), it's rough-and-tumble, with gentrified bits, and is definitely not touristy. Neighborhoods here include **Whitechapel** (EC1) and **Spitalfields** (E1), where you'll find an art gallery, Georgian houses, and Petticoat Lane market. **Clerkenwell** (EC1) and **Farringdon** (EC4) are not really East End—they're trendy, with restaurants. In fact, Clerkenwell is so trendy, it's become a dining, shopping, drinking, hanging, art- gallery destination in itself. Spitalfields, too, has spawned a youthful art subculture that's fast dominating the neighborhood. Check them out....The **Docklands** (E14), London's newest section, was reclaimed from industrial wasteland. A weird place. Adjacent **Canary Wharf** (E19) is a megabucks postmodern fake town containing Europe's tallest office tower, shops, and a concert hall.

North London: Here you'll find **Regent's Park** (NW1), which is not only a big green park that contains the zoo, but also the bordering streets, including Marylebone, with Madame Tussaud's. **Camden Town** (NW1) has the vast

The Thames's turbid waters

Many of England's most hallowed sporting events take place on the Thames, though few foreigners know of them. Who has ever heard of **Dogget's Coat and Badge Race**, for instance? It's a 280-year-old July boat race from Chelsea to London Bridge (to the pub of the same name), and it's actually the oldest event in British sport. English social calendars have the **Henley Royal Regatta** in Oxfordshire inked in for late June, as well as the **Oxford and Cambridge Boat Race** on the first Saturday in April. In the latter, the two ancient Ivy League of England universities send their best rowing eights to do battle on the Thames for what is nowadays known as the gin- sponsored **Beefeater Cup**. The Hammersmith Mall is a good vantage point for the race. The previous Saturday, there's a far lesser known, far more spectacular professional version of this, when about 420 eights row the **Head of the River Race**. Another water event, held two weeks after that, which, despite being the world's toughest canoe race, is even more obscure, is the three-day, 125-mile **Devizes to Westminster International Canoe Race**. Devizes is a cute town in Wiltshire. The race ends up at Westminster's County Hall at around 9 a.m. Monday.

DIVERSIONS | INTRODUCTION

Camden Lock market; it's a grungy youth mecca. Mainly residential **Islington** (N1), which borders on Clerkenwell, has restaurants and the Almeida Theatre. It's indicative of changing times that this arty area was the stamping ground of Labor prime minister Tony Blair, who sold his house for £615,000 when he came to power. Thatcher hailed from suburban Grantham. **Hampstead** (NW3) is a quaint, expensive hilltop village, hemming a vast heath.

South of the River: This evolving area first attracted Londoners to the **South Bank** (SE1), an arts complex that includes the National Theatre. Great views. **Bankside** (SE1) comes next, the site of the new Tate Gallery, the OXO Tower and its surrounding activity, and the Globe Theatre…. **Butler's Wharf** (SE1) has the Design Museum, "Gastrodrome," and Tower Bridge; **Brixton** (SW2) is a funky neighborhood for West Indian culture, youth, and some drugs.

Getting from Here to There

London is usually described as being a good walking city, but you must add a coda to that: It's great to walk from, say, St. James's up Bond Street and across Regent Street to Soho, but it's a day's hike to go on foot from Chelsea to Regent's Park. It's a very big place. Also, the climate has not been exaggerated in folklore: You may find your entire stay is too damp and chilly to enjoy even a window-shopping stroll. However, using your trusty *A to Z*, walking is still the best way to see the details that make London a fun city.

Taking a bus costs the same as the tube in money, but it can cost you much more time, especially during rush hour. The scarlet double-decker bus, however, is one of those features that scream "London," and when you're not in a hurry, the top deck provides the cheapest and best tour, especially for seeing residential nontourist neighborhoods. All you need to do is stay on the bus and when you've had enough, cross the street and take the same route back to where you started. Bus routes, of which there are some 300, are somewhat tough to decipher (pick up free maps at Travel Information Centres). The stops are marked by concrete posts, each with a white or red sign on top and a rectangular one at eye level. A white sign means the bus stops automatically; at a red "Request" stop, you have to stick out your arm to flag a bus down. The rectangular sign shows the major stops on the route. Pay the conductor, or (usually) the driver/conductor, as you board; tell him or her where you're going and you'll be told how much to pay.

"N"-prefixed buses are Night Service buses. They cost more and run less frequently—and it should be noted that one-day Travelcards are not valid on the Night Bus network.

The tube, a.k.a. the underground (but never called the subway by locals), is far easier than the buses to negotiate—once you've decoded the system's rather beautiful, stylized map (unchanged since Harry Beck designed it in 1933), usually posted on station walls at just the points where you need to consult it. Get your own free map from any station, along with a booklet that explains the ticket price system. As with buses, you can buy tickets for individual journeys, but you'll spend as much (£1.40 to £4.30) making one round trip—or "return"—as you would buying a **Travelcard**. The card works for buses and tubes (after 9:30 a.m. weekdays), and costs from £3.60 for a day. From £4.80, the **LT Card** is good for early risers because it's valid as long as the tubes are running—which is from 5 a.m. to about midnight. You can also get weekly and monthly Travelcards, and the **Visitor's Travelcard**, which you can buy only in the U.S. or Canada, for three, four, or seven days ($25, $33, and $53 respectively). Basically it's the same as the LT Card, with a booklet of discount vouchers thrown in. Get it from your travel agent or at BritRail Travel International (1500 Broadway, New York, NY 10036, tel 212/382–3737). Finally, a new discount scheme being run by London Underground allows you to

Pomp and circumstance
*Your basic London ceremony is the **Changing of the Guard** at Buckingham Palace, which gets really busy, even though they do it every day in summer at 11:30 a.m. (September through March, it's every other day, and heavy rain stops play). It may be a tourist cliché, but you cannot see a busby (the guards' fetching fur hats) anywhere else in the world. Another cliché of royal London is the **Crown Jewels**, housed in the **Tower of London**. Also at the Tower, and free, though you have to plan ahead, is the **Ceremony of the Keys**, a hilarious 10 p.m. locking-up ritual that has used the same script and costumes every night for 700 years (for tickets, send a stamped, self-addressed envelope, preferred dates, and number in your party to: The Resident Governor and Keeper of the Jewel House, Queen's House, HM Tower of London EC3). "Halt! Who comes there?" demands the Sentry. "The Keys," answers the Chief Yeoman Warder. "Whose keys?" asks the Sentry. "Queen Elizabeth's keys," answers the CYW, whereupon the Sentry dispenses with grammar and announces: "Pass. Queen Elizabeth's keys and all's well."*

DIVERSIONS — INTRODUCTION

buy a *carnet* of tickets—10 one-way tickets for £10, instead of £14. This makes sense if you're only using the tube once or twice a day, because the tickets have unlimited validity.

You have to take a taxi (a.k.a. a "black cab," although they're not always black) at least once during your stay in London, just for the experience. Unlike taxi drivers in most cities, London cabbies have "The Knowledge"—they must pass an exhaustive exam to get their license, for which they memorize every single cul-de-sac, one-way system, and clever backstreet route in the entire metropolitan area. Many are immensely proud of their encyclopedic memories and will regale you with information about the sights you pass. Taxis have chuggy diesel-powered motors, doctored-up steering that enables them to make U-turns on a dime, and signs that say "Sit well back in your seat for safety and comfort." They cost £1.40 for the first 528 yards, or 108 seconds, then 20p per 264 yards or 54 seconds, with surcharges of 10p to £2. A short ride—say from Harrods to the Dorchester—costs about £3.50, plus (15 percent) tip; something longer—say the Savoy to the V&A—will be at least double and is very dependent on London's erratic traffic flow. A taxi is available when the yellow For Hire sign on the roof is lit—though try an unlit one when desperate; sometimes they cruise without the light to skip drunks. Taxis have a way of not being there when you need them. When that happens, unlicensed **minicabs** come in handy. Minicabs belong to privately owned car services and must be ordered by phone or by stopping in at the office, since they can't be hailed on the street. The free phone number 0800/654321 connects you with the nearest minicab operator—or look for a flashing orange light by the side of many of London's busier streets. Restaurants will usually call their pet service for you; fares may be about 20 percent lower than black cabs, but be prepared to bargain and give directions.

The Lowdown

Is this your first time?... Where should you point your camera so that everyone knows you were in London? These places may be corny and crammed with visitors, but they are essential London sights. Start with the **Tower of London,** and to get an idea of the sheer age of this city, ogle the Beefeaters and the Crown Jewels. Next to that is the familiar silhouette of **Tower Bridge,** clad in Portland stone to make it seem as old as the neighboring Tower, though it is several centuries younger. Three more of the big sights are also strung along the banks of the Thames: **St. Paul's Cathedral**, **Westminster Abbey**, and the **Houses of Parliament**. The latter includes probably the most famous thing of all, the Clock Tower, better known as **Big Ben**. The adjacent Westminster Abbey was founded by Edward the Confessor in 1067 and was the structure around which London grew. St. Paul's, with its distinctive dome, is the great architect Sir Christopher Wren's masterpiece. If you had to choose only one museum, one art collection, and one park, you should make it the **British Museum**, the **National Gallery**, and **Hyde Park**, although you ought to also throw in one of the great Victorian museums of South Kensington—probably the **V&A**, which is almost never given its full title, the Victoria & Albert. It's not very cool to be fascinated by royalty, but, let's face it, we all are. Therefore you must look at the not especially beautiful **Buckingham Palace** (now actually open sometimes for limited tours) and catch the Changing of the Guard. Also, you'd better see **Trafalgar Square**, another of those London landmarks you've seen in a million establishing shots in movies and on TV.

London's special moments... It's small things and details that arrest the attention and take the breath away, and these have done it for us: the **Holland Park** peacocks' bedtime, when the big blue birds flap into the trees, screeching in their special way, while the sun sets over the ruins of the Jacobean mansion. Sneaking in to swim the **Serpentine** after midnight during a heat wave. Pacing the Glass Gallery walkway at the **V&A** on a day without school parties, or looking down on Waterhouse Way—the great hall at the **Natural History Museum**— when it's swarming with children. **Trafalgar Square** at 2 a.m. in December (when the giant Danish fir tree's up and lit), waiting for a night bus. The romantic bleakness of the **Thames** during misty gray weather, preferably far downstream. London's lovely when new segues into old, especially if you come upon an ancient thing when you weren't looking for it—like the **Temple of Mithras**, or parts of the **Roman walls** near the Museum of London, or the (not ancient) ghost of the rose window of **Winchester House**, on Clink Street by St. Mary Overie Dock. The very best London moments come out of just happening on odd little lanes and garden squares, mews and mansions, noticing details and watching life go on. If time is limited and you want the picturesque highly concentrated, try the **Inns of Court** and **Hampstead**.

Only in London... The most screamingly London activities have history, a special relationship with the weather, and are taken for granted by the locals. Qualifying on all counts is a **trip down the Thames**, starting at Westminster Pier, passing St. Paul's and the Tower on the left, the South Bank Centre on the right, and going under Tower Bridge to **Greenwich**. Disembark there and see the one and only **Prime Meridian**—the line which the whole world uses without a thought—from which all time is measured. Parks exist elsewhere, but few cities have palaces across the lawn. **St. James's Park** has two— the Buckingham Palace façade and the back of St. James's, while **Kensington Gardens** and **Kew Gardens** have an eponymous palace apiece. For assessing the current state of eccentric English behavior, **Speaker's Corner** is the lodestone, though a visit to **Sir John Soane's Museum** illustrates how London-style unconventionality looks when taken to its natural conclusion. **18 Folgate Street** shows the same thing, but being the brainchild of an American, suggests that London may be more a state of mind than a collection of historic buildings.

What if it's raining?... And it probably is raining (nobody lives in England for the climate). Museums are the obvious thing to do, and the **British Museum** (often known as the BM) is big enough—it has about 100 galleries—to keep you indoors all day. So is the **V&A**, but here you can do more than just look—this enterprising museum of decorative arts runs short drawing and painting courses attended by everyone from total beginners to art-school professors. Or you could just pig out at the V&A's Sunday morning jazz brunch and read the papers. Take in the Glass Gallery first, because it's so full of reflected light, you'll forget the awful weather. At the other end of town, the **Saatchi Gallery** is a good rainy-day place, since its acres of white space and red-hot contemporary works form their own micro-environment....But not nearly so effectively as the **London Aquarium**, where you are immersed in the waters of the world without getting damp. Afterwards, have a (bad) coffee in the cafe, and watch the rain teeming on the Thames, with the Houses of Parliament behind. Two art-laden houses in which to forget the gray clouds are that eccentric wonderland **Sir John Soane's Museum**, and the 18th-century version, the **Wallace Collection**. Satisfy a different sense during lunchtime concerts at the churches of **St. John's Smith Square** and **St. Martin-in-the-Fields**. (At the latter, descend to the crypt for the **London Brass Rubbing Centre** and fashion your own souvenir.) For some unpredictable and occasionally ghoulish live theater, drop in on a trial at the **Old Bailey**, the principal criminal courts of the land. Visiting the **Commonwealth Institute** is like fantasizing a round-the-world trip—the 51 independent members of the Commonwealth run from Vanuatu to Tuvalu, Kiribati to the Solomon Islands, and here they all are in hand-painted dioramas and displays of grocery packets and car tires representing exports. For my money, the best parts of this sweet museum are those that never got out of the '60s—though the first floor is now an interactive extravaganza, complete with a Malaysian helicopter ride, which is sure to beat anyone's rainy-day blues. If you must shop, the department stores are obviously good, but better still are the **Piccadilly Arcades** (see Shopping), which pre-date the oldest mall by about 150 years and are rather more posh. Have afternoon tea nearby, because it's always best in the rain.

When the sun shines... Anything you do in London on a warm, sunny day is enhanced at least 100 percent, since everyone's idiotically happy (this doesn't apply to heat waves, when complaints soon set in), but a **Thames boat trip** is the best of all. Take one downriver from West-minster to the Tower, or to **Greenwich**, but think twice before committing to a long (about three-hour) upstream trip—to **Hampton Court** or **Richmond**—since there are great stretches of nothing to look at. The **Regent's Canal** is fun, whether on foot or by canal barge; the prettiest parts are between **Camden Lock** (by the markets) and **Regent's Park**, and at **Little Venice**—an expensive, little-visited area of big white houses. The Canal Cafe Theatre (see Entertainment) can be your destination—or maybe you're here on the first weekend in May for the water fes-tival, the **Canalway Cavalcade**, a celebration with boat pageants, craft stalls, and a teddy bears' picnic (Blomfield Road, Little Venice, W9). The **London Zoo** is where everyone with children congregates on sunny days. Avoid it. Go instead to the recently renovated **Ham House** in

Richmond instead, with its great 17th-century gardens, or to the exquisite **Chelsea Physic Garden**, both in neighborhoods that cry out for aimless strolling. Or stay in **Regent's Park** and buy tickets for Shakespeare (usually one of the comedies) at the open-air theater. Another open-air theater is secreted in exquisite **Holland Park**, on a stage fashioned from the ruins of a Jacobean mansion blitzed in the Blitz. It stages opera and dance, all to the sound of peacocks screeching. For a theatrical experience without script, go to **Speaker's Corner**, by Marble Arch, where anyone is welcome to stand on a soapbox and hold forth. You may be lucky enough to catch a memorable loony—sunny days attract them.

The oldest things... London's very oldest thing has nothing to do with London, or with the person it's named after. It is the Egyptian obelisk by Victoria Embankment, **Cleopatra's Needle**, and it's around 3,500 years old. Younger, but still ancient, are two of the **British Museum**'s best treasures, the fourth-century **Mausoleum of Halicarnassus**, one of the Wonders of the Ancient World, and the controversial **Elgin Marbles**, carved on the Parthenon frieze in Athens in about 440 B.C. and named after the English earl who saved them from ruin in the early 19th century. They should now go back to Greece, say the Greeks—and many Brits. Only about 200 years younger than Cleopatra's Needle is the **Sarcophagus of Seti I**, which the fun-loving architect of the Bank of England, Sir John Soane, bought for a song and installed in his basement. His house, now **Sir John Soane's Museum**, outdoes the sculpture. As for indigenous things, you can see parts of London's Roman walls in and around the **Museum of London**, as well as the third-century **Temple of Mithras**, which was unearthed about 50 years ago. It's a little strip of history, although there's nothing but a boring set of foundations to look at. A better example of ancient/modern juxtaposition is the rose window of **Winchester House**, palace of the Bishops of Winchester until 1626, built into the St. Mary Overie Dock development adjacent to the bishops' old jail, now a museum called **The Clink**. Down in the law enclave, on High Holborn, you'll find London's oldest (1586) Elizabethan black-and-white half-timbered building, the **Staple Inn**, where wool traders were lodged and their commodity weighed and traded. Times have changed; now it's Ye

Olde Smoke Shoppe. The oldest part of the famously old **Tower of London** is the **White Tower**, which was the tallest building in London on its completion, in 1097.

The newest... The tallest building now is Cesar Pelli's 50-story tower at 1 Canada Square, the centerpiece of London's weirdest square mile, **Canary Wharf**. Modeled on an American downtown, this business district was reclaimed from slums as part of the 1980s redevelopment of the Docklands, but it never really fit in or took off; it makes for a really offbeat outing, from deserted mall to riverside pub. The newest train line in town, the Jubilee line extension, is the way to get there. Or see it all from the **Docklands Light Railway**. **Shakespeare's Globe Museum** is, in one sense, so new it's only just finished, but it's also London's oldest stage: a reconstruction of the Bard's "wooden O" on its original site (give or take a few yards), using original materials and building techniques. This great and slightly moonstruck idea of American film director Sam Wanamaker's has—incredibly—now become reality. Also just finished is the new **British Library**, which was originally supposed to open in 1991; it finally made it in 1997, when enough major design traumas were solved to decant 18-million-odd books into this orange-brick edifice by King's Cross Station. Many dislike the building intensely. A new(ish) building that everyone does like is the **Lloyd's Building**, most dramatic when seen at night. Its architect, Sir Richard Rogers, was also responsible for the Centre Georges Pompidou in Paris; he's adored in England. Clearly, however, the newest thing in London is the millennium...

The Millennium... London is the home of **Greenwich**, Greenwich is the home of time, and it's thanks to time that we have a millennium to celebrate at all. It is hardly surprising then to find the city chock-full of new and updated attractions to mark this auspicious anniversary. At press time only a handful of these had opened, most of which (countdown clocks) will be obsolete by the time this tome reaches your hands. The biggest and most celebrated, however, is the **Millennium Dome.** The Dome is situated in Greenwich (accessible by the Jubilee Line and the Docklands Light Railway-DLR) and promises great things. There are 14 themed zones celebrating British ideas and technology and examining the choices facing humankind in the 21st century and beyond—work, play, body, mind, beliefs, and the environment feature strongly. In the center of the Dome a show featuring 2,000 performers will play several times a day. Frankly, information on the Dome could fill a guidebook all by itself, so discover all you need to know at the official web site (www.dome2000.co.uk). Also worth a mention is the British Airways–sponsored **London Eye**, a 135-meter-high (450 feet) Ferris wheel—the largest observation wheel in the world—which will offer 30-minute "flights" on the South Bank of the Thames. For information on the countless other new millennium attractions, contact the London Tourist Board, which publishes a document called "London Millennium City," with further listings (London Tourist Board's "London Line 2000": 09068/66-33-44; www.LondonMillenniumCity.com).

Don't bother... Although it is an essential building to see from the outside, there's no reason to shell out close to a tenner to go inside **Buckingham Palace**. Since the Queen now has to pay taxes and Windsor Castle (which she much prefers) nearly burned down, she's opened her London digs to the public, though they've been a little cheap with the room selection—all you see are the most public of the public chambers: the State Dining Room, the Throne Room, the White Drawing Room (where the family firm congregates before appearing in public). Not the prettiest of palaces or the oldest (it dates from 1703), Buckingham Palace has been heavily remodeled and has only housed the monarch since Victoria moved in in 1837. **Madame Tussaud's** consistently appears on the top visitor volume list at about number 3, and there's a permanent line outside. This is a complete mystery. Inside are lifesize wax models of famous people and historic figures wearing their own clothes—which could be cute if this place didn't charge the greediest admission in all of London. Admittedly, Tussaud's also offers the Spirit of London animatronic "time taxi" ride, which isn't bad, and the Chamber of Horrors murderers' gallery is always a laugh. Also charging a high admission, and only intermittently worthwhile, is the **London Zoo**. We don't want to be mean to the dear zoo, which nearly had to close because of falling ratings, but things are a little tired in Regent's Park. The famous Elephant Pavilion, Penguin Pool, and Aviary are not as arresting as in their 1960s prime; there's no giant panda anymore; the new Children's Zoo's pathetic; and we're still waiting for the rest of the promised new stuff (a rain forest with tropical storms, for instance). However, when you yearn to look a gorilla in the eye, and want to be inches from a Bengal tiger's fangs (behind glass), the zoo is still great. Do go if you're here with young kids. Finally, **Harrods** as a tourist destination is overrated. Harrods is a shop. (See Shopping.)

Go out of your way for... If it's royal residences you're after, you can't get a better one than **Hampton Court Palace**, closely associated with our most colorful king—'Enery the Eighth, of the six wives and the weight problem, who moved in in 1525. The last monarch to call it home was poor George III, who decamped to Kew to go mad in relative peace. See one of the world's best privet mazes, the just-restored Tudor kitchens, the Great Hall, the Banqueting House, and—what you can't see at Buckingham Palace— the State Apartments, all in a beauteous Thames setting. It'll take the whole day, being 20 miles out of London, further still than Richmond. Ah, Richmond. **Richmond Park** is quite the wildest in London (well, near London), complete with herds of deer; you can go horseback riding here, or biking, or use it as an excuse for a few pints at the Cricketers, which is like a real village pub. Here also are two stately homes almost facing each other on opposite banks of the Thames: **Ham House** and **Marble Hill House**. At the opposite end of town, and not too much of a trek if you're staying in the West End, is **Hampstead**, a pricey village (think Marie Antoinette) high on a hill, with quaint cottages and Georgian mansions, expensive boutiques, **Keats House** and the Everyman Cinema (see Entertainment), branches of the Gap and McDonald's (how the residents hate that), and surprisingly bad restaurants. Hampsteadites are represented in Parliament by the Oscar-winning former actress Glenda Jackson, which should give you an idea of the tone up here. Some of the best things are the other wild park, **Hampstead Heath**, all rolling hills and dells and ancient woods, which leads to **Kenwood House**, worth seeing for two reasons: the Iveagh Bequest of paintings (Gainsborough, Rembrandt, Turner, Van Dyck, and Vermeer) and summer concerts at the open-air bowl—with tea at the cafe an important adjunct. The best and oldest necropolis in London is barely known by Londoners themselves: It's the 77-acre **Kensal Green**

Cemetery, best seen on the first Sunday of the month, when you can descend to the catacombs, guided by fanatic local historians dressed in black, who also point out the last resting places of novelists Thackeray, Trollope, and Wilkie Collins.

Inspiring spires... You don't have to be a believer to love London's churches. Many of the most loved are the work of the great architect so closely associated with London, Sir Christopher Wren, who rebuilt 51 of the 87 churches destroyed in the Great Fire of 1666. Twenty-five remain, plus, of course, his masterpiece, **St. Paul's Cathedral**. We'll leave it to other guides to do the exhaustive Wren tour, but here are a couple from the Wren stable. The usefully central **St. James's Piccadilly** was his last (1684) and his favorite; its spire, hit by the WWII Blitz, is now fiberglass. Learn to read the tarot, or hear a Handel recital here—the acoustics are angelic. **St. James's Garlickhythe** (with St. Michael Queenhithe and Holy Trinity-the-Less, to give it its full name) also has recitals, Tuesday lunchtimes, under Wren's highest ceiling (apart from St. Paul's). It's a handy stop en route to Shakespeare's Globe across the river and the adjacent **Southwark Cathedral** (more recitals here). A lesser building than Westminster Abbey, it's London's second-oldest church, with parts of its 12th-century self still intact. Shakespeare worshiped here, and his brother Edmund is buried here. It's also the only church with its own pizza cafe. The Cafe-in-the-Crypt at **St. Martin-in-the-Fields** is pretty good, too, and the church itself is fab. This one will look familiar to New Englanders, since James Gibbs's 1726 design—a sort of classical temple with a spire appended—was taken and run with by the early colonists; there are clapboard versions of it from Connecticut to Maine. The music program here is the best, apart from the June music festival at an exquisite church hardly anyone visits: Sir Nicholas Hawksmoor's 1728 **Christ Church Spitalfields**. Admittedly, it will hardly ever be open, until restoration is finished in the next few years, but go see the gorgeous colonnaded portico on a Brick Lane outing.

Who lived here?... The Bloomsbury Group still haunts London and exerts permanent fascination over the London intelligentsia. Virginia Woolf, the Bells and Dora Carrington, T. S. Eliot and E. M. Forster, John Maynard

Keynes, Lytton Strachey et alia lived, wrote, and regarded themselves highly in Bloomsbury. See the group plaque in, yes, **Bloomsbury Square**, and individual residences all over—e.g., **46** (Woolf, the Bells, Keynes) and **51** (Strachey) **Gordon Square**; and **52 Tavistock Square** (the Woolfs). All over town you'll see these blue plaques—cerulean ceramic disks that enable you to do your own dead-celeb spotting, and the "Blue Plaque Guide" is worth getting if you're serious about this. There are about 400 stuck on the house fronts of those who "enhanced human welfare or happiness." Some enjoy more than a plaque—like Charles Dickens, who lived in almost as many houses as he drank in (every London pub claims his patronage), though only one survived to become the official **Dickens House.** On the way to **Keats House** in Hampstead (where the young poet wrote "Ode to a Nightingale," only to expire two years later), you can visit with the Couch of Couches, behind which the father of psychoanalysis practiced, at the **Sigmund Freud Museum**. At **221B Baker Street**, Sherlock Holmes didn't ever actually live—it's the Abbey National Building Society's offices now—but there is a hokey **Sherlock Holmes Museum** that has appropriated the famous address, though it's really at number 237. The best former residence in all of London belonged to somebody you've probably never heard of, but don't miss **Sir John Soane's Museum**. The architect of the Bank of England, among other buildings, Soane had a wacky sense of humor, perfect taste in art, and the sensibility of a fairground proprietor. His house is full of higgledy-piggledy crazy perspectives, thousands of pieces of statuary, an ancient sarcophagus in the basement (for which he once threw a two-day party), an art gallery with fold-back walls, stained glass, and a joyous atmosphere. It simply must be seen.

Their Majesties live here... It's too early to say whether Diana's former home, **Kensington Palace**, is becoming the number-one place of pilgrimage, but signs are that the almost domestically scaled abode—which is still Princess Margaret's London address, but hasn't harbored a monarch since Victoria decamped from here to Buckingham Palace at her accession (1837)—is going to top the popularity hit parade (just like *Candle in the Wind 1997* did). K.P.'s none-too-successful run as primary royal residence started with the Bill and Hill of English monarchs, William and Mary (1689–1702). William fell off his horse and died of

pleurisy; Mary succumbed to smallpox; Queen Anne suf-
fered a fatal apoplectic fit due to overeating; so did George
I (he OD'd on melons); and poor George II met the most
ignominious Kensington Palace end—he burst a blood
vessel while on the royal commode. But by far the most
embarrassing monarch was "Farmer George," George III,
the mad one. He succumbed to lunacy and died at **Kew
Palace**, the most intimate and domestic and the least vis-
ited of all London's palaces, though lots of visitors stroll
around its gardens. We've already accused **Buckingham
Palace** of being the most boring of royal residences, but if
by some miracle you manage to wangle an invitation to
one of HRH's garden parties, you'd see it differently—
these are the best gardens in London. The Queen is in, by
the way, when the royal standard is hoisted, and is never
there when the place is open to tourists. Previous palaces
are much more fun: We've already mentioned the **Tower of
London** and **Hampton Court**, but we've not said a word
about another piece of Henry VIII's real estate, **St. James's
Palace**, the sweetest and smallest of all, and the one to
which visiting dignitaries are still sent. The catch is that it's
a completely private palace—all you can see is its redbrick
Tudor façade and some side views. You can't see the current HRH's gardens, but you can see her horses and
coaches at the **Royal Mews**. The present queen, however,
has nothing to do with the **Queen's House** in Greenwich,
which was designed by the great Inigo Jones for James I's
queen, Anne of Denmark. The first Classical building in
Britain, it is important and exquisite. Inigo Jones was also
responsible for all that remains of yet another of Henry VIII's
palaces—the one he died in—**Banqueting House**, the only
surviving bit of the labyrinthine Whitehall Palace, which
burned to the ground in 1698. **Windsor Castle** nearly
burned down, too, in 1992. You'll need an entire day for the
excursion to this place, reputed to be Elizabeth II's favorite of
her modest homes and now all back in working order, thanks
to funding by…you.

Modern art… Art lives. It starts in the national collections,
continues in galleries mounting exhibitions of new work,
and culminates in commercial spaces, avant-garde *boîtes,*
and independent dealerships. The **Tate Gallery** holds by
far the most important and extensive modern collection
in London, with too much art to be on display at one
time—they're constantly rehanging the stuff to give it all

a fair show…until the new Tate opens, when you'll be able to see it all. For now, be content here with the most famous works on perennial show. The **Hayward Gallery** in the South Bank Centre is also a major public space, with changing shows favoring sculpture and installation. Neither is especially known for taking risks, though the Tate causes an occasional outcry when it buys a controversial work (most infamously when it invested in Carl André's *Bricks*—a block of bricks). The **ICA** and the smaller but creatively curated **Serpentine Gallery** are nearer the cutting edge, but to see what's being produced by the latest generation of British artists, go to the **Saatchi Gallery**, whose advertising-maven founders were early champions of Damien Hirst and Rachel Whiteread, among other near household names. Ditto the East End **Whitechapel Gallery**, always worth the trek, with major shows and lecture series and a good cafe. Among newer outlying spaces, the **South London Gallery** and **gasworks** are worth checking out for exciting artists not yet sanctified by the establishment, especially the former. But if you want one neighborhood for unplanned, aimless gallery-hopping, then head to Notting Hill, where many tiny independent galleries around the Portobello and Goldborne Roads have led to a little scene like New York's SoHo. Way the hell out in the East End (combine it with the Whitechapel and the **Lux Cinema,** which promotes arthouse films and young filmmakers), the radical **Camerawork** is a standout for photography. Convenient to Covent Garden is the consistently excellent **Photographers' Gallery**, while the **Barbican**, the **National Portrait Gallery**, and the foyer of the **Royal Festival Hall** often feature photography exhibits.

The old masters… The world does not need another guide to the **National Gallery**, so we'll just point you in that direction and leave you to it. The adjacent **National Portrait Gallery** is not to be sniffed at, though it's smaller and has many obscure faces among the familiar figures. In this museum, who is represented is of more interest than how, and so some of the work is egregiously bad. That can't be said for the **Royal Academy**, housed in the imposing Burlington House, and center of the British art establishment—except during the annual Summer Exhibition, which consists of thousands of works, many unsolicited and chosen by committee in "auditions." The 1997 show, entitled *Sensation,* caused one, being a roundup of the young Brit artists (Damien Hirst, Sarah Lucas, Jenny Saville, Dino and Jake Chapman, Rachel Whiteread, etc.) whose in-yer-face style shocks the establishment, and was now, for the first time, in the establishment's establishment. Change at last, unlike at the wonderful **Courtauld Institute,** which still has the most impressive Impressionists and Post-Impressionists, plus the odd Rubens—speaking of which, don't miss the Rubens ceiling at **Banqueting House**. For viewing pleasure and fewer crowds, try the exquisite **Wallace Collection**, where the Fragonards, Bouchers, and Canalettos are displayed *in situ,* as if the Marquesses of Hertford who collected them were about to stroll by. Ditto the small, eccentric collection of paintings, starring several from Hogarth's Rake's Progress series, at **Sir John Soane's Museum**, with countless statues and architectural fragments and *objets* bursting the walls of this amazing house. Soane also designed what was London's first public art gallery, the practically perfect **Dulwich Picture Gallery**, little changed since its 1811 opening, right down to its parkland surroundings—a mere 12-minute train ride from Victoria for Tiepolo, Canaletto, Gainsborough, Rembrandt, Van Dyck, Poussin…and all for free on Fridays.

Art alfresco… Avert your eyes when passing the paintings hung along the sidewalks on Sundays at Green Park's Piccadilly border and the Bayswater Road edge of Hyde Park, unless you like paintings on velvet and watercolors of big-eyed kittens. But do keep an eye out for the ubiquitous statues on London streets. A random sampling: Hubert le Sueur's equestrian *Charles I* (on Trafalgar Square near Whitehall), reerected by his son, Charles II, nearly on the spot of his father's execution; *Oliver Cromwell*, who was responsible for that execution; Rodin's *The Burghers of Calais* (nearby, in the Victoria Tower Gardens); and a 600-year-old *Alfred the Great* (though nobody's quite sure of the exact date—Trinity Church Square SE1). Kensington Gardens has three famous sculptures: a rather splendid bronze horse and rider titled *Physical Energy;* a whimsical bronze *Peter Pan,* near the home of his creator, J. M. Barrie; and another children's favorite, the *Elfin Oak,* carved from a tree. The following are more obscure: *William Huskisson,* the first man to be killed by a train, confusingly dressed in a toga (Pimlico

Gardens); the pretty blue column of the *Thames Water Surge Shaft* kinetic water barometer—functional art at its finest and funnest (Shepherd's Bush Roundabout W11); the granite bedouin tent *Tomb of Sir Richard Burton* (the Victorian explorer, not the actor).

Won't bore the kids... That *Elfin Oak* statue stands just outside a much-loved playground in **Kensington Gardens**. You'll find a similar one in most parks, but the appropriately named **Holland Park Adventure Playground** is among the best. More touristy things that children like include the **London Zoo**, though it isn't much different from any other zoo; the **Royal Mews**, with all its ornate coaches; and the **Tower of London**, especially the gory parts. An expensive ticket, but worth the investment for older or tougher children, is the **London Dungeon**, a sort of extrapolation of the Tower's aforementioned gory bits crossed with Madame Tussaud's. Give overpriced **Madame Tussaud's** a miss, skipping next door instead into the **Planetarium**, with its laser shows and brand-new star projector. You'll think it better than the **Trocadero Center**'s plasticky high-tech shows; the kids may disagree. In similar vein, try steering them straight past the scary **Namco Station**, which sits outside the **London Aquarium**'s shop, its horrible lights blinking, disco music on a loop, video games bleeping. Ugh to London's least welcome new thing. The **Aquarium**, by contrast, is quite adorable, though Sea World alumni will probably scoff. It's small scale, but it takes you deep into its watery world. The museums to pick are: the **Natural History Museum** (especially the Creepy-Crawlies Gallery, the animatronic deinonychus, and the rain forest), and the next-door **Science Museum** (the computer and outer-space stuff is genius). Also a hit are the **London Transport Museum**, where you can climb all over old double-deckers and tube cars, and the far-off **Horniman Museum**, with its bee colony and musical instrument collection. Smaller kids will prefer the V&A's **Bethnal Green Museum of Childhood**, way out in the East End but so worth the trek—it has the world's biggest toy collection, including loads of fabulous dollhouses. If that's too far for you, try the quirky, labyrinthine **Pollocks Toy Museum**. **Greenwich** makes a great day out, not least because of **The Millennium Dome;** but you should save Greenwich town for another day—the Dome is so huge that it's impossible to do the other, smaller sights justice without a second visit. Arrive by boat, and save the *Cutty Sark* for last, because it's the children's favorite, though kids also like seeing the Prime Meridian, from which the world's time is measured, at the **Old Royal Observatory**—you can stand with one foot in each hemisphere. You can do a canal day, too, taking a **canal barge trip** from Little Venice to the zoo. You may be in luck and find the **Puppet Theatre Barge** is in town.

Photo ops... Essential tourist shots start with Trafalgar Square's **Nelson's Column**, which is the official center of London, or at least of the tourists mobbed by pigeons around its base. The rest of the shots you'd expect—Big Ben, Westminster Abbey, and Westminster Bridge (if its repairs are finally finished, which is unlikely)—you can buy on postcards. Well OK, shoot Big Ben from **the Aquarium's walkway**—because you'll probably be there in any case. But then why not look for something more subtle? The Chelsea Pensioners who live in Wren's stunning Palladian **Royal Hospital**, a retirement home for ex-soldiers, are just as picturesque as the Beefeaters, in their red-and-gold frock coats; then whiz over to the **Monument**, Wren's memorial to the people burnt in the Great Fire. Run up the 311 steps and snap a view from the top. In late May, bring lots of color stock to capture the great tumbling banks of rhododendrons in **Kensington Gardens**, **Holland Park**, and **Kew Gardens**. Get out a zoom lens for the façade of the **Natural History Museum**, with its intricate arches of fauna—extinct creatures to the right, living ones to the left. If, like John Lennon, you've wondered how many holes it takes to fill the **Albert Hall**, take a shot of this curious circular, domed Victorian building just off Kensington Gardens, then point your camera across the street toward the **Albert Memorial**, that ridiculously ornate love token from Victoria to her prematurely dead consort, now sparkling in brand-new gold leaf after at least a decade of restoration. Forget nearby Harrods—go instead to **Fortnum & Mason** (see Shopping) and get a shot of one of the city's sweetest clocks, featuring automata of the founders shaking hands on the hour.

A day of grunge... The **Thames Barrier** almost qualifies as part of this day, but we're looking more for the disreputable here. These are things to do when it's raining relentlessly, or for any day if you're under twenty. **Camden Lock** is the Seattle-in-the-late-'80s of London: It's a flea market that ate a neighborhood. On weekends, the High Street's crawling with whatever that slacker demographic's called now; other days, you can still get tattooed, pierced, or drunk, or buy a pair of cheap boots before installing yourselves in a smoke-hazed former Irish pub with a pool table. The other youth-centric neighborhood is in and around the **Portobello Market** in Notting Hill. More multicultural and cultural than Camden, it has small art galleries, ceramics, and ethnic artifact shops interspersed with vintage clothing and antiques. If you want true sleaze, **King's Cross** is the seediest part of town—prostitution, drug dealing, the lot. The nasty stuff happens around the British Rail Station, but there's another scene emerging behind it in the warehouses—a youthful, artsy one. Check listings for the current state of play. This day must end with a gig, for which you should consult the Nightlife chapter.

A day of romance... Whatever else you do, you must take tea, and no ritual is more genteel than the **Waldorf Tea Dance**. If performing the tango and the quickstep between scones hasn't yet become the fashion again, it soon will. You must also take a walk—perhaps along the **banks of the Thames** around Embankment, or on the south side along Bankside, going as far east as Tower Bridge and timing things to end up at **Le Pont de la Tour** (see Dining) for cocktail hour and oysters from the raw bar. Any park is also good, especially in summer after dark, and there's something very appealing about London's squares, with trees in the middle and maybe a row of Georgian houses around it. Try 18th-century **Kensington Square** (take Derry or Young streets off Kensington High Street), or the even older—laid out around 1670—**St. James's Square**, from which you could explore the wonderful perfumers and shaving-accoutrement emporia and shirt shops of Jermyn Street. Drop into the **National Gallery** and restrict yourself to the romantic works, like Velasquez's *The Toilet of Venus* (you'll recognize her when you see her), Constable's *The Hay Wain* (so bucolic), and perhaps some Canalettos, then on to the **Tate Gallery** for the splendid Turners in the Clore Wing. An evening stroll in **Hampstead** might segue into a show at the Everyman—one of London's last repertory cinemas, and a sweet old-fashioned place (see Entertainment).

DIVERSIONS | THE LOWDOWN

Alternatively, spend all day at the **Porchester Baths**, having massages and sweating in the steam rooms.

For gardeners... Serious horticulturalists should seriously consider coming to London in late May for the **Chelsea Flower Show**, one of the world's foremost flower shows. Failing that, try to be here in summer, when all the parks have flower beds stuffed full of color. In **Regent's Park**, St. Mary's Rose Garden is scented and formal, while **Holland Park** has its Dutch Garden, where the first dahlias in England grew in the late 18th century. With 60,000 plant species, **Kew Gardens** has something flowering in every season, and it also has the pair of spectacular 19th-century greenhouses, the Palm House and its corollary the Temperate House, which boasts the world's biggest greenhouse plant—a Chilean wine palm rooted in 1846. An even bigger greenhouse than those two is the 1987 Princess of Wales Conservatory, with its 10 separate climates. **Columbia Road Market** (see Shopping) has just the one English climate, but you can fantasize planting your ideal English garden among the overflowing, blooming stalls here and buy horticultural accoutrements to take home. Garden historians should under no circumstances miss **Ham House**, with its meticulously restored 17th-century grounds; they should also allow time to get to **Hampton Court** for the Elizabethan Knot Garden, the Great Vine, the maze, and the topiary—not to mention the only show that rivals Chelsea. Talking of Chelsea, the **Chelsea Physic Garden** is exquisite and educational in equal measure—medicinal plants are grown here alongside the country's oldest rock garden. There's one more stop on the itinerary: the **Museum of Garden History**, housed in a deconsecrated church and featuring another 17th-century knot garden for those who failed to get to Hampton Court.

For the impecunious... Get on a bus, climb the stairs to the top deck, show your Travelcard, and sit back for the least expensive grandstand tour in the land. Good bus routes include the **94** or **12**, for Hyde Park on the north side, Oxford and Regent streets, Piccadilly Circus, Trafalgar Square, and more; the **11** for Chelsea through to Knightsbridge, the City via Westminster; the **74** for the South Ken museums through Hyde Park corner past Lord's cricket ground to the zoo; and the **29** from Victoria or Piccadilly Circus through Bloomsbury and the British Museum to Camden Lock. Bus maps are free from major tube stations. Or else you could splash out and board a sightseeing bus. Outside Green Park tube stop is the best place to get one. They travel around The Sights, allowing you to hop on and off at will. You must be sure to have a **White Card** if you're going in anywhere—it entitles you to three or seven days of unlimited museum and gallery hopping, good at the following: Barbican, Courtauld, RA, and Hayward galleries, and at least eight museums, including Design, London Transport, London, Moving Image, Natural History, V&A, Science, and the museums of Greenwich. Pick one up at any of the above or at Tourist Info centers. They cost £16 for three days, £26 for seven days; family cards (two adults and four kids under 17) cost £32 for three days, £50 for seven days. Some of the best museums in town are free, too: the **British Museum**, the **National Gallery**, and the **Tate** charge no entrance fees, and there are always exhibitions up in the foyers of the **Royal Festival Hall** and the **National Theatre**, too (see Entertainment). If it's late June, look in *Time Out* magazine for news of the student degree shows, where you get the chance to buy work straight from the hands of art-schoolers at ridiculously low rates—the **RCA** (Royal College of Art, next to the Royal Albert Hall) is especially recommended. Lunchtime classical recitals in churches are another great delight of London to look up in the listings, and most are free or bargains. Hang around **Covent Garden** to see the buskers perform, too—if it's summer, the piazza may even feature a particularly juicy Pavarotti- or Domingo-laden opera production beamed onto giant screens, courtesy of the Royal Opera House. **Street markets** (see Shopping) are probably the best free shows of all, though; those and just walking. Traveling by foot is especially entertaining because you will get lost and you will find yourself in the mewses and alleys and streetlets with which London is crammed.

Go east... There's a strong argument that the East End is the true London, following the truism that a real Cockney must be born within the sound of Bow Bells (at St. Mary-le-Bow church). The "Melrose Place" of England, "Eastenders"—a cult in certain Stateside circles—is set here in the fictional, but recognizable, Albert Square. And this is Jack the Ripper land (take a Ripper walking tour if you must—there are loads of them). The neighborhoods of the east are gritty, so don't expect a smooth tourist patina. The major museum, the **Bethnal Green Museum of Childhood,** an outpost of the V&A, is a good excuse to head east, especially with kids in tow. There are several city farms nearby for them, too—**Spitalfields City Farm** has the works: sheep, goats, cows, horses, pony rides, and summer barbecues. Ask about the horse-and-cart local history tour. Instead of Tobacco Dock, which sounds fab with its pirate ships and crafts fairs but turns out to be one of the most depressing malls you've ever seen, go to **Spitalfields Market** (see Shopping), where there are great sports facilities and a little opera house, a farmer's market and good crafts shops. It's near Hawksmoor's **Christ Church,** which you should probably not make a special trip to see, since it's usually closed, but do check the concert schedule and watch for the two music festivals—this is a treat. Last but not least is one of London's most surprising and evocative museums, the **Geffrye Museum,** which contains a series of period rooms done with a Hollywood movie–scale attention to detail and authenticity. Unlike the stately homes you normally have access to, these interiors are domestic, so you get a powerful sense of how people lived. It's really out of the way but worth it if your interests tend at all toward popular and cultural history. Easier to reach (right next to the tube) is the **Whitechapel Gallery,** most certainly worth a special trip for anyone with an eye for the big-name and up-and-coming artists of now (plus it's got a pretty good cafe). From there, stroll down to the **Whitechapel Bell Foundry** to see the birthplace of the Liberty Bell (yes, that one) and Big Ben. Or nearly see— you can't go into the actual foundry, but you can buy a handbell and look at a cute little exhibit. The classic thing to do around here is to spend Sunday at the markets. Chief among them are **Brick Lane** and **Petticoat Lane**—which are adjacent to each other—and **Columbia Road Flower Market** (see Shopping for details). The last one is not much use for souvenirs, but it's full of local color and then some—and some of the shops that open only on market day (Sunday) are also well worth a gander. **18 Folgate Street** is the home of eccentric California-born Dennis Sever, who shares it with a ghostly fictional family named Jervis; once a month he leads the audience on a silent tour of the house to appreciate its style but above all to conjure up the atmosphere of Olde Worlde London. The

Georgian house is in perfect period style, outdoing the Geffrye Museum in authenticity, since Sever actually lives there, without electricity but with a butler in 18th-century livery.

The wild west... There's nothing wild about west London, actually, except for the neighborhood known as Notting Hill, which denotes the square mile or so around Portobello Road, the hippest part of the whole city. There is, however, plenty to keep you occupied in this quadrant, with many parks, great big beautiful (mostly Victorian) covetable houses, and shopping. The shopping is concentrated in expensive **Knightsbridge**, where **Harrods** is, and on into the Brompton Cross area of South Ken. (See Shopping for more on Knightsbridge's stores.) Walking around here will make you feel un-put-together unless you dress for it. You can enter **Hyde Park** from here, to visit the **Serpentine Gallery** or take a rowboat out on the Serpentine Lake. Heading west, the park becomes **Kensington Gardens**, whose Round Pond is a magnet for model-boat enthusiasts. Stay on the Knightsbridge (south) side of the park, walk it west, and you reach the road called **Kensington Gore** (which is what fake blood is called on British movie sets); turn south off it down Exhibition Road, and you're in what Albert, consort-of-Victoria, hoped would be a cultural fairyland, an Albertopolis of erudition and edification. His schemes were never fully realized—this boulevard down to the **Natural History** and **Science museums**, and the later **V&A**, is something of a wasted opportunity (try to get a coffee here and you'll understand). The Millennium Fund just might change all this. There's more shopping to be had on the formerly famous **King's Road**, the main drag of Chelsea, but it's long lost its louche edge. Chelsea today is best for strolling around, noticing all those north-facing oversize picture windows—the studios of the original bohemian artists who put Chelsea on the map late last century. These are now among the most expensive pieces of real estate in town. Visit **Carlyle's House** if you want to see how literary Victorians lived. Also here are the **Chelsea Physic Garden** and Wren's **Royal Hospital**. Way west off the tourist route, but worth it if you're in the mood, is the **Kensal Green Cemetery**.

Northern lights... The rival to that older necropolis is **Highgate Cemetery**, which is about as far north as you can go without leaving London. You've also heard a lot about Hampstead, which is joined to it at the hip, and has the edge for quaintness. Both are wonderful wandering neighborhoods, and there is, of course, **Hampstead Heath** to complete the package. Also there's Waterlow Park bordering on Highgate Cemetery, **Kenwood House**, **Keats House**, and much shopping in Hampstead village. Going down south—literally down the hill—you reach Camden Town, that youth mecca of markets and pubs and cheap leather jacket shops, which borders on **Regent's Park** (see Getting Outside), where the **London Zoo** is located. In Camden is the recently relocated **Jewish Museum**, where, as you'd imagine, the history of the Jewish in Britain is illustrated. From **Camden Lock** (see Shopping), you can stroll along the canal towpath in either direction—west to Little Venice (and the zoo) or east to King's Cross. There's the little **London Canal Museum** down that way if you want to learn more about the rather fascinating British waterways and the way of life they support.

Pearlies
After a big shipment of Japanese pearl buttons arrived in London in the late 18th century, street vendors from this area began sewing them onto their clothes. Fashion became identity in the early 19th century, when the vendors formed the Pearly Kings and Queens Association to meet the challenges they faced from those who would have them put off the streets. The original Kings were elected to help protect the vendors. The Kings and Queens still exist, as do the pearlies, but their roles are rather ceremonial now, and they act more as a loose charity than as a sort of street vendors' union.

The deep south... Ignore any South of the River snobbery and lame jokes you encounter (don't forget your passport, etc.)—there really is life across the Thames. **Shakespeare's Globe Museum** is finally finished, but still evolving. Catch one of the productions on the open-air stage in summer. Eventually, the new **Tate Gallery**, replacing the one in Pimlico, will be its neighbor. There's a rather vibrant putative arts scene emerging in the cheaper, bigger spaces south of the river—the **South London Gallery** could be called its hub, but check others listed in *Time Out* under "Alternative Spaces." After gallery-hopping, you could head to **Tower Bridge**, or lunch in one of the "Gastrodrome" restaurants (see Dining), or visit the **Design Museum**. Back upstream, the **South Bank Centre** is still vibrant and fun, fun, fun, after all these years—London's biggest arts complex, housed in a set of Brutalist-style buildings by Denis Lasdun (about to be covered in Richard Rogers's glass canopy, if the funding comes through) that have weathered into classic London landmarks. Between the Globe and the Olivier theaters, don't ignore **Southwark Cathedral**, as most people do. And **Battersea Park** is a charmingly different sort of place to visit—a place that will show you the echt atmosphere of South London like no museum can. See if you can't spot Battersea metamorphosing into the new Chelsea, with bars, shops, restaurants, and very, very young residents—hence "Nappy valley" for the area behind the Victorians along the south side of the park.

Street scenes... **Brixton** is the nearest thing to Caribbean culture in London and a magnet for the young and hip, though it helps to have a local show you around. **Notting Hill** is the posher version, and even hipper. It's *the* place—here are galleries, restaurants, gewgaw shops, antiques shops, clothes shops, all clustered around the hub of **Portobello Market** (see Shopping) and the formerly rasta ganja-dealing, now restaurant- and cafe-laden **All Saints Road**. You may hear people refer to this area as West Eleven, which is simply its post code. The three-day **Notting Hill Carnival**, held over the August Bank Holiday weekend, is the ultimate London street party; West Indian culture rules here, but it's eclectic. It once had a reputation for trouble, but the worst you'll have to deal with anymore is the crush of thousands of revelers. **Camden Town** is less groovy and cool, being more populated with high school kids and wannabes than are the Portobello environs, but it's not dissimilar. A million miles more touristy, and also dead central, is **Covent Garden**. Every single visitor to London swarms to the piazza, especially in summer, and actually, it's not too bad there—with its cobbled streets and picturesque converted market building, it's just a big ole mall. Nearby is **Leicester Square**, home of large movie houses and a backpackers' mecca. In London, which tends to close down early, it's nice to see so much life at night, and Leicester Square never gets too quiet. Next to that is **Soho** (see Nightlife).

Unwinding... When it's all been too, too much, try these relaxing diversions. London's best and finest-looking yoga school is the **Notting Hill Gate Life Centre**, where a very bendy staff teach various levels mainly of the energetic Vinyasa technique. Iyengar devotees should try the **Maida Vale Institute of Iyengar Yoga**. Head to **Bodywise** for a one-on-one refresher if you're already started on the Alexander Technique—others can get massaged (whether reiki-ed, shiatsued, or craniosacral-ed) at this East End holistic health center. If you're a fan of that other conscious body-realignment therapy, Pilates, the **Belsize Studio** won't disappoint.

The Index

Banqueting House. Inigo Jones (1573–1652) designed this Palladian hall, all that remains of Henry VIII's Whitehall Palace, which burned down in 1698. Charles I commissioned the Rubens ceiling in tribute to his father, James I.... *Tel 0207/930–4179. Westminster Embankment, Charing Cross tube stop. Open Mon.–Sat. 10–5. Closed Easter, Christmas, and at short notice for government functions (call first).£* **(see pp. 104, 106)**

Barbican. This mega arts complex is famed for being ugly and labyrinthine, but it's useful for the gallery, the theaters—this is home to the Royal Shakespeare Company—and the concert halls.... *Tel 0207/638–4141; Box Office*

0207/638–8891. Silk St. EC2, Moorgate/Barbican tube stop.
Open Mon.–Sat. 9 a.m.–11 p.m., Sun. noon–11 p.m. Ø
(see p. 105)

Belsize Studio. The Pilates body-alignment therapy is taught and practiced here.... Tel 0207/431–6223. 74a Belsize Lane NW3, Belsize Park tube stop.   **(see p. 116)**

Bethnal Green Museum of Childhood. The V&A's outpost focuses on all things small—dollhouses to teddy bears—illustrating the history of play.... Tel 0208/980–2415. Cambridge Heath Rd. E2, Bethnal Green tube stop. Open 7 days (except Fri.) 10–5:30, Sun. 2:30–5:50; closed May 1, Christmas, Jan. 1. Ø   **(see pp. 107, 112)**

Big Ben. The nickname for the bell contained in the Clock Tower of the Houses of Parliament, often applied to the clock and tower as well. You can go on a tour, but you need a proven interest in horology.... At the Houses of Parliament, Westminster tube stop. Ø   **(see p. 95)**

Bodywise. A holistic health center in the East End offers various massages, yoga, osteopathy, homeopathy, and other therapies, and classes in the Alexander Technique.... Tel 0208/981–6938. 119 Roman Rd. E2, Bethnal Green tube stop.
(see p. 116)

British Library. The new home of every book that's ever been published in England is now available for use, but not by you unless you can prove you have a good reason.... St. Pancras Rd. NW1. Ø   **(see p. 99)**

British Museum. The national collection of man-made objects from all over the world—some as old as humankind—fills 2.5 miles of galleries. Highlights are the Egyptian Rooms, including the Rosetta Stone and many mummies, and the Elgin Marbles.... Tel 0207/636–1555. Great Russell St. WC1, Russell Sq. tube stop. Open Mon.–Sat. 10–5, Sun. noon–6 p.m. Closed Good Friday, Christmas, Jan. 1. Ø
(see pp. 95, 96, 98, 111)

Buckingham Palace. The queen's London home has a limited opening for visitors, with the State Rooms open a couple months a year. Get in line early.... Tel 0207/839–1377.

THE INDEX

DIVERSIONS

Buckingham Palace Rd. SW1, Green Park tube stop. Open Aug.–Sept. daily 9:30–4 p.m. (ticket office opens 9 a.m.). ££ **(see pp. 95, 100, 104)**

Camerawork. An East End gallery with a political conscience, it shows the latest in "lens-based media".... *Tel 0208/980–6256. 121 Roman Rd. E2, Bethnal Green tube stop. Open Thurs.–Sat. 1–6 p.m., Sun. 12–5. Ø* **(see p. 105)**

Canal Barge Trips. Cruise the Grand Union and Regent's canals by barge, from Little Venice or Camden Lock to the zoo.... *Jason's Trip, tel 0207/286–3428, and London Waterbus Co., tel 0207/482–2660. Operates daily April–Oct.; Sat. and Sun. Nov.–March; call for details.* **(see p. 108)**

Canary Wharf. Futuristic new business district fashioned from a once-decrepit loop of the Thames called the Isle of Dogs.... *Tel 0207/418–2000 (general information), 0207/418–2783 (arts and events). Cabot Place E14, Canary Wharf tube stop. Ø* **(see pp. 91, 99)**

Carlyle's House. This pretty Queen Anne house, home of 19th-century author Thomas Carlyle and his witty poet wife, Jane, was a hub of Victorian literary life.... *Tel 0207/352–7087. 24 Cheyne Row, SW3; Sloane Sq. tube stop, and 11, 19, or 22 bus. Open April–Oct. Wed.–Sun. and bank holidays 11–5. Closed Good Friday. ££* **(see p. 113)**

Chelsea Physic Garden. An exquisite and educational garden of medicinal plants, herbs, shrubs, and flowers including England's first rock garden, dating from 1673.... *Tel 0207/352–5646. 66 Royal Hospital Rd. SW3, Sloane Sq. tube stop, and bus 11, 19, or 22. Open April–Oct., Wed. 12–5 and Sun. 2–6 (during Chelsea Flower Show, daily noon–5). £* **(see pp. 98, 110, 113)**

Christ Church Spitalfields. Nicholas Hawksmoor's 1729 masterpiece is one of only six London churches by the great associate of Wren's. Currently under renovation, its opening times are limited; for information on opening and services, call the rectory. The Spitalfield's Festival puts on classical concerts in June and December.... *Tel 0207/247–7202 (rectory), 0207/377–0287 (festival information). Commercial St. E1, Liverpool St. tube stop. Ø (concerts ££)***(see pp. 102, 112)**

Cleopatra's Needle. This granite obelisk, dating from about 1475 B.C., was given to the British by the viceroy of Egypt (named Mohammed Ali) in 1819.... *Victoria Embankment Gardens, Embankment tube stop. Ø* **(see p. 98)**

The Clink. The jail of the Bishops of Winchester's palace is now a black-walled dungeon museum, including a history of prostitution in the "Southwark Stews" and a reconstruction of a 1690 debtors' cell complete with Rat Man (a man who eats rats).... *Tel 0207/378–1558. 1 Clink St. SE1, London Bridge tube stop. Open 10–6, summer 10–10. Closed Christmas, Jan. 1. £* **(see p. 98)**

Commonwealth Institute. Dioramas upstairs create a lovable anachronistic tour around the 51 Commonwealth countries, with added arts events, all housed in a wacky blue copper-roofed building. The institute is being totally renovated and will not fully reopen until 2002.... *Tel 0207/603–4535. 230 Kensington High St. W8, High St. Kensington tube stop. Open Mon.–Sat.; call for times during renovations. Closed Christmas and Jan. 1. £.* **(see p. 97)**

Courtauld Institute. Impressionists and Post-Impressionists star in Somerset House, with plenty of Old Masters to back them up.... *Tel 0207/848–2526. Strand WC2, Holborn tube stop. Open Mon.–Sat. 10–6, Sun./holidays 12–6; closed Easter, Christmas, Jan. 1. £* **(see p. 106)**

Cutty Sark. One of the Greenwich delights, this handsome tea clipper is evocative of the seafaring life and has a wicked collection of figureheads.... *Tel 0208/858–3445. Cutty Sark for Maritime Greenwich Docklands Light Railway. Open 10–5 daily. Closed Easter, Christmas, Jan. 1. £* **(see p. 108)**

Design Museum. A temple to domestic and small-scale commercial design, from Corbusier chairs to the Coke bottle, this south-of-the-river museum (across Tower Bridge) always has special exhibitions on tap.... *Tel 0207/378–6055. Butler's Wharf SE1, Tower Hill tube stop. Open Mon.-Fri. 11:30–6, weekends 12–6. £* **(see p. 115)**

Dickens House. The house where he wrote *Nicholas Nickleby* and *Oliver Twist,* and finished *Pickwick Papers,* is a shrine to the great novelist.... *Tel 0207/405–2127. 48 Doughty St.*

WC1, Russell Sq. tube stop. Open Mon.–Sat. 10–5. £
(see p. 103)

Dulwich Picture Gallery. Reopens May 2000 after extensive renovation. Britain's first purposefully built art gallery, designed by Sir John Soane, has some 300 works on display, all Old Masters.... *Tel 0208/693–5254. College Rd. SE21, West or North Dulwich BR. Open Tues.–Fri. 10–5, weekends and holidays 11–5. Free on Friday. £* **(see p. 106)**

18 Folgate Street. Once a month, in a meticulously authentic early-18th-century house, Dennis Severs leads a small audience on a silent tour, breathing the atmosphere of Olde London.... *Tel 0207/247–4013. 18 Folgate St. E1, Liverpool St. tube stop. House open first Sunday of month. Performances first Monday of each month. Booking is required. ££* **(see pp. 96, 112)**

gasworks. One of South London's alternative gallery spaces.... *Tel 0207/582–6848. 155 Vauxhall St. SE11, Oval tube stop. Open Fri.–Sun. 11–6. Ø* **(see p. 105)**

Geffrye Museum. In a row of 18th-century almshouses, this perfect museum re-creates the sitting room of England from 1600 to 1950.... *Tel 0207/739–9893. Kingsland Rd. E2, Liverpool St. tube stop. Open Tues.–Sat. 10–5, Sun. and bank holidays 12–5. Ø* **(see p. 112)**

Greenwich. As well as being home to the Millennium Dome, this riverside town has many attractions—the *Cutty Sark* (see above), the Royal Naval College, and the Royal Observatory (see below). Get there via boat (see Thames boat trips, below) or the Docklands Light Railway.... *Island or Cutty Sark for Maritime Greenwich DLR stations or North Greenwich tube stop for the Dome.* **(see pp. 97, 99, 107)**

Ham House. This Stuart stately home, dating from about 1610, has 17th-century furniture and gardens; it's just been restored.... *Tel 0208/940–1950. Ham St., Richmond, Surrey, Richmond tube stop. Open April–Oct. 1–5 (closed Thurs. and Fri.). Gardens only 10:30–6. £* **(see pp. 97, 101, 110)**

Hampton Court Palace. Henry VIII's stunning Thames-side palace satisfies every royal fantasy—see everything from the King's Apartments to the Tudor kitchens, and maybe a royal ghost. The 1714 yew maze is famous.... *Tel 0208/781– 9500. East Molesey, Surrey, Hampton Court BR. Open March–Oct. Mon. 10:15–6, Tues.–Sun. 9:30–6; Oct.–March Mon. 10:15–4:30, Tues.–Sun. 9:30–4:30. Closed Dec. 24–26, Jan. 1. ££* **(see p. 101)**

Hayward Gallery. The art department of the South Bank Centre stages about five exhibitions of modern work per year.... *Tel 0207/261–0127. Belvedere Rd. SE1, Waterloo tube stop. Open daily 10–6 (until 8 p.m. Tues.–Wed.). Closed between exhibitions. £* **(see p. 105)**

Horniman Museum. An anthropological museum of great charm, best known for its bee colony and its 1,500 musical instruments.... *Tel 0208/699–2339. 100 London Rd. SE23, Forest Hill BR. Open Mon.–Sat. 10:30–5:30, Sun. 2–5:30. Ø* **(see p. 107)**

Houses of Parliament. "The mother of all parliaments" takes place in Charles Barry and Augustus Pugin's mid-19th-century neo-Gothic pile, complete with the famous Clock Tower (Big Ben). It's possible to visit both the House of Commons and the House of Lords in session, but the lines are long.... *Tel 0207/219–3000. St. Margaret St. SW1, Westminster tube stop. Open Mon. and Tues. 2:30–10, Wed. 9:30 a.m.–10 p.m., Thurs. 11:30–7:30, Fri. 9:30–3. Closed Easter week, May 1, July–Oct., three weeks at Christmas. Ø* **(see p. 95)**

ICA. The Institute of Contemporary Arts is secreted in a Nash terrace on the pink road and houses much arts action, with galleries, two small movie theaters, and a theater.... *Tel 0207/930–3647. The Mall, SW1, Charing Cross tube stop. Gallery open noon–7:30 (Fri. until 9 p.m.). £* **(see p. 105)**

Inns of Court. Legal London is still centered around the four Inns of Court: Gray's Inn, Lincoln's Inn, Middle Temple, and Inner Temple, the earliest part of which is the 12th-century Temple Church (not open to the public).... *Tel 0207/936– 6000. The Strand WC2, Temple EC1, Chancery Lane, Temple or Chancery Lane tube stops. (Law courts) Mon.–Fri. 9–4:30. Ø* **(see p. 90, 96)**

Keats House. The poet lived two years of his short life here in handsome Hampstead; today it also houses the Keats archives.... *Tel 0207/435–2062. Keats Grove NW3,*

THE INDEX

DIVERSIONS

Hampstead tube stop. Open Mon.–Fri. 10–6, Sat. 10–5, Sun. and holidays 2–5 (Nov.–March, opens at 1 p.m. week-days). Closed one hour at lunch; closed Easter, Christmas, Jan. 1. Ø **(see pp. 101, 103, 114)**

Kensal Green Cemetery. London's oldest necropolis (from 1833) is atmospheric and beautiful to behold; it contains the remains of Wilkie Collins, Thackeray, Trollope, and other great Victorians.... *Tel 0208/969–0152; 0207/402–2749 for tours. Harrow Rd. W10, Kensal Green tube stop. Open Mon.–Sat. 9–5:30, Sun. 10–5:30; tours March–Oct. Sat. and Sun. 2:30, Oct.–Feb. Sun. 2 p.m.; catacomb tours first Sunday of month. Donation requested.* **(see pp. 101, 113)**

Kensington Palace. The state apartments contain the pos-sessions of the Stuart and Hanoverian monarchs who called it home, the Court Dress Collection, and a re-creation of Victoria's childhood home. This being Diana's former home, the books of condolence have found their place of rest here.... *Tel 0207/937–9561. Kensington Gardens W8, High St. Kensington tube stop. Open daily 10–5 (10–4 in winter). ££* **(see p. 103)**

Kenwood House. A Robert Adam masterpiece, this Neoclassical villa on a heavenly hillside near Hampstead Heath holds the Iveagh Bequest, which has some important paintings, and the Hull Grundy Jewelry Collection. The lake-side concert bowl opens summertime.... *Tel 0208/348–1286. Hampstead Lane NW3, Archway or Goldens Green tube stop, and 210 bus. Open daily April–Sept. 10–6; Oct 10–5; Nov.–March 10–4. Closed Christmas Eve and Day. Ø* **(see pp. 101, 114)**

Kew Gardens. The 300-acre Royal Botanic Gardens grow 40,000 kinds of plants, and feature art galleries, a visitors' center, and—especially—the Victorian crystal-palace glasshouses, which make this a perfect day trip.... *Tel 0208/940–1171. Kew, Richmond, Surrey, Kew Gardens tube stop. Open daily 9:30–dusk. Closed Christmas and Jan. 1. £* **(see pp. 96, 108, 110)**

Kew Palace. There's even a royal palace in the gardens—the littlest and most picturesque one of all, where King George III lost his marbles.... *Tel 0208/332–5189. Kew,*

Richmond, Surrey, Kew Gardens tube stop. Open April–Oct. 11–5:30. £ **(see p. 104)**

Lloyd's Building. One of London's few amazing modern buildings, this 1986 inside-out glass-and-steel tower, headquarters of the venerable Lloyd's of London, is recognizably Sir Richard Rogers's (Paris's Pompidou Center architect).... *Tel 0207/327–1000. 1 Lime St. EC1, Monument tube stop. Closed to visitors.* **(see p. 99)**

London Aquarium. For Londoners, it's an especially surreal experience to penetrate the bowels of the former County Hall (seat of the Greater London Council) to find...fish! There aren't any really big ones, but there are luminous jellyfish, strokeable rays, an almost-real rain forest, a deep Atlantic pool of hound sharks and conger eel—and all set out on a downward spiral with marine sound effects and eerie subaqueous light.... *Tel 0207/967–8000. County Hall, Westminster Bridge Rd. SE1 7PB, Westminster tube stop (across bridge). Open 10–6 year-round. ££* **(see pp. 96, 107)**

London Brass Rubbing Centre. The crypt of St. Martin-in-the-Fields provides paper, metallic waxes, and instructions on how to rub your own replica of historic brasses.... *Tel 0207/930–9306. Trafalgar Sq. W1, Charing Cross or Leicester Sq. tube stop. Open Mon.–Sat. 10–6, Sun. noon–6. Closed Easter, Christmas, Jan. 1. Charge for rubbing.* **(see p. 97)**

London Canal Museum. This small museum in a former ice-storage house illustrates the life of the waterways of England.... *Tel 0207/713–0836. 12–13 New Wharf Rd. N1, King's Cross tube stop. Open Tues.–Sun. 10–4:30. £* **(see p. 114)**

London Dungeon. Ghastly and gory exhibits of torture and treachery, mostly from the Middle Ages, appeal greatly to horrid children. Complete with the "Jack the Ripper Experience".... *Tel 0891/600–0666. 28–34 Tooley St. SE1, London Bridge tube stop. Open daily April–Sept. 10–5:30; Oct.–March 10–4:30. Closed Christmas. ££* **(see p. 107)**

London Transport Museum. Better than it sounds, this has lots of hands-on stuff that kids like.... *Tel 0207/*

THE INDEX

DIVERSIONS

379–6344. 39 Wellington St. WC2, Covent Garden tube stop. Open daily 10–6, Fri. 11–6. Closed Christmas. ££
(see p. 107)

London Zoo. About 8,000 creatures call this home. You can get real close to the big cats, watch the penguin feeding, and ride a camel—all the usual stuff, but in a pretty setting.... *Tel 0207/722–3333. Regent's Park NW1, Camden Town tube stop. Open daily March–Sept. 10–5:30; Oct.–Feb. 10–4. Closed Christmas.* ££ **(see pp. 97, 100, 107, 114)**

Lux Cinema. This 120-seat cinema shows obscure films, hosts festivals, and showcases new talent; it also includes the first electronic art gallery in the United Kingdom and impressive projections.... *Tel 0207/684–0201. 2–4 Hoxton Sq. N1, Old St. tube stop.* £ **(see p. 105)**

Madame Tussaud's. A Frenchwoman learned to make wax-work people by fashioning death masks of aristocrats during the French Revolution, then inflicted this museum of the frozen famous on London. Expect to stand in line forever.... *Tel 0207/935–6861. Marylebone Rd. NW1, Baker St. tube stop. Open Mon.–Fri. 10–5:30, Sat.–Sun. 9:30–5:30. Closed Christmas.* ££ **(see pp. 100, 107)**

Maida Vale Institute of Iyengar Yoga. For Iyengar yoga classes, just as the name promises.... *Tel 0207/624–3080. 223a Randolph Ave. W9, Maida Vale tube stop.*
(see p. 116)

Marble Hill House. Built in the Palladian style for George II's mistress, Henrietta Howard, this Thames-side villa, nearly opposite Ham House, offers summertime concerts and teas in the Coach House.... *Tel 0208/892–5115. Richmond Rd., Twickenham, Richmond tube stop. Open daily April–Oct. 10–6; Nov.–March 10–4. Closed Christmas.* £ **(see p. 101)**

The Millennium Dome. Possibly the largest tourist attraction of all time is in Greenwich, home of time itself. With too many events and exhibitions to list, the Dome aims to be the spectacle to end all spectacles.... *Tel 0208/293–8375 (information), 0870/606–2000 (tickets). Greenwich SE10, North Greenwich tube stop.* £££ **(see pp. 99, 107)**

Monument. Christopher Wren's tower commemorates the terrible destruction wrought by the Great Fire of 1666. Climb the 311 steps for an iron-caged view of the City.... *Tel 0207/ 626–2717. Monument St. EC3, Monument tube stop. Open April–Sept. Mon.–Fri. 9–5:40, Sat.–Sun. 2–5:40; Oct.–March Mon.–Sat. 9–3:40. £* **(see p. 108)**

Museum of Garden History. The Tradescant Trust, named after great botanist John Tradescant (1570–1638), runs this museum in a deconsecrated church, complete with a 17th-century knot garden and the tomb of Captain Bligh of the *Bounty*.... *Tel 0207/401–8865. Lambeth Palace Rd. SE1, Lambeth North tube stop. Open March–Dec. Mo.n–Fri. 10:30–4, Sun. 10:30–5. Admission free; donations welcome.* **(see p. 110)**

Museum of London. This chronologically arranged museum gives the background to what you've seen outside. Highlights include a street of Victorian shops in the basement and a Great Fire diorama.... *Tel 0207/600–3699. 150 London Wall EC2, St. Paul's tube stop. Open Tues.–Sat. 10–5:30, Sun. noon–5:50. Closed Christmas, Jan. 1. £* **(see p. 98)**

National Gallery. The national collection of art is suitably impressive, full of familiar masterpieces. The Sainsbury Wing contains the early Renaissance collection, but the whole place spans 700 years, up to 1920.... *Tel 0207/839–3321. Trafalgar Sq. WC2, Charing Cross tube stop. Open Mon.–Sat .10–6, Sun. 10–6, Wed. 10–9. Closed Easter, May 1, Christmas, Jan. 1. Ø* **(see pp. 95, 105, 109, 111)**

National Portrait Gallery. Next to the National Gallery, this intimate and likeable museum, recently renovated, features portraits of the famous—and the forgotten—from medieval times to now.... *Tel 0207/306–0055. St. Martin's Place WC2, Charing Cross tube stop. Open Mon.–Sat. 10–6, Sun. 12–6. Closed Easter, May 1, Christmas, Jan. 1. Ø* **(see p. 105)**

Natural History Museum. Almost as big as the world it depicts, this is one of the best museums around, with its many renovated galleries.... *Tel 0207/938–9123. Cromwell Rd. SW7, South Kensington tube stop. Open Mon.–Sat. 10–5:50, Sun. and holidays 11–5:50. Closed Dec. 23–26. Kids free. ££* **(see pp. 95, 107, 108)**

Nelson's Column. The geographical center of London is this 145-foot granite column from which E. H. Baily's 1843 Admiral Lord Nelson keeps watch.... *Trafalgar Sq., Charing Cross tube stop. Ø* **(see p. 108)**

Notting Hill Gate Life Centre. Classes in Vinyasa yoga, Pilates, and tai chi offer a way to relax here.... *Tel 0207/221–4602. 15 Edge St. W8, Notting Hill Gate tube stop.* **(see p. 116)**

Old Bailey. Crowned by a gilded statue of Justice, this incarnation of England's Central Criminal Court was built in 1907 on the site of notorious Newgate Prison.... *Tel 0207/248–3277. Public gallery entrance at Newgate St., St. Paul's tube stop. Public gallery open Mon.–Fri. 10–1 and 2–4:30. No children under 14. Ø* **(see p. 97)**

Old Royal Observatory. This 1675 Wren-designed museum calls itself "the place where time begins," and it does not exaggerate. Here's where Greenwich Mean Time is measured from, and here's the Prime Meridian, which bisects the world.... *Tel 0208/858–4422. Greenwich Park SE10, Island Gardens DLR. Open daily 10–5. Closed Christmas. ££* **(see p. 108)**

Photographers' Gallery. Conveniently central place to see top shows of 20th-century photographic art.... *Tel 0207/831–1772. 5 Great Newport St. WC2, Leicester Sq. tube stop. Open Mon.–Sat. 11–6, Sun. 12–6. Ø* **(see p. 105)**

Planetarium. See the Star Show under this recently refreshed dome, in tandem with its neighbor, Madame Tussaud's, or on its own. There are outer-space exhibits too.... *Tel 0207/935–6861. Marylebone Rd. NW1, Baker St. tube stop. Shows every 40 minutes, Mon.–Fri. 12:20–4, Sat.–Sun. 10:20–5. Closed Christmas. ££* **(see p. 107)**

Pollocks Toy Museum. A pair of 19th-century houses are crammed to the beams with every conceivable Victorian toy.... *Tel 0207/636–3452. 1 Scala St. W1, Goodge St. tube stop. Open Mon.–Sat. 10–5. £* **(see p. 107)**

Puppet Theatre Barge. When it's open, this Little Venice floating marionette show is a treat for toddlers, with fairy tales, rhymes, and songs.... *Tel 0207/249–6876. Blomfield Rd. W9, Warwick Ave. tube stop. Call for times. ££* **(see p. 108)**

Queen's House. The first Classical house in England, designed by Inigo Jones for the Stuart Queen Anne of Denmark, is one of the delights of Greenwich.... *Tel 0208/858–4422. Romney Rd., Greenwich, Island Gardens BR. Open April–Sept. daily 10–5; Oct.–March, Mon.–Sat. 10:30–5:30, Sun. 2:15–4. Closed Christmas, Jan. 1 ££* **(see p. 104)**

Royal Academy. Eighteenth-century Burlington House is the venue for whichever major art show is in town, plus the vast and unruly Summer Exhibition.... *Tel 0207/300–8000. Piccadilly W1, Piccadilly Circus tube stop. Open 10–6. ££*
(see p. 105)

Royal College of Art (RCA). Designed by Hugh Casson, the building is worth a look from the outside; in fact you can rarely get inside.... *Tel 0207/590–4444. Kensington Gore W8, South Kensington tube stop. Ø* **(see p. 111)**

Royal Hospital. The retirement home Charles II founded for his best soldiers, designed by Wren, still houses some 400 quaintly costumed ex-servicemen, "Chelsea Pensioners." Parts are open to the public, more when it's Chelsea Flower Show time.... *Tel 0207/730–0161. Royal Hospital Rd. SW3, Sloane Sq. tube stop, and 211 or 239 bus. Open Mon.–Sat. 10–1 and 2–4, Sun. 2–4 (closed Sun. Oct.–March). Closed national holidays. Ø* **(see pp. 108, 113)**

Royal Mews. Not all the queen's horses are here, but many are, alongside her ceremonial fairy-tale coaches and carriages.... *Tel 0207/799–2331. Buckingham Palace Rd. SW1, Victoria tube stop. Open Mon–Thur 12–3:30 (Aug and Sept, 10:30–4). £* **(see pp. 104, 107)**

Saatchi Gallery. All the young turks of the British art scene are snapped up by the older turk advertising and media maven, Charles Saatchi, to be shown off in this glorious white-on-white space.... *Tel 0207/624–8299. 98a Boundary Rd. NW8, Swiss Cottage tube stop. Open Thurs.–Sun. noon–6. £* **(see pp. 96, 105)**

St. James's Garlickhythe. One of Wren's City churches, notable for its concerts.... *Tel 0207/236–1719, Garlick Hill EC4, Mansion House tube stop. Concerts: call to confirm. Ø*
(see p. 102)

St. James's Piccadilly. Another Wren church with a concert program, this one is improbably supplemented by various new-agey events, plus a crafts market and a cafe.... *Tel 0207/387–0441. Piccadilly, Piccadilly Circus tube stop. Call for hours. Admission free at lunchtimes; call for details.*

(see p. 102)

St. John's Smith Square. Yet another church with concerts, this one deconsecrated and next to Conservative Party head-quarters.... *Tel 0207/222–1061. Smith Sq., Westminster tube stop. Admission varies; call for details. ££* **(see p. 97)**

St. Martin-in-the-Fields. Not another one? Yes, another one, albeit the daddy of all churches-with-music, being the home of the famous gothic music combo, the Academy of St. Martin-in-the-Fields. The James Gibbs church is well worth visiting in its own right.... *Tel 0207/839–8362. Trafalgar Sq. W1, Charing Cross tube stop. Open Mon.–Sat. 10–6, Sun. noon–6. Admission charges sometimes apply; call for details. £* **(see pp. 97, 102)**

St. Paul's Cathedral. Wren's undoubted masterpiece is instantly recognizable as one of the defining buildings of the London skyline and should not be missed. Bribe the kids with the Whispering Gallery and its magic acoustics.... *Tel 0207/236–4128. EC4, St. Paul's tube stop. Open for sightseeing Mon.–Sat. 8:30–4, for worship Mon.–Sat. 7:30–6 and Sun. 8–6. £* **(see pp. 95, 102)**

Science Museum. Neighbor of the Natural History Museum, this is similarly popular with kids who love the interactive stuff and the cool Space Gallery and Flight Lab.... *Tel 0207/938–8000. Exhibition Rd. SW7, South Kensington tube stop. Open daily 10–6. ££* **(see pp. 107, 113)**

Serpentine Gallery. In the middle of Kensington Gardens is this space for avant-garde, modern shows.... *Tel 0207/ 402–6075. Lancaster Gate tube stop. Open 10–6. Closed between exhibitions. Ø* **(see pp. 105, 113)**

Shakespeare's Globe Museum. The late American film direc-tor Sam Wanamaker brought into being this ambitious pro-ject to re-create Shakespeare's original theater and add an overdue London center for Bard worship and study. Events and performances supplement the exhibition.... *Tel 0207/*

902–1500. New Globe Walk, Bankside SE1, Mansion House tube stop. Open Oct.–March 10–5; March–Oct. call for times. Closed Christmas. ££ **(see pp. 99, 114)**

Sherlock Holmes Museum. A hokey tourist trap cashes in on the fictional detective, but it's probably magnetic to addicts for the address alone.... *Tel 0207/935–8866. "221B" Baker St., Baker St. tube stop. Open daily 9:30–6. Closed Christmas.* ££ **(see p. 103)**

Sigmund Freud Museum. Where the father of analysis spent his final months—see The Couch, personal paraphernalia, and Freud events.... *Tel 0207/435–2002. 20 Maresfield Gardens NW3, Finchley Rd. tube stop. Open Wed.–Sun. noon–5. Closed Easter, Christmas, Jan. 1.* £ **(see p. 103)**

Sir John Soane's Museum. One of London's most wonderful museum experiences, the architect of the Bank of England's house is full of ancient sculpture, mad perspectives, juicy colors, and art, art, art. It makes you smile.... *Tel 0207/ 405–2107. 13 Lincoln's Inn Fields, Holborn tube stop. Open Tues.–Sat. 10–5. Closed Christmas, Jan. 1, and bank holidays.* Ø **(see pp. 96, 97, 98, 103, 106)**

South Bank Centre. Home of the Royal National Theatre, the National Film Theatre, MOMI, the Hayward Gallery, Royal Festival Hall, and other concert halls.... You're bound to end up here at least once. See Entertainment for more details.... *Tel 0207/928–2252. South Bank SE1, Embankment tube stop.* Ø **(see p. 115)**

South London Gallery. Hip youngsters show art here.... *Tel 0207/703–6120. 65 Peckham Rd. SE5; 12, 36, 171, or P3 bus. Open Tues.–Fri. 11–6 (until 7 p.m. Thurs.), Sat.–Sun. 2–6.* Ø **(see pp. 105, 114)**

Southwark Cathedral. London's second oldest church, after Westminster Abbey, is where Shakespeare worshiped, his brother Edmund is buried, and the founder of Harvard College was baptized. Look out for concerts.... *Tel 0207/ 367–6700. Montagne Close, London Bridge tube stop.* **(see pp. 102, 115)**

Speaker's Corner. Sunday afternoons, the northeast corner of

Hyde Park welcomes anyone with anything to say and a soapbox to stand on.... *Marble Arch tube stop.* **(see pp. 96, 98)**

Spitalfields City Farm. As it sounds, this is a farm in the middle of the East End, complete with cows, sheep, goats, and ducks, pony rides for kids, and summer barbecues.... *Tel 0207/ 247–8762. Weaver St. E1, Shoreditch tube stop. Open Tues.–Sun. 9:30–5:30. Call for tour information and closing times. Admission free, but charged for tours.* **(see p. 112)**

Staple Inn. Central London's oldest surviving Tudor (1586) half-timbered house was once the wool staple, where that commodity was weighed and traded.... *High Holborn. Holborn tube stop.* **(see p. 98)**

Tate Gallery. Britain's modern collections are vast, and not all on show at once—not until the new Tate is completed (scheduled for 2000). More than just modern work is here: The Tate holds the national collection of British painting from 1500 to now, plus the Turner collection, housed in the separate Clore Gallery.... *Tel 0207/887–8000. Millbank SW1, Pimlico tube stop. Open daily 10–5:50. Closed Christmas. Admission free; charged for special exhibitions.* **(see pp. 104, 109, 111, 114)**

Temple of Mithras. Mithraists preferred Christ's third- and fourth-century rival, the Persian god of light, Mithras, though it took archaeologists a while to figure that out from the foundations they unearthed here in 1954.... *Queen Victoria St., Mansion House tube stop.* **(see pp. 95, 98)**

Thames Barrier. Resembling a silver stretched-out version of the Sydney Opera House, the world's largest movable flood barrier will rise when needed to protect the city—the exhibition here tells how. There are riverside walkways.... *Tel 0208/305–4188. Unity Way, Woolwich SE18, Charlton BR. Open Mon.–Fri. 10–4, Sat.–Sun. 10:30–4:30. Closed Christmas. £* **(see p. 108)**

Thames Boat Trips. From April to October, many boats ply the Thames, most departing from Westminster Pier or Charing Cross Pier. Destinations downstream are the Tower, Greenwich, and the Thames Barrier, while the longer upstream trips end up at Richmond, Kew, and Hampton Court.... *Call for schedules (Westminster Pier to: Greenwich,* *tel 0207/930–4097; the Tower, tel 0207/930–9033; the Thames Barrier, tel 0207/930–3373; Kew Gardens, Richmond, and Hampton Court Palace, tel 0207/930–2062).* **(see p. 97)**

Tower Bridge. "Harry," an animatronic Victorian bridge worker, tells the story of the famous drawbridge, complete with the architect's ghost and a miniature music-hall show. Fab walkway views, too.... *Tel 0207/403–3761. Tower Bridge SE1, Tower Hill tube stop. Open daily April–Oct. 10–6:30; Nov.–March 9:30–6. Closed Christmas. ££* **(see pp. 94, 115)**

Tower of London. A prime sight, where London's history is oldest and bloodiest. The 900-year-old palace has the Beefeaters, countless firearms and suits of armor, and, of course, the Crown Jewels.... *Tel 0207/709–0765. Tower Hill EC3, Tower Hill tube stop. Open Mon.–Sat. 9–6, Sun. 10–6 (closes 5 p.m. Nov.–Feb.). Closed Christmas, Jan. 1. ££* **(see pp. 94, 99, 104, 107)**

Trafalgar Square. The geographical center of London has Nelson's Column and the National Gallery, and is also the hub for night buses and pigeons.... *Charing Cross tube stop Ø* **(see p. 95)**

Victoria and Albert Museum. The V&A is the national shrine of the decorative arts, with everything from the Shakespeare-immortalized Great Bed of Ware to last year's Lacroix and Comme outfits in the famous dress collection. Don't miss the glittering new Glass Gallery.... *Tel 0207/942–2000. Cromwell Rd. SW7, South Kensington tube stop. Open daily 10–5:50. Closed Christmas, Jan. 1. £* **(see pp. 95, 96, 113)**

Waldorf Tea Dance. Nothing is more bizarrely British than a three-course afternoon tea with a fox-trot on the side. Even more bizarrely, it's not touristy. Jacket and tie must be worn by the gentlemen.... *Tel 0207/836–2400. Waldorf Hotel, Aldwych WC2, Holborn tube stop. Open Sat. 2:30–5, Sun. 4–6:30. Tea costs £25, or £28 with a glass of champagne. £££* **(see p. 109)**

Wallace Collection. Four generations of Marquesses of Hertford assembled this exquisite collection of European paintings, Sèvres porcelain, Italian majolica, and Renaissance gold, all housed in a late-18th-century mansion. Don't miss Frans Hals's *Laughing Cavalier.... Tel 0207/935–0687. Hertford House, Manchester Sq. W1, Bond St. tube stop. Open Mon.–Sat. 10–5, Sun. 2–5. Closed Easter, May 1, Christmas, Jan. 1. Ø* **(see pp. 97, 106)**

Westminster Abbey. London's other ur-sight (along with the Tower), this Gothic church was founded by Edward the Confessor in 1067, on the site of a Saxon church. Inside are the Coronation Chair, on which six centuries of monarchs have been crowned, Poets' Corner, and many beautiful chapels, tombs, and monuments. Prepare to queue.... *Tel 0207/222–5152. Parliament Sq. SW1, Westminster tube stop. Open 9–4:45 Mon.–Fri. (nave & cloisters); royal chapels open Mon.–Fri. 9:30–4:45, Sat. 9:30–2:45, Sun. 2–5. £* **(see p. 95)**

Whitechapel Bell Foundry. The place where Big Ben and the Liberty Bell (yes, the cracked one) were forged, this working foundry has a little exhibition; phone and book to view the foundry.... *Tel 0207/247–2599. 34 Whitechapel Rd. E1, Aldgate East tube stop. Open Mon.–Fri. 8:30–5:30. Closed public holidays. Exhibition is free but foundry visits are charged. ££* **(see p. 112)**

Whitechapel Gallery. An excitingly curated space where group and solo shows of notable contemporary work are mounted in an Art Nouveau building.... *Tel 0207/522–7878. Whitechapel High St. E1, Aldgate East tube stop. Open Tues.–Sun. 11–5 (Wed. until 8pm). Closed Christmas, Jan. 1, between exhibitions. Ø* **(see pp. 105, 112)**

Windsor Castle. The queen's favorite weekend home—and the world's largest inhabited castle—makes for a classy day trip. See the State Apartments, St. George's Chapel (restored after the fire of 1992), royal carriages, and Queen Mary's Doll's House. The town of Windsor is cute, too.... *Tel 0175/383–1118. Windsor, Berkshire, Windsor & Eton Central BR. Open March–Oct. 10–5:30, Nov.–Feb. 10–4 (3 p.m. last admission). Closed for some state visits (call first). ££* **(see p. 104)**

Diversions in and Near the City

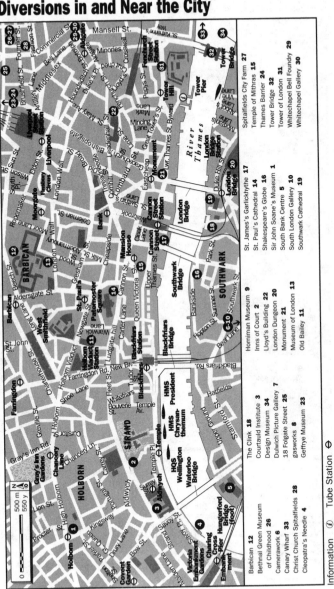

Barbican **12**
Bethnal Green Museum
 of Childhood **26**
Canarywork **6**
Canary Wharf **33**
Christ Church Spitalfields **28**
Cleopatra's Needle **4**

The Clink **18**
Courtauld Institute **3**
Design Museum **34**
Dulwich Picture Gallery **7**
18 Folgate Street **25**
gasworks **8**
Geffrye Museum **23**

Horniman Museum **9**
Inns of Court **2**
Lloyd's Building **22**
London Dungeon **20**
Monument **21**
Museum of London **13**
Old Bailey **11**

St. James's Garlickhythe **17**
St. Paul's Cathedral **14**
Shakespeare's Globe **16**
Sir John Soane's Museum **1**
South Bank Centre **5**
South London Gallery **10**
Southwark Cathedral **19**

Spitalfields City Farm **27**
Temple of Mithras **15**
Thames Barrier **24**
Tower Bridge **32**
Tower of London **31**
Whitechapel Bell Foundry **29**
Whitechapel Gallery **30**

Information ⓘ Tube Station ⊖

Central London Diversions

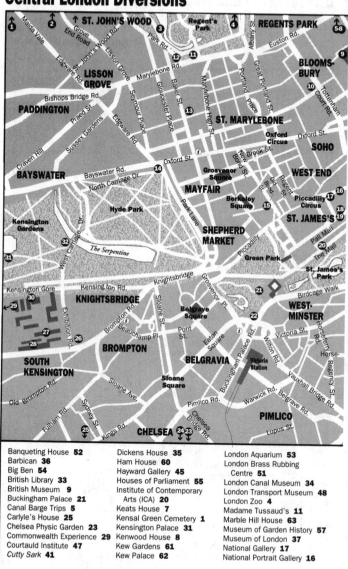

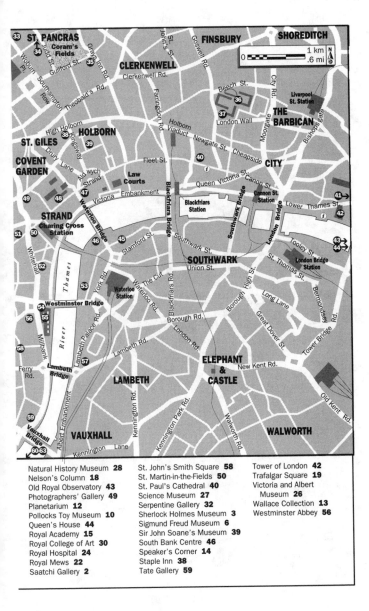

4

outside

If a Londoner
claims not to
work out at all,
believe it. The
aerobic Eighties
did hit town, but
then regular

vigorous exercise immediately regained its former English image of being punitive and faintly embarrassing. Now things have settled down somewhere between the two extremes. Games (you'd call them sports), however, are very popular, at least in theory, but although many Londoners indulge in tennis, squash, cycling, golf, etc., they do try not to wear the right clothes. Horse pursuits, cricket, and the burgeoning American sports—especially softball—are exceptions, where the correct kit is key. You'll be surprised by the dearth of physical activity in all those acres of park. You'll see a trickle of joggers and bladers, miniature packs of cyclists, and a few team games (many more on summer weekends), but even in those parks most conducive to sportif fun, the players amount to a mere fraction of the volume in, say, Central Park. This does mean more space for you....

The Lowdown

Parks to get lost in... The biggest by far are outlying **Richmond Park** and **Hampstead Heath**. Wild Richmond Park, in the upriver town of Richmond (reachable by British Rail or riverboat; see Diversions), even has a herd of deer, but its sports appeal is limited to horseback riding and biking; outside of Regent's Park, this is true of most of London's parks. Hampstead Heath, in the upscale north London neighborhood of the same name (Hampstead tube stop), is all rolling hills and dells and ancient woods, good for long contemplative walks. On summer evenings, you can pretend you're the poet Keats, who lived nearby, and sit under a tree listening for a nightingale's liquid warbling. In the center of town, **Hyde Park** and its neighbor (there's no dividing line), **Kensington Gardens**, are not at all small, and include Kensington Palace and the Serpentine Gallery, as well as lesser sights like the Italian Gardens and the Round Pond and a living grotto of green (near the Palace) that turns shrieking yellow in laburnum season. Farther out, but still central, is **Regent's Park**, medium-size (for London—that's huge for elsewhere) but impossible to get lost in, because it's encircled by a road and has a vast open space in the middle that makes it prime for sport. The London Central Mosque, due west, is an ever-visible navigation aid: See the sunset over its golden dome. The most heavenly of the heavily planted, landscaped, and manicured parks is **Kew Gardens**, far upstream (reachable via British Rail or riverboat—see Diversions). Wander through its great Victorian conservatories and their microenvironments from desert to rain forest, have a brush with the tropics under the palm trees, or spend an hour waiting for a fly to land in one of the carnivorous plants.

Perfect petite parks... Locals will swear their own green patch is the best, but they're lying unless they're from **Holland Park**. These grounds of a ruined Jacobean mansion are crammed with goodies, viz: an open-air theater mounting full-scale operas; a restaurant; a youth hostel; tennis courts; an adventure playground for kids; flocks of peacocks, guinea fowl, and Canadian geese; a Japanese water garden; a cricket pitch; an art gallery; rose gardens and rhododendrons; and the Commonwealth Institute. It's really pretty, too. If you're hitting the tourist trail in town and need respite, **St. James's Park** and, across The Mall, **Green Park**, are the obvious solutions, with the former the hands-down winner for scenery (lake, ducks, bandstand), and the latter having nothing but a weird new Canadian Air Force WWII memorial (southeast corner by Constitution Hill) and nice daffodils. The **Chelsea Physic Garden**, with its antique rock garden and medicinal herbs, is gorgeous. Be sure to get afternoon tea from the lovely volunteer ladies, then go say hi to the nattily dressed Chelsea Pensioners on the Royal Hospital grounds. Up north, between Regent's Park and the Heath, is pretty **Primrose Hill**, with panoramic skyline views, while even farther north is a bizarre slice of countryside, in the shadow of gasometers, on a street that's half light-industrial and half red-light, called **Camley Street Nature Reserve**. It's only worth visiting if you're at Camden Lock or doing a canalside walk, but it's guaranteed never to have appeared in a previous guidebook. This disreputable (and then some) neighborhood was going to be Europe's biggest building site until the plans fell through, and now it's spawning ever more interesting arts activity. It was the site of many a legendary "warehouse party" of the Ecstasy-enhanced late '80s.

Green escapes from tourism... Vest-pocket-size, but useful for the West End, are the squares **Berkeley**, where the nightingale sang, and **Grosvenor**, where the U.S. Embassy stands. From Trafalgar Square, head to the Thames for **Embankment Gardens**, or nip across the Hungerford Bridge (for trains and people only) to **Jubilee Gardens** for a peerless view, and summer events. From Westminster Abbey, visit Rodin's *Burghers of Calais* at **Victoria Tower Gardens**, on the riverbank just south of the Houses of Parliament. For a quick fix of green during a South Ken museum marathon, penetrate the heart of the **V&A**, where there's a surprising cloister garden. If you're not doing the museum, tell the ticket sellers and they should waive the donation "fee"—or you can walk brazenly past them. If you're at the British Museum, you're near the best hidden park of all: **Lincoln's Inn Fields** (if you're at Sir John Soane's Museum, you're in it), surrounded by the beautiful 17th-century courts of law. Farther north is the seven-acre **Coram's Fields**, next to which Charles Dickens lived (see his house at 48 Doughty Street) and drank (try the Lamb on Lamb's Conduit Street). **Covent Garden** is dense and annoying, but find escape in the secret garden behind the "actors' church," St. Paul's.

Best central jogging... Any Park Lane, Piccadilly, or St. James's hotel has **St. James's** and **Green parks** on the doorstep, which together provide one of the most scenic running tracks anywhere. A Green Park perimeter run is 1 mile, or you can start on Piccadilly, cross Green Park due south, and then run all around the St. James's lake and north back across Green Park for a 2-mile run. You'll pass the back door of St. James's Palace and the front gates of Buckingham Palace, and meet many species of ducks. If you're staying, say, at the Lanesborough or the Halkin, **Hyde Park** is your locale, as it is from any of the Knightsbridge hotels; starting from Hyde Park Corner, you'll find a loop right around the Serpentine, crossing its bridge and returning on the south shore, 2.5 miles long. Extend that into **Kensington Gardens** to circle around the northern section of the lake called the Long Water and you've clocked 3 miles. To run the entire 4.5-mile perimeter of both parks, follow the east and west paths, both called Broad Walk, the Carriage Drives on the north side, and the riding path, Rotten Row, on the south. Increase the cardio-intensity by running on the sandy horsetrack, but don't do this early in the morning, when the Household Cavalry exercise their hundreds of steeds. For an unusual and scenic 1-mile route, head out to Hammersmith to run from Hammersmith Bridge along the Upper, Lower, and Chiswick malls (nothing to do with shopping—rhymes with "pals").... If you'll never run alone, London's several running clubs welcome visitors, especially the long-established **Hash House Harriers**. Hyde Park is also the mecca for blading, which is fast catching on in London. Watch the poseurs by the Round Pond in Kensington Gardens or hire blades by the hour/day from any of the hire shops on Queensway, the road at the north end of the gardens. Most of these spots also offer tuition per hour by outrageously toned young'uns.

Balls... You're not going to be able to participate in the British national sports, **cricket** and **football**. ("Football" means soccer, but nobody calls it that. What Americans call football is known here as American football.) Both sports are played weekends in Regent's Park by teams of varying levels of seriousness; football's played in fall and winter, cricket starts in late spring. Cricket is relaxing to watch, however, even if you can't make head or tail of its rules; watch amateur games in Regent's Park, or more picturesquely in Holland Park, where there's a designated Cricket Lawn, with a tea room adjacent. Professional cricket is played at Lord's and the Oval (see Entertainment). In Regent's Park and also in Hyde Park, each spring you'll find a phenomenon of the last eight years or so—a ball game you'll be far more familiar with: **softball**. Teams are organized, but bring your mitt and you'll probably be able to pick up a game, especially Sundays in the middle of **Regent's Park**. Other softball parks include **Battersea** and **Clapham Common**. The standard's getting pretty good, especially since most serious teams include American expat ringers, who imported skills that have now been thoroughly absorbed. *Time Out* lists finals in the various leagues; the men's fast-pitch team the **Zoo Crew** and the coed slow-pitch **London New Zealand** are worth catching. The **Seymour Leisure Centre** (tel 0207/723–8019, Seymour Place W2) has a hall that accommodates many sports, from badminton to five-a-side football, from circuit training to, yes, basketball; there's also a serious amateur b-ball league sponsored by Budweiser. The games are played indoors, and though you're welcome to watch, you can see better at your local college gym. **Baseball** is played in Britain, but really badly. If you're any good, you'll probably be a welcome ringer, but you'd have to be desperate, because most teams are based in the suburbs. Two sports you can play here, and not at home, are **Australian Rules Football** and **Camogie**. The rules in the former are apparently very loose—this is like gridiron crossed with mud wrestling (look in *Time Out* for the latest team details). **Camogie** (call the Islington Camogie Club, tel 0207/272–1374) is the most Irish of sports, somewhere between hurling, lacrosse, and field hockey. **Field hockey** is called hockey here, and hockey is called **ice hockey**; on Hampstead Heath, there's a high-standard hockey pickup game you're welcome to join that's been going on every Sunday since WWII (about 300 yards past Whitestone Ponds; to the right, near the TV antenna. Bully-off at 3 p.m.).

Horsing around... The English really like messing around with large quadrupeds, and you can do it with them, either in the center of town or, in a bigger way, by taking a tube to the end of a line. In **Hyde Park** is **Rotten Row**, a sand-track artery with various sand-track arterioles, which has been handy for showing off an equestrian wardrobe and a perfect seat (that's your form on horseback) since Charles II laid it down. The name Rotten Row is probably a corruption of *route du roi*, in reference to that same king. Both **Ross Nye** (tel 0207/262–3791, 8 Bathurst Mews W2) and **Hyde Park Riding Stables** (tel 0207/723–2813, 63 Bathurst Mews W2) can mount you and send you off into the park, albeit not unaccompanied, not dressed in jeans, not Western style, and not at a gallop. It's a pretty formal affair, riding in London, and if you've never ridden English saddle, be prepared for a shock—it's utterly different and far more complex than Western saddle, though experienced wranglers should get the hang of the basics pretty fast. The **London Equestrian Centre** (tel 0208/349–1345, Lullington Garth N12) is a good place, even for beginners; all new riders get a half-hour assessment lesson. **Trent Park Equestrian Centre** (tel 0208/363–8630, East Pole Farm, Bramley Rd. N14) has the dual advantages of being on the end of a tube line (get the Piccadilly to Oakwood) and having acres of "green belt" protected countryside to ride around in in addition to two international-sized indoor schools. You'll leave the city far behind. Hard hats and shoes with heels are a requirement to ride in the U.K.; stables can usually furnish you with a riding helmet.

Teeing off... There are many fine courses in England, and world-class ones in Scotland; in London itself, however, the pickings are slim. Next door to Trent Park Stables is **Trent Park Golf Club** (tel 0208/367–4653, Bramley Rd., Southgate N14, Oakwood tube), about the only full-scale 18-hole round of golf so accessible to downtown. There are also two 18-hole public courses that are reputed to be quite good, a bit farther out at **Richmond Park** (tel 0208/876–1795, Roehampton Gate SW15); they can get mobbed, however, with all London's golfers. To pacify your addiction, try **Regent's Park Golf School** (tel 0207/724–0643, in Regent's Park, near the zoo), where you can schedule a lesson or just putt around on the small greens—including indoor ones—or drive in the ranges.

On the water... You can watch rowing on a stretch of the Thames from Hammersmith to Putney, but you can't easily do it yourself—real Oxford and Cambridge Boat Race–style rowing and sculling clubs are exclusively members-only. From a hut on the Lido, you can take out a recreational rowboat on the Serpentine during the months of April through September. Though it's a bargain (around £5 an hour to rent a boat), it is really just a pale imitation of river sculling. Sailing, believe it or not, is available in London on the Thames—at **Westminster Boating Base** (tel 0207/821–7389, 136 Grosvenor Rd. SW1) and in the 'burbs, on a big reservoir in the 23-acre **Lee Valley Park** (tel 208/531–1129, Banbury reservoir, Harbert Rd., Chinsford).

In the swim... Thanks to the climate, water is a natural element for the English, and there are consequently loads of public swimming pools in London, though surprisingly few hotels have pools. The best pools among the hotels we list in Accommodations are at **Grosvenor House** and **Kensington Close**; **Dolphin Square**'s is the most atmospheric, and often the emptiest, while the pool at the **Regent** is small and perfectly formed. Two unlisted (by us) hotels with spectacular pools are the **Meridien** (tel 0207/734–8000, Piccadilly, W1), whose megabucks health club is run by the swanky spa Champneys (which charges the megabucks membership of £110–275 per day, including lunch and a variety of pampering treatments), and the **Knightsbridge Berkeley** (tel 0207/235–6000, Wilton Place, SW1), with a roof that peels back to expose its elysian pool. If your hotel is poolless, search out a public pool—on the whole, they're well maintained and sparkling clean, though the chlorine level is high and the changing rooms are communal. The **Oasis** (tel 0207/831–1804, 32 Endell St. WC2) has two pools, including a not particularly beautiful outdoor one, and it couldn't be more central, but every office worker near Covent Garden seems to be there at lunchtime. A better outdoor option is the **Serpentine** Lido pool (Hyde Park W2, open May–September), with a chlorinated section. Join the mad Serpentine Swimming Club for a dip in the Serpentine itself at 6 a.m. every single day of the year; get on TV when they break the ice in the year's first freeze. Of course you don't need to join the club to swim here; it's open all year. As far as public indoor pools go, **Swiss Cottage** pool (tel 0207/483–4324, Winchester Rd. NW3) is one of the biggest (37 yards long) and conveniently next to the Swiss Cottage tube stop, but it gets crowded; the **Chelsea** pool (tel 0207/352–6985, Chelsea Manor St. SW3) is handy for aqua-addicts staying in the west. **Seymour Leisure Centre** (tel 0207/723–8019, Seymour Place W2) has a good, long, four-lane lap pool just a 15-minute walk from Marble Arch. Watch out for aqua-aerobics times, though—the Seymour Centre is well known for its fitness classes. You can also get your scuba diving certification here. You'd need a good reason to head all the way out to the enormous **Crystal Palace National Sports Centre** (tel 0208/778–0131, Ledrington Rd. SE19), and what better one than a game of underwater hockey? A.k.a. Octopush, this involves teams of six flicking a rubber squid along the pool bottom. It's a serious sport—just ask the reigning Southsea men's team or the sport's development officer (tel 01252/712–632).

Climbing the walls... London offers no mountains but several opportunities to learn to climb them—rock climbing and mountaineering are popular here, and Brits even win medals at it. Oldest and finest of the climbing centers is indoors at **Mile End Climbing Wall** (tel 0208/980–0289, Cordova Rd. Bow E3, Mile End tube). It's hidden deep in the East End (call for directions) but is worth the trek for rock fans, since there are faces with many features—for bouldering (traverse climbing), competition climbing (with moveable holds), high up, medium, easy, impossible, and completely upside-down climbing. There are lessons, and it's all extremely inexpensive. The newest wall is outdoors at the **Westway Sports Centre** (tel 0208/969–0992, 1 Crowthorne Rd. W10, Latimer Road), with a 15-meter tower, a 12-meter pyramid, and 30 meters of traversing wall. Both cost around £5 a day and offer lessons. One more wall is the 70-footer at north London's **Sobell Sports Centre** (tel 0207/609–2166, Hornsey Rd. N7, Finsbury Park), an all-around sports facility that offers plenty to do.

Downhill racing... What's that other mountain sport? Skiing! Why on earth would you attempt this in London? Because you can! At the **Hillingdon Ski Centre** (tel 01895/237069, Gatting Way, Uxbridge) there's a 170-meter main slope, floodlit for night skiing. There is no snow.

On ice... Time was, the Thames froze solid enough to situate a fair on top of it for the duration of winter. Even in the 1960s, the winters were reliably cold enough for the Round Pond in Kensington Gardens to be London's unofficial skating rink. Now, however, we must rely on a handful of artificially frozen rinks, of which **Queens Ice Skating Club** (tel 0207/229–0172, Queensway W2) is the largest, most central, and best known. There are disco evenings, classes, skate hire, but no ice hockey—for that you'd have to go way out to the 'burbs for a chance at playing (hockey skates are never allowed on regular rinks). If you're desperate, you can substitute stupid games like brushball (which is just what it sounds like), some of which aren't even played in skates, at the fall-and-winter-only **Broadgate Arena** (tel 0207/588–6565, 3 Broadgate EC2) in a swanky City business development. Broadgate, London's only outdoor rink, is small—as is the indoor rink at the **Sobell Sports Centre** (tel 0207/609–2166, Hornsey Rd. N7, Finsbury Park).

Getting fit indoors... London's hotels are not necessarily equipped with the kind of gym you expect for the rates they charge; see Accommodations for the few that offer exercise facilities. If a workout is essential to your well-being, try the following multipurpose gyms offering temporary memberships or drop-in rates. The trusty **Central YMCA** (tel 0207/637–8131, 112 Great Russell St. WC1), like every Y, is very well equipped, though frill-free. The bustling **Seymour Leisure Centre** (tel 0207/723–8019, Seymour Place W2, Marble Arch tube) has a gym, badminton, and morning-to-evening classes in the Move It program (the funk class, especially if Julie Corsair is still around, is a party). **Jubilee Hall** (tel 0207/379–0008, 30 the Piazza WC2, Covent Garden tube) actually feels swankier and more expensive than the public facility that it is; you can do tai chi or Thai kickboxing before your step class here. The still tonier **Gym at the Sanctuary** (tel 0207/240–0695, 12 Floral St. WC2, Covent Garden tube), attached to the women-only day spa of the same name (but operated separately), is a good place for women to sweat unobserved by Schwarzeneggers. The **Albany Fitness Centre** (tel 0207/383–7131, St. Bede's Hall, Albany St. NW1, Great Portland tube) is fun and full of weight-training hardware for would-be Schwarzeneggers, in a deconsecrated church. For dance classes, **Pineapple** (tel 0207/836–4004, 7 Langley St. WC2, Covent Garden tube) tends toward the aerobics, hip-hop, jazz side, as well as tai chi, while **Danceworks** (tel 0207/629–6183, 16 Balderton St. W1, Bond Street tube) has everything from ballet to salsa at all levels from beginner to pro, plus various aerobics innovations, like "Garage-Jam!" aerobics; professional dancers who need to take a class might try **The Place** (tel 0207/388–8430, 17 Dukes Rd. WC2, Euston tube), attached to the London Contemporary Dance School. Tennis players should gravitate toward two new indoor tennis centers built for the public, to bring the game out of the posh exclusive clubs: the **Islington Tennis Centre** (tel 0207/700–1370, Market Rd. N7), is a bit remote, though five minutes' walk from the Caledonian Road tube; and the **Westway Sports Centre** (tel 0208/969–0992, 1 Crowthorne Rd. W10), is nearer to downtown and close to the Latimer Road tube. For squash, head for **Finsbury Leisure Centre** (tel 0207/253–2346, Norman St. EC1), **Portobello Green** (tel 0208/ 960–2221, 3–5 Thorpe Close W10, Ladbroke Grove tube), or the **Sobell Sports Centre** (tel 0207/609–2166, Hornsey Rd. N7, Finsbury Park tube). Isola Akay's wonderful west London boxing gym housed in a church, **All Stars Gym** (tel 0208/960–7724, 576 Harrow Rd. W10; call after 5 p.m.) welcomes all contenders to its two-hour, no-contact KO circuit; it's the friendliest (stay for tea and biscuits after) and most challenging workout in town.

ping

If you ask us—

and you did—

London is one of

the world's great

shopping cities.

Sure, it's full of

the international

chain stores that make it difficult to discern which country you're in, but there are depths below that scummy surface—and some of the home-grown clothing chains are actually pretty good. Prices aren't the lowest, and the dollar–sterling exchange rate periodically makes shopping London fiendishly expensive, but you make up for that with quality and selection.

What to Buy

Get antiques, or just lust after them. If you're not rich, trawl flea markets and so-called junk shops for treasure. Stock up on books—antiquarian, out-of-print, and those written by European and British writers without a U.S. publisher—then lug them home. Some of the world's best porcelain and china is indigenous to England—Royal Doulton, Spode, and Wedgwood spring to mind—and London's good for rustic European tableware, too. Buy clothes here. The big European designers have at least a store each, as do the Americans, but British designers you may not have heard of will surprise you, and they're perfectionists with the finish. Traditional English tailoring is famous, of course. Savile Row (it rhymes with "gravel") is the apogee, but look at the less exorbitant (but still not cheap) huntin', shootin', and fishin' outfits, elements of which work with any wardrobe. Ralph Lauren, eat your heart out. At the other extreme, look for street clothes—London's been famous for funky since the mods put Carnaby Street on the map. The word "crafts" conjures images of crocheted granola Birkenstocks, but really means acres of exciting, handmade design wares that you can only find here. Also buy tea—loose leaf, not bags—and a teapot and strainer. Other food gifts and treats are cheeses, especially whole mini-cheddars and stiltons, and the oatcakes to accompany them; then there are pork pies, Thornton's special toffee, and anything from Marks & Spencer, Waitrose, or Sainsbury's (in order of decreasing poshness) for the packaging. This is a nation of gardeners. If you share that obsession, get paraphernalia here.

Target Zones

There are so many shopping districts; here's a whizz through. The **West End**'s artery is the busiest street in town: **Oxford Street**, with chain stores and tacky closeout stores, plus good department stores and two swanky fashion streets on the edge (**South Molton Street** and **St. Christopher's Place**). Around the corner is **Bond Street** (New, segueing into Old), famous for top-dollar clothes, art, jewelry. **Savile Row**, **St. James's**, and the arcades of **Piccadilly** (the sine qua non of window shopping) also count as West End, as does **Regent Street** (for big stores **Liberty** and **Hamleys**, and the little streets around **Soho** and **Carnaby Street**, full of T-shirts and sneakers, plus more interesting designer-type boutiques. **Covent Garden** is sort of counted as West End, but is a very fruitful shopping district in its own right. It has all the better clothing chains, plus market stalls, and many little boutiques, with the bookstores of **Charing Cross Road** and **Cecil Court** on its border. A 20-minute ride north on the 24 or 29 bus, **Camden Town** has its huge teenage street market, the **Lock**, but also available in its shops are plenty of vintage clothes, Indian brassware, denims, funky hats and boots, kilims, and silver jewelry. Keep going north and you hit **Hampstead**, a picturesque way to shop the best clothing chains. You wouldn't make **Upper Street**, **Islington** your shopping destination unless you were antiquing in **Camden Passage**, but if you happened to be in the neighborhood at the Almeida Theater, you would find many interesting small shops, mostly clothes and housewares. In the west, **Knightsbridge** is the ultimate destination, with London's most famous store, **Harrods**, plus every European designer represented in shops strung along **Sloane Street** and **Brompton Road**. Keep going, and you reach **Brompton Cross**, with its cluster of very fancy fashion and interiors shops. North of Knightsbridge, you'll hear Kensington's main drag shortened to **Ken High Street**. It has most of the chains, plus the interesting curve of **Ken Church Street**, where antiques are expensive but of museum quality. More egalitarian antiques are found farther north, in and around famous **Portobello Road**—not just a market, but a way of life. Explore the neighborhood for fashion designers just starting out, stuff for interiors, and young, affordable artists. One more westerly destination is **Chelsea**. The **King's Road** has been past its prime for years, though it's okay for midpriced antiques and the better clothing chains, and has a **Waitrose** reputed to be a good place to shop both for groceries and for a date. Its nether reaches, around **World's End**, where the designer Vivienne Westwood has her shop, are better.

Bargain Hunting

You can make London much less expensive by applying three main strategies: shopping the sales, hitting markets, and (for clothes) seeking out resale stores. The sales seasons are traditionally January and June, although these are moveable feasts that leak further into December and July every year. Lots of shops also have a permanent sale rack. We list resale shops, but look in the *Evening Standard*, and in *Time Out*'s "Sell Out" section for news of designers' "warehouse sales" or showroom clearances. Look below for how to do markets and what to get there. By the way, here the phrase "It's on sale" doesn't mean the price has been reduced, it just means you can buy it.

Trading with the Natives

Certain rituals familiar to every American shopper are mysteries to Brits. The layaway is not done, for instance (how long are you staying anyway?), and you may find assistants less attentive than you're used to. Londoners don't wish to know how a stranger thinks this looks on them and whether it goes with their new jacket. You won't see "We Ship Anywhere" signs either. Big stores will ship, but otherwise you're usually on your own, though your hotel may help. Places that ship are usually set up for instant VAT refunds as well (see below). Delivery in London is also the exception rather than the rule, and usually costs extra. As you would expect, bargaining for a lower price is not done in regular shops, though haggling can pay dividends in street markets.

Hours of Business

There is less and less uniformity to the hours a shop keeps, since Sunday trading laws have relaxed, and Londoners are getting more demanding. Traditional opening hours are 9 to 5 or 6, with one half-day closing (almost an extinct practice in London, but still found in the provinces) and one day with extended hours, usually Thursday till 7 or 8 p.m. Most shops these days open on Sundays, which is often the busiest day. They are currently allowed a six-hour window—could be 10–4 or 11–5 or 12–6.

Sales Tax

England's sales tax is called **Value Added Tax**, or **VAT**, and it runs at a greedy 17.5 percent on so-called nonessential goods. You can get it refunded by filling out a form at the time of purchase, which you then take, with the goods and receipts, to customs at Heathrow. For this reason, always shop with your passport. Some shops have a minimum (about £30 and up), some don't want to do it at all, and some have big long lines. If you have something shipped, you can get an on-the-spot VAT refund.

The Lowdown

The big stores... Of Oxford Street's three department stores, **Selfridges** is the best, and is getting better, because they're pouring money into a major sprucing-up program. The Food Hall and the fashion departments were first to be thoroughly revamped. (By the way, clothing is the core merchandise at all of these stores, unless otherwise indicated.) Still on Oxford Street, pass by **Debenhams**, the Kmart to Selfridges' Macy's, perhaps dropping in for a squint at **Jasper Conran**'s bargain "J" line, plus other designers' diffusion lines, then head to **John Lewis** (loveable for its motto, "Never Knowingly Undersold") and its excellent fabrics, notions, and haberdashery. Around the corner, in Regent Street, **Dickens & Jones** is the flagship of the nationwide House of Fraser group, which is not generally known for fashion leadership. This store, however, tries really hard with its prices in the middle range, and its great sales. Nearby is irresistible **Liberty**, which started as an Oriental bazaar and still maintains an Eastern bias in certain exotic corners of its mahogany and stained-glass interior. Down Bond Street, find slightly odd **Fenwick**, a store that often attempts to be all things to all people but isn't, except in the underwear department. The lord of department stores is **Fortnum & Mason**. It's the queen's grocer, and you shouldn't pass up the food halls with liveried servers and towers of teas, preserves, handmade chocolates, and cans of turtle soup. But go upstairs, too, for the least frenetic cosmetics counter in town and many matronly clothes. Mega-successful nationwide chain **Marks & Spencer** is the hamburger of shops, universally known and loved. Every Londoner has Marks 'n' Sparks knickers (panties, that is), sweaters, and an addiction to some item from the food ranges. In the west, **Peter Jones** is more of a sociological phenomenon than a store, the spiritual home of the Sloane Ranger and purveyor of school uniforms. The great store of the west, though, is **Harvey Nichols**, home of practically nothing but fashion—but what clothes! And what prices. Nearby is **Harrods**. What do you want us to say? That it's overrated? Overpriced? Over? Well, it isn't, it's wonderful. This London landmark and its 230 departments do attempt to live up to the store motto "Omnia, Omnibus, Ubique" (everything for everyone, everywhere).

Rattling the chains... Instead of the Gap and other places you can patronize chez vous, sport local styles. Look like a teenage clubber in iridescent minis and day-glo rubber Ts—shop **Top Shop**, **Miss Selfridge**, and (for more formal occasions), **River Island** and **Oasis,** the best of the cheapies. Best of the best for the generation formerly known as X, though, is **Warehouse**, where stock moves so fast, it's blurred. Some stuff there suits the older girly too, but better is **Jigsaw**, where things don't fall apart as quickly as at most chains. Everyone goes to **Marks & Spencer** for underwear, but it's an open secret that Marks 'n' Sparks gets fancy designers to consult on bigger garments, and there's much to discover in the formerly frumpy superchain. A very *short* chain, but best of all for quality, and being on target aesthetically, is **Whistles**.

The big names... The shop with the mostest has to be **Browns**, from which owner Joan Burstein has led London into the appreciation and assimilation of tasty clothes for many years. Here are Galliano, Demeule-meester, Ozbek, Rykiel, Karan, Tyler, Gigli, Sander, Muir, etc., etc. Other places where you can compare and contrast multiple makers include the tiny Knightsbridge **À La Mode**, which favors the Americans and the Belgians. Best for young Brit designers, of the edgy, envelope-pushing sort—like those famous few who stormed Paris (McQueen, Galliano, McCartney)—but we daren't name names for fear that they'll have their own flagship store by now and we'll look stupid. All designers you've ever heard of are in London somewhere, but highlights among those (non-British ones) with whole shops include **Prada**, **Dolce & Gabbana,** and **Comme des Garçons**. **Armani** and his **Emporio** are everywhere, while the memory of **Gianni Versace** is kept alive in an over-the top rococo marble folly on Bond Street. For less cash outlay than at any of the above, shop **Joseph** for enticing ranges of mostly French-made and mono-chrome separates, including the almost-cult-pants New Yorkers are snapping up.

Homegrown talent... The British Isles once produced great writers, but now it's better at clothes. You may know that her ladyship **Vivienne Westwood** is one of the world's most inventive and most copied designers, but you should see her clothes close up—they're exquisitely tailored as well. (Wear her son's wares from **Agent Provocateur** underneath.) Easier to handle, though, are **Betty Jackson**'s slightly offbeat classics. Also check out this pair of designers who do the riding-clothes–country-tweeds–rumpled-linens look better than anyone: **Margaret Howell**'s clothes last forever; Irishman **Paul Costelloe** does the Irish version with *lots* of linen. See **Mulberry** for the most staid versions of this look, and next door to that, the secret of certain well-dressed, anti-fashion mature women, **Paddy Campbell**, who makes timeless fitted suits and separates. **Paul Smith** is the menswear king for suits with a sense of humor, plus accessories and tons of shirts, with a limited women's range too. The other terribly famous (and deservedly so) menswear man is the clothes **Conran**, Jasper, who also dresses women. **Nicole Farhi** also swings both ways. She's London's Donna Karan. On the opposite bank, wearing work clothes in denim with something clingy, rhinestoned, and small, and a well-cut jacket, stands **Katharine Hamnett**. And, on the wilder shores, look at **Koh Samui** and **Urban Outfitters** for street style.

For riot grrls and boys... Except for the abovementioned stores, streetwear stays out of the limelight and is found, yes, on the street—in market stalls, thrift stores (called charity shops here), and rummage sales (jumble sales). However, to approximate a London look, try the following: the **Duffer of St. George** has the Chelsea boot-boy kitted out in vaguely threatening style; riot girls wear it too. **The Dispensary** edits other people's lines—some from the U.S.—and makes their own to dress you not too outrageously, while **Johnsons** has been going forever, whether in or out of fashion, with its teddy-boy suits and boots. **Kensington Market** is one-stop shopping for teenage clubbers, down to the tattoo and haircut. However, as this edition goes to press, the market is in danger of closing down. A campaign to save this, one of London's best-known youth shopping experiences, is under way—but be sure to call ahead to avoid disappointment. Just opposite, for those aficionados of New York City style, is London's own **Urban Outfitters,** complete with record shop, vintage and new clothes, and some of the hippest home-furnishing ideas and gizmos on the planet. As for flea markets, **Camden Lock** is the biggest, but before you plunge in, pause at **Holt's Footwear,** which has been providing 20-hole Docs for punk feet for over a century. It's a cramped, not necessarily freundlich, cash-only shopping experience, but every Brit band, Beatles to Madness to Pulp to Cornershop, was shod here. Next head to the Westway on Friday morning or Saturday all day for the clothes part of **Portobello.** Nearby is the number-one fetishwear center, **Skin Two,** which specializes in rubber.

Labels for less... We mentioned in the intro how you should check listings in the *Standard* and *Time Out* for warehouse sales, and call the showrooms too. Some other sources: **Labels For Less** is **Browns'** outlet store, while Burberrys outlet store is called **Burberrys.** **Whistles** also has one, not far away. Both **Vivienne Westwood** and **Paul Smith** have permanent sale stores. Of London's consignment and used-designer-clothing shops, the best are Hampstead's **Designs** (for the Escada and Genny type of woman—the German well-pressed look), **Designer Secondhand Store** (a little hipper, with some Versace, Rifat Ozbek, and Paul Smith), and the Knightsbridge **Pandora** (big and well known, with wodges of Alaïa, Armani, Karan, and even Chanel). For designers who are no longer designing, there's nowhere better than the incredible **Steinberg & Tolkein.** The basement here is like a funky version of the V&A Dress Collection where everything's for sale, with a ton of affordable tat alongside the Jacques Fath and historic Chanel pieces from the days of Coco herself. Nowhere except the **Antique Clothing Shop,** that is. The catch is, you have to be here Friday or Saturday for a riffle through Snady Stagg's bulging rails of '30s tea dresses, flapper gowns, cricket sweaters, and frock coats.

For sir, with $$$... The famous tailors of Savile Row are moving with the times...a bit. **Richard James** is a newer face, who cuts with nontraditional cloths like denim, as well as the suitings one would expect. At 1 Savile Row is the quintessential, ultimate bespoke tailor, **Gieves &**

Hawkes (that's a hard "G"), which started with Admiral Nelson and graduated to Hugh Grant's Oscar-night suit. Get your shirts made where the Prince of Wales and Warren Christopher get theirs, **Turnbull & Asser**. A Savile Row suit will take maybe six weeks and at least three fittings, will not cost less than £1,000, and the tab may be almost double that. A minimum order half-dozen bespoke shirts with shell buttons and collar stays of bone will set you back £600–£900. If you're not in that tax bracket yet, try **Favourbrook** for a brocade weskit, or vest, in one of their many dandy fabrics, or an entire silk-brocade dandy's suit. Nearly all these tailors will also make to measure for women.

Cutting costs... The tailoring skills of London designers have long been appreciated in the world of fashion. Surprisingly, a tailored suit (or just one that has been altered) need not cost a bomb. **Keith Watson** has been tailoring on Carnaby Street for the last 30 years, and one of his suits (for sir or madam) will set you back only £350-odd (plus fabric). Another tailor with an impressive celeb client list is **Jackie Palmer,** with wedding outfits (for the whole team) a specialty. **Mr. Eddie** and his crew can knock up a suit in a few days if you're in a hurry—but do expect to pay a bit more for your haste. **Geoff Slack** will also work on a tight schedule—whether fashioning full-scale wedding dresses or duplicates of your favorite T-shirts. Geoff is also never happier than when working with "fetishistic" fabrics—latex wedding dress, anyone? If the outfit you love doesn't fit like a glove, you need **Couturière,** inexpensive but excellent alterations by Japanese-born Takako Sato, whose skill with a needle is legendary. It's all sewn by hand—and her English is respectable, too!

Your own crown jewels... The actual crown jewels are watched over by **Garrard**, where you can order your personal collection any way you like it, or try out the royal-looking work of **Theo Fennell**—his ecclesiastical goldsmithery is quite distinctive. But, let's face it, you're probably looking for something a little less *real*. The most outrageously rhinestoned of **Butler & Wilson**'s wares fool nobody none of the time and are irresistible to human magpies, especially the crown brooches and earrings; there's also great classic French gilt and a lot of jet. If you really do require an actual crown, **Slim Barrett** is your man. His stone-encrusted coronets and tiaras are fashion-victim favorites. But for something to wear on a daily basis, visit with **Dinny Hall** (who works mostly in silver), see the jewelry departments at **Liberty** and **Harvey Nichols**, or check out the score of young designers at **Janet Fitch**.

Gifts that scream London... Janet Fitch is a great gift source for your modern and design-conscious friends, and the diamanté crown pieces from **Butler & Wilson** are cute British gifts, or get a St. Paul's dome in umbrella form from the **Museum Store**. There are racks and racks more of the essential English accessory at the gorgeous Victorian brolly (umbrella to you) emporium **James Smith & Sons**, where you can also get shooting sticks (a portable seat), silver-topped canes, Mary Poppins parrot-top umbrellas, and riding crops. Our favorite scarves come from genius **Georgina von Etzdorf**, whose *devoré* velvets and hand-printed silk chiffons and opulent satins are much copied but never equaled. For gifts in quantity, for the entire office, perhaps, get orchid or banana tea from **The Tea House**, or Twining's Earl Grey (the best) from **R. Twining & Co.**, with its little tea museum on the company's original premises; or go for smoky Lapsang Souchong and the New York blend (made to brew with New York water—really) from **Fortnum & Mason**, which is one-stop shopping for the entire gift list. Smellies are not boring gifts when they come from **Penhaligon's**, where you'll have a blast uncorking crystal flacons and sniffing precious waters. William Penhaligon was Victoria's court barber, and the same Blenheim Bouquet he blended is sold still. **Rococo** has Earl Gray tea chocolate bars, while **Thornton's** is forever coming up with gimmicky candies. If there's nothing London-themed right now, get some Special Toffee, which is the best there is—plus there's a Thornton's in Heathrow (this side of the gates) for emergencies.

Guy gifts... For jocks and tomboys (i.e., guys of both genders), London's got every accoutrement—also for Bond, James Bond, who could have bought bugs, counter-bugs, Coke-can safes, and cigarette-lighter cameras at **Spycatcher**. Real cigarette lighters can be picked up at **Davidoff Cigars**, which is really more for cigar smokers, with wall-to-wall Havanas in its walk-in humidor. Those who prefer an indigenous English sports souvenir will fare best at **Lillywhite's**, the amazing sports department store. Football gear, including the jerseys of all London teams, plus those of the glamorous Italian *Serie* A and other Euro footy players, is at **Soccer Scene**, while British boxers (one of the few sports for which the English supply stars) get their hands wrapped at **Lonsdale**.

Remarkable markets...

Bermondsey is for serious antiques collectors. It's where dealers buy, but early, very, very early—before dawn. **Camden Passage** has a picturesque setting, with its alleys and little shops, in which the prices are higher than on the stalls. Finds are also still possible among the 2,000-odd dealers at the most famous market, **Portobello Road**. The antiques are concentrated at the Notting Hill end; they give way to fruit-and-veg, to the flea under the Westway (great vintage clothes), then into the nether reaches of Goldborne Road, where it's all junk and rummage, character, and the important pit stop, the **Lisboa Portuguese bakery. Brick Lane** has antiques too, but you'll have to sift. It has great atmo, this East End Sunday agglomeration of *stuff*—cassettes, work tools, candies, leather jackets, wallets—and provides you the best chance of catching old market trader's banter and maybe rhyming slang. For a "real" market bang in the West End, you can't beat the fruit and vegetable traders of Soho's **Berwick**

Cockney Rhyming Slang

If you wander the East End of London, you may hear a few odd word pairings that are meant to substitute for things related only inasmuch as they rhyme. For example: whistle+flute=suit, or Brahms+Liszt=pissed (=drunk, not angry), or apple+pear=stair. These are sometimes boiled down to just the first word, which then produces sentences such as, "Nice whistle, matey," meaning, "That is an elegant suit." Years of Ealing comedies and My Fair Lady have convinced much of the world that these constructions, called Rhyming Slang, are a secret language of the Cockneys. In fact, the rhyming slang used by some Londoners is really a form of wordplay common among traders in the 18th century and found as well in Australia and in the States. Its continued presence on English radio and television shows in this century has given it a prominence based more on regional identity than on actual use, much like the famous Brooklyn accent in New York.

SHOPPING | THE LOWDOWN

Street, so good that chefs shop there. For the diametric opposite, try **Camden Lock**—heaven to some (most under 20), hell on wheels to others. Another famous market is **Petticoat Lane**, which is really a lot of tat nowadays and is surpassed by its neighbors **Brick Lane** and the totally contrasting, covered **Spitalfields Market**, whose Sunday greenmarket is a breath of the country.

Very old things... London has rich antiques pickings in shops and at auction, as well as at the markets mentioned above. It's one area where a price tag is a mutable thing, and haggling is advisable. Annual antiques fairs—of which the three biggies are the **Grosvenor House**, the **Chelsea**, and the **British Antique Dealers' Association**—attract international buyers and carriage trade alike. Several collections of stalls under one roof—sort of permanent versions of those—are best bets for casual purchases. In the King's Road are two big ones: **Antiquarius** and **Chenil Galleries**. Between those and the West End **Grays**, you'll probably score a hit. If not, try the **London Silver Vaults** for a set of Edwardian fruit knives, **Hope & Glory** for its stock of affordable commemorative china, the wonderful **Gallery of Antique Costume & Textiles**, which also makes its own reproduction 18th-century vests and coats, or **The Button Queen** for something to jazz up your jacket.

Money's no object... A tasteful way to splash some cash around would be to commission one of those British designers at **OXO Tower** to make you the *objet* of your dreams. Such transactions can be more complex and emotional than even the kind of bespoke Savile Row experience offered by **Gieves & Hawkes** or the hipper version chez **Richard James**. Speaking of which, only Hong Kong rivals London as a place to achieve perfect head-to-toe tailoring—and Hong Kong lacks the class of the bowler hat capital. **James Lock** is your guy for that hat, except that Mr. Lock himself expired around the early 18th century, after making Admiral Lord Nelson's titfers (tit-for-tat: hat). Your platinum cards will want to leave St. James's when they see the beautiful, security-guard-patrolled Burlington Arcade, where the **Irish Linen Co.** has some of the world's finest pure white sheets, and which leads to Piccadilly. Show them the bathroom fittings heaven that is **Czech & Speake** before crossing that street to Mayfair, with its Old Masters (**Marlborough Fine Art**—you don't have to buy), jewelers (**Asprey**), and the finest purveyor of porcelain and crystal, **Thomas Goode & Co.**

Money's too tight to mention... For those without means who yet aspire to the pristine Irish linen sheets and English bone china tea service, **The Linen Cupboard** and **Harrods' Sale** were invented. Alternatively, forget the whole aspirational thing and creatively go to **Neal Street East** for an enormous selection of Asian imports for the home, to **Columbia Road Market** for stuff to enhance the yard, and to **The Stencil Store** for supplies to do the wall art at which the English are curiously expert. Cheap gifts that look expensive are easy. The **Tea House** supplies tea and "teaphernalia," as they call it; **Marks & Spencer** has good things to wear, and its food department packages so gorgeously, you could make a gift of a TV dinner.

For bookworms... London's literary legacy lives on in bookstores of all sizes. In the West End resides vast and impossible to understand **Foyles**; its near neighbors are **Dillons** and handsome **Hatchards**, where they're really helpful, and the original **Waterstone's**, which cloned itself all over London. Those are the best big ones, but look for the countless little specialty stores. Around book heaven Charing Cross Road, browse several varieties of **Zwemmer** (the art store is especially fine) and the self-explanatory **Dance Books**, among others. There are shops stocked as exhaustively as sections of the British Library, such as **French's Theatre Bookshop**, with every English-language play; beautiful, wood-paneled **Daunt Books** for travel tomes; **Stanford** for the accompanying maps and guides; and **Sportspages** for the obvious. Antiquarian books are a famous commodity of this town, though nowadays try **Any Amount of Books** at no. 62. If you need a specific out-of-print title, go to **Skoob**; for a rarity or a signed first edition, investigate the world-class dealer **Bernard Quaritch**, who quotes prices in dollars.

For aural obsessives... London's been the world's vinyl capital since the Beatles, and now that everyone's got CDs (which are ridiculously expensive here), it still is. For club music that always did and still does hit the streets in 12-inch single form, this city's number one. Try **Trax** for Euro dance (trance, house, Balearic), while the chief place for jungle is Chelsea's **Section 5**. For jazz, the near-legendary **Mole Jazz** is better than it ever was in its new and larger place—it's kept up with the times on the CD front, too. The Portobello **Honest Jon's** has a Blue Note collection that's sublime, plus a good secondhand section, and many new CDs. As you would guess from its name, that other Soho institution **Reckless Records** stocks only vinyl, and only secondhand at that, with rock, soul, and jazz the main genres.

For the green thumb... London is frustrating for American gardeners, since you can't take the plants home. Ideas and inspiration, however, are free. **The Chelsea Gardener** and the **Camden Garden Centre** are the city's two best outdoor emporia, with climbers and rosebushes to die for, free advice, and accessories. Ditto the pots of **S & B Evans** at the unmissable **Columbia Road Market**, which is itself full of wrought iron, terra-cotta, and wooden accessories.

Small fry... Convert fractious kids into shopping experts by showing them the five floors of **Hamleys**, the "world's biggest toy store" (or is that Toys "R" Us?). Smaller and maybe better is **Humla**, a cult among grandmas, for the gorgeous European garments and wooden toys at remarkably ungreedy prices. Older girls find heaven at **Hennes**, a Scandinavian chain that does high fashion cheap—and has great kids' clothes, too. If you forgot to bring something, classy British chain **Mothercare** is fine for baby equipment and toddler stuff. Wooden and traditional toys, teddies, dolls, stationery, and games are London finds. Try well-stocked **Tridias**, or if that isn't enough, take them to nearby **Harrods**, whose phantasmagorical Toy Kingdom is the kind where the plush lions are life-size and roar. Owners of dollhouses will remember **Kristin Baybars** all their lives, so it's worth the trek.

For gastronomes and epicures... For gifts in bulk, Prince Charles has obligingly done a Paul Newman—he sells packs of his own brand; the disarmingly delicious Duchy Originals oatcakes and ginger biscuits fill every carry-on bag. The whole baby stilton cheese for the oatcakes should be got from **Paxton & Whitfield**, the cheese shop of cheese shops since 1797 (no Monty Python references please), or the **Neal's Yard Dairy**, in which everything is from the British Isles, or made on the premises, and you can ask for tasters. Neal's Yard products are among the epicurian riches of **Tom's**. This may stretch your credulity, but Tom is yet another Conran: brother of Jasper the clothesdesigner, and son of Sir Terence, whose "Gastrodrome" by Tower Bridge provides smoked fish and seaweed bread, French charcuterie, fruit vinegars, Tuscan olive oils, homemade English chutneys, and more, in four separate shops. Of these, the **Oils and Spice Shop** is the most things-to-take-home oriented. There's also the newer **Bluebird** food emporium on the King's Road. **Fortnum & Mason**, as you know by now, also fulfills this role. Get cans of brown windsor, truffled foie gras, thick-cut marmalade with Scottish whisky, the anchovy paste in decorative ceramic jars called Patum Peperium Gentleman's Relish, and English mustard, but not, as a persistent myth has it, red ants in chocolate.

For sweet teeth... Almost as exotic as Fortnum's fictional sweetmeat are certain of master chocolatier Gerard Ronay's handmade fillings, like his award-winning smoked lemon. They are available at **Selfridges**. Chocoholics dedicated to quality will enjoy **Rococo** on the King's Road, a cocoa paradise run by the founder of the Chocolate Society. Anyone preferring quantity will favor the many branches of **Thornton's**—for Belgian fresh cream truffles, children's novelty shapes in creamy milk and sickly white chocolate, and the aptly named Special Toffee, which is chewy, buttery caramel, not brittle like the "English toffee" of Heath Bars.

The Index

All shops are closed Sunday, unless otherwise indicated.

Agent Provocateur. Joe Corré's snottily supergroovy boudoir boutique. Get the transparent tangerine nylon with kingfisher lace–trim bra you've been looking for.... *Tel 0207/439–0229. 6 Broadwick St. W1, Oxford Circus tube stop. Open Mon.–Sat. 11–7.* **(see p. 155)**

À La Mode. Opposite Harrods is this tiny *boîte* stocking the hottest designers for wardrobe investments.... *Tel 0207/584–2133. 36 Hans Crescent, SW1, Knightsbridge tube stop.* **(see p. 154)**

Antiquarius. A long-established collection of antique dealers, with art deco especially notable.... *Tel 0207/351–5353. 131– 141 King's Rd. SW3, Sloane Sq. tube stop.* **(see p. 160)**

Antique Clothing Shop. This secret address is the dog's bollocks for exceptional pieces 1880–1970. Kate bleedin' Moss shops here, so go figure.... *Tel 0208/964–4830. 282 Portobello Rd. W10, Ladbroke Grove tube stop. Open Fri.–Sat. 9–6 or by appointment.* **(see p. 156)**

Any Amount of Books. Take this secondhand (as opposed to antiquarian) store on book row literally.... *Tel 0207/ 240–8140. 62 Charing Cross Rd. WC2, Leicester Sq. tube stop. Open Mon.–Sat. 10:30–9:30, Sun. 10:30–8:30.* **(see p. 161)**

Asprey. Jewelry, silver, leather goods, crystal, and bone china exquisitely served by this swanky gift emporium.... *Tel 0207/493–6767. 167 New Bond St. W1, Bond St. tube stop. Open Mon.–Fri. 9–5:30, Sat. 10–5.* **(see p. 161)**

Bermondsey Market. Join the serious antiques collectors and trade professionals here at dawn (take a flashlight). If you go later, you miss the choicest pieces and the best atmosphere. *Bermondsey Square SE1, Borough tube stop. Fri. 5 a.m.–noon.* **(see p. 159)**

Bernard Quaritch. Fine rare manuscripts and antiquarian volumes, priced in dollars *and* pounds. Know what you want before you go.... *Tel 0207/734–2983. 5–8 Lower John St. W1, Piccadilly Circus tube stop. Closed Sat.*
(see p. 161)

Berwick Street Market. Soho's fruit and vegetable market serves local color in every sense; bargain prices too. *Berwick and Rupert streets W1, Leicester Sq. tube stop. Open Mon.–Sat. 9–6.* **(see p. 159)**

Betty Jackson. With her kind cuts, interesting textures, and extraordinary color combos, Jackson's women's collection is always a hot seller.... *Tel 0207/589–7884. 311 Brompton Rd. SW3, South Kensington tube stop.* **(see p. 155)**

Bluebird. Sir Terence "omni" Conran has yet another gastro enterprise here in Chelsea, with huge *traiteur* and grocery, faux market stalls, restaurants (see Dining). Worth a miss if you don't want to feel manipulated.... *Tel 0207/559–1000. 350 King's Rd. Sloane Sq. tube stop.* **(see p. 163)**

Brick Lane Market. For our money, this is the most fun Sunday market—from bric-a-brac and antiques to bikes and bagels, it's best early. *Brick Lane, east to Cheshire St., north to Club Row. Shoreditch tube stop. Open Sun. 6 a.m.–1 p.m.*
(see pp. 159, 160)

British Antique Dealers' Association Fair. The newest of the big fairs happens in late March.... *Tel 0207/589–6108 for information. 20 Rutland Gate, SW7 1BD.* **(see p. 160)**

Browns. One-stop shopping if you live for fashion and have healthy plastic. All known designers live in connected shops, with Browns' own label providing missing links. Don't forget **Labels For Less** at no. 50.... *Tel 0207/491–7833. 23–27 South Molton St. W1, Bond St. tube stop.* **(see pp. 154, 156)**

Burberrys factory shop. East End outlet store for the famous plaid-lined quintessentially Brit macs for tourists, and related clothing and paraphernalia.... *Tel 0208/985–3344. 29–53 Chatham Place E9, Bethnal Green tube, then 106, 253 bus. Open Mon.–Fri. 11–6, Sat. 10–5, Sun. 11–5.* **(see p. 156)**

Butler & Wilson. Come out dripping with diamanté, multicolored rhinestones, gilt, and jet, but still managing to look chic.... *Tel 0207/409–2955, 20 South Molton St. W1, Bond St. tube stop; tel 0207/352–8255, 189 Fulham Rd. SW3, South Kensington tube stop.* **(see pp. 157, 158)**

The Button Queen. An array of clothes closers—from antique, precious, and collectible to wacky, handmade, and plain useful.... *Tel 0207/935–1505. 19 Marylebone Lane W1, Bond St. tube stop. Sat. closes 1:30 p.m.* **(see p. 160)**

Camden Garden Centre. This gardenlike outdoor store is a living catalog for the green-thumbed.... *Tel 0207/485–8468. 2 Barker Dr., St. Pancras Way NW1, Camden Town tube stop. Open Mon.–Sat. 9–5, Sun. 10–4.* **(see p. 162)**

Camden Lock. The labyrinthine 25-year-old maze in warehouse and railway buildings both historic and fake 'round the Regent's Canal gets beyond busy on sunny Sundays. *Camden Lock, Chalk Farm Rd., all down Camden High St. NW1, Camden Town, Chalk Farm tube stop. Open Sat., Sun. 10–6; limited stalls daily 9:30–5:30.* **(see pp. 156, 160)**

Camden Passage. Twice-a-week antiques market still offers the odd bargain. Shops augment stalls.... *Tel 0207/359–9969. Camden Passage, Upper St. N1, Angel tube stop. Open Wed. 8 a.m.–1 p.m., Sat. 10–3.* **(see p. 159)**

Chelsea Antiques Fair. Twice a year (March and September), dealers of pre-1830 pieces congregate at the Old Town Hall, King's Rd.... *Tel 01444/482514 for info. Sloane Sq. tube stop.* **(see p. 160)**

Chelsea Gardener. The toniest of garden stores, with multitudes of ideas to steal, and yard accessories to buy.... *Tel 0207/352–5656. 125 Sydney St. SW3, Sloane Sq. tube stop. Open Mon.–Sat. 10–6, Sun. 11–5.* **(see p. 162)**

Chenil Galleries. This sister to Antiquarius has higher price tags and more serious pieces.... *Tel 0207/351–5353. 181–183 King's Rd. SW3, Sloane Sq. tube stop.* **(see p. 160)**

Columbia Road Market. Heaven for flower fans, gardeners, or people with a spare Sunday morning, this is the cut-flower, bedding-plant, and yard-accoutrement bargain center of Europe. *Gosset St. to the Royal Oak pub E2, Old St. tube stop. Sun. 8–1.* **(see pp. 161, 162)**

Comme des Garçons. Rei Kawakubo's structural, collectible art clothes are augmented by her more affordable lines.... *Tel 0207/493–1258. 59 Brooke St. W1, Bond St. tube stop.* **(see p. 154)**

Couturière. Inexpensive but highly skilled alterations. Let Takako Sato make the outfit you love fit you like a glove.... *Tel 0207/493–1564. 2nd Floor, 22 Brook St. W1, Bond St. tube stop.* **(see p. 157)**

Czech & Speake. Mecca for bathroom-hardware fanatics desirous of Italian brushed-steel faucets.... *Tel 0207/439–0216. 39c Jermyn St. SW1, Piccadilly Circus tube stop.* **(see p. 161)**

Dance Books. Also magazines and memorabilia for balletomanes. *Tel 0207/836–2314. 9 Cecil Court WC2, Leicester Sq. tube stop.* **(see p. 161)**

Daunt Books. This handsome galleried shop covers travel worldwide. *Tel 0207/224–2295. 83 Marylebone High St. W1. Baker St. tube stop.* **(see p. 161)**

Davidoff Cigars. Mainly Davidoff, but all the rare breeds are carried here, plus European packaged varieties in all cigar sizes are sold by appropriately snotty gents.... *Tel 0207/930–3079. 35 St. James's St. SW1, Green Park tube stop.* **(see p. 158)**

Debenhams. Not London's most exciting department store, but this part of the Burton Group empire keeps prices on the low side, and contains a few designer surprises, including Jasper Conran's "J" collection.... *Tel 0207/580–3000. 334–338 Oxford St. W1,. Bond St. tube stop. Open until 8 p.m. Wed.–Fri.* **(see p. 153)**

Designer Secondhand Store. The Hampstead version of Designer Source, straighter of label (Mugler and Muir, not Ozbek and Westwood), and a tad friendlier.... *Tel 0207/431–8618. 24 Hampstead High St. NW3, Hampstead tube stop. Open Sun. 10:30–6.* **(see p. 156)**

THE INDEX

SHOPPING

Designs. This other Hampstead designer secondhand shop is the more staid of the two (Prada and Donna Karan), but everything is scrupulously as-new.... *Tel 0207/435–0100. 60 Rosslyn Hill NW3, Hampstead tube stop.* (see p. 156)

Dickens & Jones. This department store went from old-fashioned to good on fashion, especially the midprice lines on the ground (first) floor.... *Tel 0207/734–7070. 224–244 Regent St. W1, Oxford Circus tube stop. Open till 8 p.m. Thurs.* (see p. 153)

Dillons. A helpful staff who know the comprehensive stock that characterizes this bookstore by the University of London.... *Tel 0207/636–1577. 82 Gower St. WC1, Goodge St. tube stop. Open Mon., Wed.–Fri. 9–7; Tues. 9:30–7; Sat. 9:30–6; Sun. noon–6. Branches.* (see p. 161)

Dinny Hall. Jeweler Dinny favors silver, turning out wearable, beautifully crafted pieces at reasonable prices.... *Tel 0207/792–3913. 200 Westbourne Grove W11, Notting Hill Gate tube stop.* (see p. 158)

The Dispensary. Four branches of this hip clothes emporium serve up the longer-lasting (i.e., well-made) model of street style—Patrick Cox's Wannabes, Schott leathers, Stüssy, and its own label.... *Tel 0207/287–8145, 9 Newburgh St. (menswear at #15) W1, Oxford Circus tube stop; tel 0207/221–9290, 25 Penbridge Rd. W11, Notting Hill Gate tube stop; tel 0207/727–8797, 200 Kensington Park Rd. W11, Notting Hill Gate tube stop.* (see p. 155)

Dolce & Gabbana. We would love to be able to afford the beautifully tailored, sexy clothes of these Italians, like Madonna can.... *Tel 0207/235–0335. 175 Sloane St. SW1, Knightsbridge tube stop.* (see p. 154)

Duffer of St. George. Perennially hip club garb from this menswear street stylist, with added sports stuff and U.S. labels (Phat Farm, Antoni & Alison).... *Tel 0207/379–4660. 29 Shorts Gardens WC2, Covent Garden tube stop.* (see p. 155)

Emporio Armani. Oh, you know what this is like. Three London branches.... *Tel 0207/491–8080. 1129 New Bond St. W1, Bond St. tube stop; tel 0207/917–6882, 57–59 Long*

Acre WC2, Covent Garden tube stop; tel 0207/823–8818, 191 Brompton Rd. SW3, Knightsbridge tube stop. Covent Garden store open on Sun.   **(see p. 154)**

Favourbrook. Brocades and damasks, silks, velvets, and embroidered linens get made into exquisite vests, jackets, and frock coats at this co-ed tailor. Perfect wedding wear.... Tel 0207/491–2337. 55 Jermyn St. SW1, Green Park tube stop.
(see p. 157)

Fenwick. Four floors of fashion. Standout departments are lingerie and a designer floor with Betty Jackson, Jean Muir, Paul Costelloe, Jasper Conran, Nicole Farhi, and Georges Rech.... Tel 0207/629–9161. 63 New Bond St. W1, Bond St. tube stop.   **(see p. 153)**

Fortnum & Mason. The ne plus ultra of grocers has the royal warrant for her very majesty, plus gifts for your entire list, and a quaint clock in front. Check out the other lovely, pricey, old-fashioned departments, too.... Tel 0207/734–8040. 181 Piccadilly W1, Piccadilly Circus/Green Park tube stop.
(see pp. 153, 158, 163)

Foyles. The biggest bookstore in town is also the least organized, but this has its charm, since it's such fun to get lost in the stacks.... Tel 0207/437–5660. 119 Charing Cross Rd. WC2, Leicester Sq. tube stop.   **(see p. 161)**

French's Theatre Bookshop. This aims to stock every play in the English language that's in print.... Tel 0207/ 387–9373. 52 Fitzroy St. W1, Warren Street tube stop. Open Mon.–Fri. 9:30–5:30, Sat. 11–5.   **(see p. 161)**

Gallery of Antique Costume & Textiles. Another shop you can treat as a museum, except you'll want to walk out with a '20s tea gown, a chenille throw, or one of the reproduction brocade vests they fashion here.... Tel 0207/723–9981. 2 Church St. NW8, Marylebone tube stop.   **(see p. 160)**

Garrard. Yet another gallery of a shop, this one studded with precious gems and laden with gold. They polish the crown jewels here.... Tel 0207/493–6767. 167 New Bond St. W1, Oxford Circus tube stop.   **(see p. 157)**

Geoff Slack. No job is too large or too small, from duplicating

THE INDEX

SHOPPING

your fave cotton T-shirt to a customized rubber bodysuit.... *Tel 0208/743–7713. Goldhawk Rd. W12. Call fo an appointment.* **(see p. 157)**

Georgina von Etzdorf. Darling of the fashion pages, Von Etzdorf produces England's most desirably opulent scarves and clothing, as well as home furnishings in precious materials.... *Tel 0207/409–7789. 1–2 Burlington Arcade W1, Piccadilly Circus tube stop.* **(see p. 158)**

Gianni Versace. This marble palace with the snootiest staff in the kingdom matches Versace's gaudy, gilt-embossed, dominatrix-wear exactly.... *Tel 0207/499–1862. 34–36 Old Bond St. W1, Green Park tube stop.* **(see p. 154)**

Gieves & Hawkes. One of Savile Row's best-known, yet also most approachable, bespoke tailors has fiendish rates, but for the best.... *Tel 0207/434–2001. 1 Savile Row W1, Piccadilly Circus tube stop.* **(see pp. 156, 160)**

Grays Antiques Market. One of those collections of collectors, based conveniently downtown, and not overpriced.... *Tel 0207/629–7034. South Molton Lane W1, Bond St. tube stop. Closed weekends.* **(see p. 160)**

Grosvenor House. For a week in June, the toniest of antiquing opportunities.... *Tel 0207/399–8100. Grosvenor House, Park Lane W1, Marble Arch tube stop.* **(see p. 160)**

Hamleys. The vastest toy shop this side of FAO Schwarz creates similar problems for parents trying to reach the exit.... *Tel 0207/734–3161. 188–196 Regent St. W1, Oxford Circus tube stop. Open Mon.–Wed. 10–6:30, Thurs. 10–8, Fri. 10–7, Sat. 9:30–7, Sun. noon–6.* **(see p. 162)**

Harrods. The one and only. Go ogle the food hall, visit the pets, covet stuff in the young-designer room, then get an olive-green-and-gold logo bag. The sales are essential.... *Tel 0207/730–1234. 87–155 Brompton Rd. SW1, Knightsbridge tube stop.* **(see pp. 153, 161, 162)**

Harvey Nichols. Here are Galliano, Dolce & Gabbana, Rifat Ozbek, Claude Montana, Jil Sander, Moschino, and oh, thousands more, including new young Brits-to-watch.... *Tel*

0207/235–5000. 109–125 Knightsbridge SW1, Knights-
bridge tube stop. Open Sun. noon–6. **(see pp. 153, 158)**

Hatchards. This wood-paneled store, with its royal warrant and
helpful staff, is a most pleasant way to stock up on reading
matter.... *Tel 0207/439–9921. 187 Piccadilly W1, Picca-*
dilly Circus/Green Park tube stops. Open Sun. noon–6.
(see p. 161)

Hennes. The hottest fashion moments frozen in cheap materials
for addicts who need high turnover, which means teenage
girls. Kids' department, too.... *Tel 0207/493–8557. 481*
Oxford St. W1, Oxford Circus tube stop; tel 0207/493–4004,
261 Regent St. W1, Oxford Circus tube stop; tel 0207/937–
3329, 123 Kensington High St. W8, Kensington High Street
tube stop. Open Sun. noon–6. **(see p. 162)**

Holt's Footwear. An institution for a century, this wee store next
to Camden tube still supplies rude boys (Madness and the
Specials shopped here) with 20-hole DMs (Doc Martens),
monkey boots and house-brand Gladiator boots.... *Tel 0207/*
485–8505. 5 Kentish Town Rd. NW1, Camden Town tube
*stop. Open Mon.–Sat. 9.30–5.30, Sun. 11–4.***(see p. 156)**

Honest Jon's. A vinyl destination for about three decades, this is
black-music central, from jazz and funk to soul and reggae,
vintage and rare, plus new CDs.... *Tel 0208/969–9822.*
276–278 Portobello Rd. W10, Ladbroke Grove tube stop.
Open Sun. 11–5. **(see p. 162)**

Hope & Glory. Commemorative china is an egalitarian antique,
easily within all pockets, as long as you don't mind a mere
Liz's Silver Jubilee mug—more exalted anniversaries have
higher prices.... *Tel 0207/727–8424. 131 Kensington*
Church St. W8, Notting Hill Gate tube stop. **(see p. 160)**

Humla. Under-eights almost welcome clothes gifts when they're
colorful fun things from here, especially when backed up by
a Humla wooden toy.... *Tel 0207/224–1773. 23 St.*
Christopher's Place W1. Bond St. tube stop. Branches.
(see p. 162)

Irish Linen Co. Delicious, pristine bed linens and home accessories made of that crunchy, rare fabric.... *Tel 0207/493–*

8949. 35–36 Burlington Arcade W1, Piccadilly Circus/Green Park tube stops. **(see p. 160)**

Jackie Palmer. Allow three weeks (ideally) for one of Jackie's gorgeous, boned, strapless dresses. (Push-up bras? Who needs 'em?) Also specializes in maternity bridal wear (?!) and men's vests.... *Tel 0207/734–0755. W1, Piccadilly Circus tube stop. Call for appointment.* **(see p. 157)**

James Lock. Hats to the gentry since 1676. A bowler costs from £175, but they also sell more modern headgear, for women too.... *Tel 0207/930–5849. 6 St. James's St. SW1, Green Park tube stop.* **(see p. 160)**

James Smith & Sons. Every umbrella under the sun, or rain. Also riding crops, shooting sticks, walking canes, and other fetishists' dreams sold in handsome Victorian premises.... *Tel 0207/836–4731. 53 New Oxford St. WC1, Tottenham Court Rd. tube stop.* **(see p. 158)**

Janet Fitch. Jewelry, bags, and *objets* are hand-picked by Ms. Fitch, who's known to have the most perfect taste in town.... *Tel 0207/287–3789. 37a Neal St. WC2, Covent Garden tube stop. Branches. Open Mon–Sat 11–7, Sun 1–6.* **(see p. 158)**

Jasper Conran. He's got no store of his own, but find his delicious women's tailored stuff at Harrods, Selfridges, Harvey Nick's, Fenwicks, and À La Mode, plus his affordable "J" collection at Debenhams. **(see p. 153)**

Jigsaw. A superior clothing chain, where the finish is finer, the fabric denser, the style hipper than its competitors in this middle price range (like Benetton, for instance).... *Tel 0207/584–6226. 31 Brompton Rd. SW3, Knightsbridge tube stop. Branches. Open Sun. noon–6.* **(see p. 154)**

John Lewis. "Never Knowingly Undersold" is a boast not bearing close scrutiny; still, this no-frills department store is pretty unbeatable for practical homemaking items.... *Tel 0207/629–7711. 278–306 Oxford St. W1, Oxford Circus tube stop. Branches.* **(see p. 153)**

Johnsons. The original source of teddy-boy gear—stovepipes, sharkskin drape jackets, Chelsea boots, at reasonable prices.... *Tel 0207/351–3268. 406 King's Rd. SW10, Sloane Sq. tube stop; branch in Kensington Market, tel 0207/937–4711.* **(see p. 155)**

Joseph. Joseph Ettedgui has had a major influence on how London dresses and furnishes for two decades. He doesn't design himself, but has an eye to buy what the English want, at mid-price. Monochrome, youthful, fitted, or knitted is the tone.... *Tel 0207/629–3713. 23 Old Bond St. W1, Green Park tube stop. Mon.–Sat. 10–6:30. Branches.* **(see p. 154)**

Katharine Hamnett. Half bad-girl, half environmental activist, Hamnett's clothes are similarly schizoid, with spandex and canvas, nicely cut jackets, and slut dresses, plus the good Hamnett Active jeans line.... *Tel 0207/823–1002. 20 Sloane St. SW1, Knightsbridge tube stop.* **(see p. 155)**

Keith Watson. One of the last of the Carnaby Street tailors, Keith has stitched for Bobby de Niro and girl band All Saints. Also responsible for Rod Stewart's tight velvet jackets in the '70s. Never mind.... *Tel 0207/437–2327. 47A Carnaby St. W1, Piccadilly Circus tube stop. Call for appointment.***(see p. 157)**

Kensington Market. This resembles a hipsters' mall, with hundreds of stalls and shops for high school kids to pose around on the weekend.... *Tel 0207/938–4343. 49–53 Kensington High St. W8, Kensington High St. tube stop. Open Sun. noon–5.* **(see p. 155)**

Koh Samui. Homegrown hipness on hangers. Half of the 20-odd label names—Clements Tibeiro, Christa Davies, Ruti Danan, Fabio Piras—have probably won their own couture house in Paris by now.... *Tel 0207/240–4280. 50 Monmouth St. WC2H 9EP, Covent Garden tube stop. Open Mon.–Sat. 11–7.* **(see p. 155)**

Kristin Baybars. Everything for the doll's house, including the doll's house—this tiny place is unrivaled.... *Tel 0207/267–0934. 7 Mansfield Rd. NW3, Gospel Oak BR. Open Tues.–Sat. 11:15–6.* **(see p. 162)**

Liberty. What started as an importer of Asian goods is the most enticing department store in town, with lovely Liberty prints, good jewelry, accessories, and fashion housed in Arts-and-Crafts grandeur.... *Tel 0207/734–1234. 214 Regent St. W1, Oxford Circus tube stop.* **(see pp. 153, 158)**

Lillywhite's. Sports nirvana, with six floors of paraphernalia, kit, and garb for the usual jock competitions, British games, and cruel and unusual activities you've never heard of. The goods are high ticket, high quality.... *Tel 0207/915–4000. 24–36 Lower Regent St. SW1, Piccadilly Circus tube stop. Open Sun. 11–5.* **(see p. 159)**

The Linen Cupboard. Bargain bedclothes; good things mixed up with tat in this chaotic shop.... *Tel 0207/629–4062. 21 Great Castle St. W1, Oxford Circus tube stop.* **(see p. 161)**

London Silver Vaults. About two-score traders have gathered under this roof since the mid-19th century. Bargains are possible.... *Tel 0207/242–3844. Chancery House, 53–64 Chancery Lane WC2, Chancery Lane tube stop.* **(see p. 160)**

Lonsdale. The place for pugilists, and for those who just imitate them—the British answer to Everlast and Reyes does a leisurewear line.... *Tel 0207/437–1526. 47 Beak St. W1, Oxford Circus tube stop.* **(see p. 159)**

Margaret Howell. Unpretentious, tailored English clothes that nod to the equestrian for men and women.... *Tel 0207/495–4888. 24 Brook St. W1, Bond St. tube stop; tel 0207/584–2462, 29 Beauchamp Place SW3, Knightsbridge tube stop.* **(see p. 155)**

Marks & Spencer. Whatever their social stratum, the Londoner shops M&S for underwear and sweaters. Clothes are inexpensive, well made, and getting more exciting by the season. The food department is equally adored.... *Tel 0207/935–7954. 459 Oxford St. W1, Marble Arch tube stop. Open Mon.–Fri. 9–8, Sat. 9–7, Sun. 12–6. Branches.* **(see pp. 153, 154, 161)**

Marlborough Fine Art. Where to shop for an Old Master—or just look like one.... *Tel 0207/629–5161. 6 Albermarle St. W1, Green Park tube stop.* **(see p. 161)**

Miss Selfridge. Hip high-school girls find constantly metamorphosing clothing here to gratify short attention spans and modest allowances.... *Tel 0207/318–3833. 40 Duke St. W1, Bond St. tube stop. Open Mon.–Wed. 10–7, Thurs.–Fri. 10–8, Sat. 10–7, Sun. 12–6. Branches.* **(see p. 154)**

Mr. Eddie. Over 35 years in the biz and another with a big celeb client list. Large stock of fabric (including Austin Powers' shagadelic velvet) means fast turnaround for a simple suit.... *Tel 0207/437–3727. 52 Berwick St. W1, Piccadilly Circus tube stop.* **(see p. 157)**

Mole Jazz. Probably the best of all London's excellent jazz stores, with a load of rare stuff and comprehensive stacks of new CDs, too.... *Tel 0207/278–8623. 311 Gray's Inn Rd. WC1, King's Cross tube stop.* **(see p. 162)**

Mothercare. One-stop shopping for baby and toddler needs; low prices, high quality.... *Tel 0207/629–6621. 461 Oxford St. W1, Marble Arch tube stop. Branches. Open Sun noon–6.* **(see p. 162)**

Mulberry. Tweed hacking jackets, cord jodhpurs (but not for riding in), leather purses, belts, and wallets, tailored separates and staid frocks—not bargain, but top quality.... *Tel 0207/ 493–2546. 11 Gees Court W1, Bond St. tube stop; tel 0207/225–0313, 185 Brompton Rd. SW3, Knightsbridge tube stop.* **(see p. 155)**

Museum Store. Collected goodies from museums around the world—reproduction ancient artifacts to arty scarves—last-minute gifts that look like you shopped your heart out.... *Tel 0207/431–7156, 4 Perrins Court NW3, Hampstead tube stop. Open Sun 11–5.* **(see p. 158)**

Neal Street East. Gorgeous gifts on a budget, many penny toys, kitchenware, and knickknacks from Asia make this not indigenous, but long-running store fun.... *Tel 0207/240–0135. 5 Neal St. WC2, Covent Garden tube stop. Mon.–Wed. 11–7, Thurs.–Sat. 10–7, Sun. noon–6.* **(see p. 161)**

Neal's Yard Dairy. Cheeses from the British Isles, many rare, unpasteurized farmhouse specials. 'Round the corner is London's best holistic-healing, herbalist, massage therapist, natural-foods center.... *Tel 0207/379–7646. 17 Shorts Gardens WC2, Covent Garden tube stop. Mon.–Sat. 9–7, Sun. 11–5.* **(see p. 163)**

Nicole Farhi. Wearable, well-made suits and separates in muted colors and natural fibers, and at medium fashionability and cost for both male and female grown-ups.... *Tel 0207/499–8368. 158 New Bond St. W1, Bond St. tube stop; tel 0207/497–8713, 11 Floral St. WC2, Covent Garden tube stop; tel 0207/486–3416, 26 St. Christopher's Place W1, Bond St. tube stop; tel 0207/235–0877, 193 Sloane St. SW1, Knightsbridge tube stop.* **(see p. 155)**

Oasis. Inexpensive, reasonably trendy clothes for young career girls. Color is a strong suit.... *Tel 0207/240–7445. 13 James St. WC2, Covent Garden tube stop. Open Mon.–Sat. 10–7 (8 p.m. Thurs.), Sun. noon–7. Branches.* **(see p. 154)**

Oils and Spice Shop. The aromatic entry in the gastro row of foodie shops in the Conran mall by Tower Bridge.... *Tel 0207/403–3434. Butlers Wharf Building, 36E Shad Thames SE1, Tower Hill tube stop. Open Mon–Fri noon–6, Sat.–Sun. 10–6.* **(see p. 163)**

OXO Tower. A neglected landmark building became a place to schmooze with and commission from designers of homewares, jewelry, etc. in their actual workshops. Related to Gabriel's Wharf, but better. See Dining for the restaurant.... *Tel 0207/401–3610. Bargehouse St. SE1, Waterloo tube stop. Open Tues.–Sun. 11–6.* **(see p. 160)**

Paddy Campbell. Campbell's suits and frocks in natural fabrics and non-hysterical cuts come off as if tailored for you, and swift alterations are indeed offered at her boutique.... *Tel 0207/493–5646. 8 Gees Court W1, Bond St. tube stop.* **(see p. 155)**

Pandora. Here is so much top-quality used designer garb that there are entire Armani and Chanel sections. Plenty of other names and labels, too.... *Tel 0207/589–5289. 16–22 Cheval Place SW7, Knightsbridge tube stop.* **(see p. 156)**

Paul Costelloe. Best known for midpriced Dressage collection of Irish linens and tweed suits. Costelloe also offers a high-fashion line.... *Tel 0207/589–9480. 156 Brompton Rd. SW3, Knightsbridge tube stop.* **(see p. 155)**

Paul Smith. The king of quirk has opened a new flagship store in the heart of hip Notting Hill, and another for the ladies with their little sprogs. Ah, bless!.... *Tel 0207/727–3553. 122 Kensington Park Rd. W11, Notting Hill tube stop.* **Women and children only:** *Tel 0207/589–9139. 84–86 Sloane Ave. SW3, Sloane Sq. tube stop.* **Original flagship store:** *Tel 0207/379–7133. 40–44 Floral St. WC2, Covent Garden tube stop.* **Sale shop:** *Tel 0207/493–1287. 23 Avery Row W1, Bond St. tube stop.* **(see pp. 155, 156)**

Paxton & Whitfield. The cheese shop of your dairy dreams is the oldest in the land, in beautiful period premises.... *Tel 0207/930–0259. 93 Jermyn St. SW1, Piccadilly Circus tube stop.* **(see p. 163)**

Penhaligon's. Gorgeous glass flacons with classic smells for your delectation. Founded by Victoria's court barber.... *Tel 0207/836–2150. 41 Wellington St. WC2, Covent Garden tube stop; tel 0207/629–1416, 16 Burlington Arcade W1, Piccadilly Circus tube stop; tel 0207/493–0002, 20a Brook St. W1, Bond St. tube stop. Wellington St. branch open Sun. noon–5.* **(see p. 158)**

Peter Jones. Where the Sloane Ranger mummy gets the cricket sweater and prep school uniform, plus her own twin-set and pearls.... *Tel 0207/730–3434. Sloane Sq. SW1, Sloane Sq. tube stop.* **(see p. 153)**

Petticoat Lane Market. Famous streets of cheap leather jackets, underwear, CDs, and old gold stalls amount to London's most famous market. Past its heyday, but still very cheap. *Middlesex/Goulston/Old Castle/Cutler Streets, Bell Lane. Liverpool St. tube stop. Open Sun. 9–2.* **(see p. 160)**

Portobello Road Market. Several markets in one, from the 2,000 antiques dealers of the Notting Hill end, past the fruit-and-veg traders, to the trendy stalls of vintage stuff under the Westway, and on into the junk of Goldborne Road. London's best, we think. *Portobello Rd. W11–W10. Ladbroke Grove or Notting Hill Gate tube stops. Antiques open Sat. 7 a.m.–5:30 p.m., general Mon.–Sat. 9–5; closes 1 p.m. Thurs.* **(see pp. 156, 159)**

Prada. Every fashion victim and fashion editor's favorite fashion fetish.... *Tel 0207/235–0008. 43–5 Sloane St. SW3, Sloane Sq. tube stop; tel 0207/647–5000, 15–18 Old Bond St., Green Park tube stop.* **(see p. 154)**

R. Twining & Co. Where Twining's tea was brought into the world is still a shop, with a tea museum-ette attached.... *Tel 0207/353–3511. 216 Strand WC2, Temple tube stop. Closed weekends.* **(see p. 158)**

Reckless Records. Here's another venerable vinyl destination, not a genre specialist, but well stocked with second-hand rock, pop, soul, jazz.... *Tel 0207/437–4271. 30 Berwick St. W1, Oxford Circus tube stop. Open daily 10–7.* **(see p. 162)**

Richard James. The groovy face of Savile Row. Preview his bespoke style—eye up the waiters at the Atlantic.... *Tel 0207/434–0605. 31 Savile Row W1, Piccadilly Circus tube stop.* **(see pp. 156, 160)**

River Island. Trendy, inexpensive fashion from this High Street chain, with the Charlotte Halton line going upmarket in suits and frocks for dressing up.... *Tel 0207/937–0224. 124 Kensington High St. W8, High Street Kensington tube stop. Open Mon.–Sat. 9–6 (Thurs. 10–7:30), Sun. 11–5. Branches.* **(see p. 154)**

Rococo. Chocoholic heaven, way beyond Hershey's, and even Valrhona—get sophisticated high-cocoa-content confections, and funny-shape novelties.... *Tel 0207/352–5857. 321 King's Rd. SW3, Sloane Sq. tube stop.* **(see pp. 158, 163)**

S & B Evans. Pots for yards, in the market for gardeners—Columbia Road.... *Tel 0207/729–6635. 7a Ezra St. E2, Old St. tube stop.* **(see p. 162)**

Section 5. Jungle is the hot beat at press time, and here is where to get it for a turntable near you.... *Tel 0207/351–6853. The Common Market, 121 King's Rd. SW3, Sloane Sq. tube stop.* **(see p. 162)**

Selfridges. A venerable department store, founded by an American. Food, fashion, and cosmetics are strong.... *Tel 0207/629–1234. 400 Oxford St. W1, Bond St. tube stop. Open Mon.–Wed. 10–7, Thurs.–Fri. 10–8, Sat. 9:30–7, Sun. 12–6.* **(see pp. 153, 163)**

Skin Two. Fetishwear, mostly rubber, with authentic Victorian-cut wasp-waist corsets and made-to-measure rubber, PVC,

and fetish-oriented giftware on the side.... *Tel 0207/ 840–0146. Unit N306, Westminster Business Sq., Durham St. SE11, Vauxhall tube stop. Call ahead for appointment.*
(see p. 156)

Skoob Books. Well-stocked secondhand book mecca, for when you know what you're after.... *Tel 0207/404–3063. 15 Sicilian Ave. WC1, Holborn tube stop. Open Sun. noon–5.*
(see p. 161)

Slim Barrett. This hip jeweler makes crowns for our times, and also home accessories.... *Tel 0207/354–9393. Studio 6, Shepeton House, 83–93 Shepeton Rd. N1, Angel tube stop. All viewing by appointment.* **(see p. 158)**

Soccer Scene. Impress your teammates back home with an Arsenal uniform, or a pair of British spikes.... *Tel 0207/ 439–0778, 56–57 Carnaby St. W1; tel 0207/437–1966 (the year the English won the World Cup), 17 Foubert's Place W1, Oxford Circus tube stop (both). Open Sun. 11–5.*
(see p. 159)

Spitalfields Market. An indoor collection of permanent stalls with a changing center—Sunday is greenmarket and crafts day.... *Tel 0207/247–6590. Commercial/Brushfield St. E1, Liverpool St. tube stop. Mon.–Fri., Sun. 11–3.* **(see p. 160)**

Sportspages. The place for that unusual cricket tome you've been hunting for, or any other brit-sport book.... *Tel 0207/240–9604. Caxton Walk, 94–96 Charing Cross Rd. WC2, Tottenham Court Rd. tube stop. Open Mon.–Sat. 9:30–7, Sun. 11:30–5.* **(see p. 161)**

Spycatcher. Espionage gewgaws.... *Tel 0207/245–9445. 25G Lowndes St. SW1, Knightsbridge tube stop.* **(see p. 158)**

Stanford. Maps, travel guides, and even globes in great abundance satisfy wanderlust.... *Tel 0207/836–1321. 12 Long Acre WC2, Leicester Sq. tube stop.* **(see p. 161)**

Steinberg & Tolkein. Museum-quality pre-1960 clothing in classy thrift-shop ambience downstairs; mountains of vintage costume jewelry upstairs.... *Tel 0207/376–3660. 193 King's Rd. SW3, Sloane Sq. tube stop. Open Mon.–Sat. 10:30–7.* **(see p. 156)**

The Stencil Store. Everything for wall art, including inspiration.... *Tel 0207/730–0728. 89 Lower Sloane St. SW1, Sloane Sq. tube stop.* **(see p. 161)**

The Tea House. More varieties of tea than you can count, plus strainers, trivets, pots, and cozies.... *Tel 0207/240–7539. 15 Neal St. WC2, Covent Garden tube stop. Open Mon.–Sat. 10–7, Sun. noon–6.* **(see pp. 158, 161)**

Theo Fennell. Gold ecclesiastical/Renaissance-inspired shapes with cabochon gems, and exquisitely detailed silver miniatures are what Fennell does best. Top dollar.... *Tel 0207/591–5000. 169 Fulham Rd. SW3, South Kensington tube stop.* **(see p. 157)**

Thomas Goode & Co. The ultimate store for bone china and porcelain, crystal glassware, and related costly goods.... *Tel 0207/499–2823. 19 South Audley St. W1, Green Park tube stop.* **(see p. 161)**

Thornton's. The confectioner that took over the U.K. started with Special Toffee (and it is), and progressed to Belgian-style cream truffles, kids' novelties, ice cream, and other goodies.... *Tel 0207/434–2483. 254 Regent St. W1, Oxford Circus tube stop. Open Mon.–Wed., Fri.–Sat. 9:30–7, Thurs. 9:30–7:30, Sun. 11:30–5:30. Branches.* **(see pp. 158, 163)**

Tom's. A Conran shop, this one from the food son-of-Terence, and a cornucopian deli it is.... *Tel 0207/221–8818. 226 Westbourne Grove W11, Notting Hill Gate tube stop. Open Sun. noon–4.* **(see p. 163)**

Top Shop. Loud clothes in a loud shop, cheap, colorful, and tight, mostly for teenagers, who find them stylish.... *Tel 0207/636–7700. 214 Oxford St. W1, Oxford Circus tube stop. Branches. Open Sun. noon–6.* **(see p. 154)**

Trax. A Soho place for Soho club–type groove music.... *Tel 0207/734–0795. 55 Greek St. W1, Tottenham Court Rd. tube stop.* **(see p. 162)**

Tridias. Toys tending toward traditional, with science sets, coloring pens, and games galore; near the big museums.... *Tel 0207/584–2330. 25 Bute St. SW7, South Kensington tube stop.* **(see p. 162)**

Turnbull & Asser. The minimum first order for customized shirts is a half dozen, from £100 apiece, but these are the world's *best* shirts. Ready-made also available.... *Tel 0207/930–0502. 71 Jermyn St. SW1, Piccadilly Circus tube stop.*
(see p. 157)

Urban Outfitters. London branch of the ultra-hip NYC lifestyle store. New and vintage clothes, music, and some of the funkiest ideas for gifts and home furnishings—all combined in a faux-warehouse setting..... *Tel 0207/761–1001. 36–38 Kensington High St. W8, Kensington High St. tube stop. Open Sun. noon–6.* **(see pp. 155, 156)**

Vivienne Westwood. The ultimate style queen, who constantly invents fashion movements and is copied by the world about three years later.... *Tel 0207/352–6551. World's End, 430 King's Rd. SW10, Sloane Sq. tube stop, then 11 or 22 bus.* **Sale Shop**.... *Tel 0207/439–1109. 44 Conduit St. W1, Oxford Circus tube stop.* **(see pp. 155, 156)**

Warehouse. High turnover for high fashion; not top quality in the finish, but far from top prices, Warehouse keeps getting better.... *Tel 0207/734–5096. 19 Argyll St. W1, Oxford Circus tube stop. Branches.* **(see p. 154)**

Waterstone's. A terribly successful and likeable chain of bookstores, many of which run readings and signings.... *Tel 0207/434–4291. 121–125 Charing Cross Rd. W1, Leicester Sq. tube stop. Open Mon.–Sat. 9:30–8, Sun. noon–6. Branches.* **(see p. 161)**

Whistles. The tiniest and trendiest of chains racks clothes by shade, has its own label, and sells European designer-wear in bright and spacious shops.... *Tel 0207/487–4484. 12 St. Christopher's Place W1, Bond St. tube stop. Branches.*
(see pp. 154, 156)

Zwemmer. Well-stocked bookstores in two arty varieties: the fine arts and photography/cinema.... *Tel 0207/240–4158, 24 Litchfield St. WC2; tel 0207/240–4157, 80 Charing Cross Rd. WC2, Leicester Sq. tube (both).* **(see p. 161)**

THE INDEX

SHOPPING

tlife

Stop the presses! London's licensing hours are changing (or so rumor has it). In order to celebrate the next century, our happy, happy government (thanks, Tone) is allegedly going to allow *us* to decide when we want to stop drinking. About blooming time. You see, once upon a time, London went to bed early or found creative ways around the anachronistic restriction on late-night partying. Please, Tony, loosen up our 11 p.m. curfew. We're probably big enough to look after ourselves now.

Alcohol is not the only fuel for a good time, of course, but Londoners—well, the British in general—prefer a wet bar to a juice bar, however modish those ginseng-guarana-spirulina cocktails might be. God knows—Londoners like to drink. Proof is provided by the ubiquity of the age-old British pub. The full title, public house, describes exactly what a good pub offers—a warm environment where many people feel at home. Music is also important to the London soul, whether, pop, jazz, indie bands, world music, or the indigenous folk traditions of the British Isles. As for clubbing and youth culture, fashion worldwide always has an eye to what young London is wearing and saying and how it's dancing in its constantly changing array of "one-nighters," warehouse parties, and restaurants *du moment*.

The Soho gay scene has helped make London friendlier than it's ever been. The hippest gay clubs here are often the hippest clubs, period. Those legendary "Summer of Love II" warehouse parties, full of technobeat and Vicks Vaporub–enhanced trance-dancing really did exist—a phenomenon yet to be equaled for pure nighttime mayhem and depravity, although, thanks to Goldie (jungle), Fat Boy Slim (big beat), and a whole host of other funsters, there's a lot of people trying to equal it every Saturday night. These revelers have spawned such cross-cultural music-led scenes as an Asian underground and ever more subdivisions of techno, drum 'n' bass, and rave. Pick up flyers anywhere hip, or be handed them as you exit somewhere sweaty, and follow the paper trail.

Sources

For an all-around picture of music, clubs, and the student scene, pick up the weekly (out Wed.; Tues. in the city center) institution, *Time Out*, whose tone is irritatingly smug, but which does a grand job of listing nearly everything there is to do. *Time Out*'s club listings aren't bad, but there are several magazines dedicated to the scene—*MixMag* is a good one—that go deeper. Better still, the weekly (out Thurs.) music papers, especially the *NME (New Musical Express)* are good for insight into the band culture. The gay scene, for both genders, is conveyed through the monthly *Gay Times* and the weekly *MX (MetroXtra)*; free papers are available in gay establishments.

Liquor Laws and Drinking Hours

If you're British, 11 p.m. has become engrained in the body as the time when the average evening out winds down. Think "Pavlov's lush." The "last orders" bell, rung in pubs at ten of eleven, and the "time" bell are the drinking-up and getting-out signals, respectively, and many drunks have been created by the need to chug-a-lug several pints during the last ten minutes' drinking time. Yet changes are afoot. Late pub–type licenses have become more common, and more places are allowed to let you drink till midnight, or even later on week-ends. Check with your favorite pub in advance. The law governing daytime drinking was lifted long ago, so you can get quietly pissed in a pub garden all afternoon if you feel like it. Separate laws apply to private clubs, restaurants, and places with a cover charge.

The Lowdown

Personality pubs... There used to be a pub for every taste, then the big breweries (landlords of most pubs) suddenly converted every dear old grungy, down-home barroom into a small Edwardian theme park, with antiquarian books by-the-mile, a fake log fire, brass rails, and stuffed owls, then stripped them down to bare floorboards, wooden tables and plain color-washed walls, with salady, Tuscan food chalked on a blackboard. Go into any **All Bar One** to see this in action. It's annoying when what one wants in pubs is authenticity. The real thing still does exist, although **Ye Olde Cheshire Cheese**, for instance, which is about 330 years old, is terribly touristy. On the other hand, its sawdust floors, low, wood-beamed ceilings, and 14th-century crypt are just the same as when Dickens drank there. Don't get too excited by that last part: Either Dickens drank nearly everywhere in London, or publicans are congenital liars.

Beards and real ale... Oh, how the British like their beer. They like it warm, they like it dark, they like it flat, they like it strong—they like it any way but cold and gassy and in a bottle. Well, most of them. In truth, millions of Londoners have acquired an American taste in beer, and Rolling Rock, Bud, et al. are omnipresent, as is Corona with a slice of lime wedged in the neck. But "real ale" is true British beer—similar to U.S. microbrewery output, yet older. Its traditional image is mixed up with men who wear sandals with socks and grow unruly beards, but it has become trendy. Try the **Jerusalem Tavern** for proof (and good ale) or go to any of the pubs with **Firkin** (a kind of barrel used in beer making) in their names, like the **Pheasant & Firkin**, and have a pint of "rail ale" with medical students in their cups, to see how popular this game really is. For good Irish stout, **The Cow** is more salubrious than echt Irish pubs along the Kilburn High Road, and it's usually good for the *craic* too.

Cruising, schmoozing, meeting (straight)... A designated singles scene really doesn't exist in London, because the unwritten rules of dating are not the same here. Exactly how, we couldn't say (these are unwritten rules), but see if you notice a difference at **Beach Blanket Babylon**, where the decor is suitably gothic for the throbbing mass of smooth-skinned (i.e., young) humanity convening weekend nights, especially in summer. If you can force someone to get you into the **Groucho**, you'll certainly see chatting-up in progress, though you'll need a strong stomach for elitism. Despite being named after the man who wouldn't join a club that would take him as a member, the most famous media-movie-journo hangout is liable to look down its nose at you unless it knows you. Precisely the opposite is true of London's two best fests: the high-summer, West Indian, **Notting Hill Carnival**; and the Celtic party in Finsbury Park, the **Fleadh**. Whatever you did tonight, whomever you met, wherever (within reason) you are, you'll probably end up having an espresso at **Bar Italia**, scoping or dishing other clubbers. The **Hanover Grand** is where you might have been, if you're young. Or, for the best sound system in London, perhaps **The End,** in which case you're probably deaf now.

Cruising, schmoozing, meeting (gay)... The earth revolves around "the Compton"—Soho's always lively Old Compton Street that underwent metamorphosis, and is now almost New Yorky in its hours and its up-frontness. As we've said, places mostly welcome a mix (permutations of gay-straight-men-women), but men are the target customers of the biggest and busiest, **The Yard**, while little **First Out** peacefully purveys caffeine and alcohol. The dyke scene doesn't really center on Soho, nor on any one place, though you can count on any and every women-only event attracting mostly gay women. The West End arts center, **Drill Hall**, runs loads of these, plus it has a girls' bar–night Mondays. It's a fair bet that that long-running one-night-a-week club will endure. Let's all hope the **Royal Vauxhall Tavern** never closes either. It's just a local, but a faggy, sometimes dykey, one with a great vibe and an amateur drag cabaret dating from way before the Lady Bunny. **Heaven** is heaven for dancing.

East meets West... but only rarely. The much media-hyped rivalry between East (Shoreditch, Hoxton, Dalston) and West (Notting Hill, Kensal, Queen's Park) is becoming something of a London joke. The truth is, both areas are fashionable and both have a range of fashionable watering holes to suit all tastes, many of which also serve excellent food. Hooray. The East, or at least this area of it, has long been a purely commercial district; this means that opening hours are less rigid for bars. Recently, however, it was reinhabited by artists craving the space of warehouse conversions, which has made the area unrelentingly fashionable. The end result is a succession of trendy, late-opening bars. Since the big-spending city slickers are absent on the weekends, there is some closure in the area, notablyon Sunday nights—so phone ahead for opening times. On Charlotte Road are the popular **Bricklayers Arms** (dress down) and the more suity **Cantaloupe** bar. Just opposite are the **Great Eastern Dining Rooms,** often filled with a buzzing crowd, especially on Fridays, and the **Home** bar, which is currently expanding to satisfy its massive popularity. In nearby Hoxton Square are the **Shoreditch Electricity Showrooms** (which is actually a bar and not a toaster shop—how *very* Shoreditch) and the **Lux Cinema** (see Diversions). When you've sampled all these you can go to the **333 Club** for a bit of a dance. Nearer the center of town is Farringdon, home to two of London's most popular nightclubs—the long-established **Turnmills** and the enfant terrible **Fabric**. Conveniently close to both of these dens is the **Match** bar, the ideal spot to meet before a night of debauchery; indeed, it is quite capable of playing host to small-scale debauchery all its own. Although Notting Hill has in recent years become overrun by rich, glamorous yuppies, the area has managed to retain a unique character, with its colorful collection of bars and restaurants, the Portobello Road Market, and

Carnival. Portobello is really the center of the action; and you could do worse than check out the **Market Bar** and **The Beat Bar.** If you head eastward a bit you will come to the ultraglam **Westbourne,** opposite the more understated **Cow.** From here, an arc to the north and west will yield **Babushka,** with its chocolate vodkas, DJs, and upstairs parties (often private, but easily gate-crashed); the new **Golborne House,** for the last word in ice-chilled cool; **The Paradise Bar,** just as chilled but not quite as cool; and lastly, **The William IV,** a saggy-armchaired heaven for Sunday lunch. Despite its reputation as a hedonistic funfest, Notting Hill and its environs are not a good place for late drinking. If you're lucky enough to know a member, the obvious choice is **The Cobden Club,** West London's answer to Soho House. If you're not so well connected but still want to stay out late, however, you could go to the **Pharmacy,** artist Damien Hirst's conceptual bar, which is a tad overpriced and decorated as, you guessed it, a pharmacy. Our tip, however, is the less pristine **Notting Hill Arts Club,** a venue that, although basically a bar, is committed to supporting other artistic endeavors—films, exhibitions, performances, and the like.

Late license... The **Atlantic Bar and Grill** began to transform London's nights when it won a 3 a.m. alcohol license back in 1993. Others followed, but the revolution—whatever you've heard—never hit. The divey **Barcelona** and its neighbor **Café Bohème** both are very central, with late licenses, but neither has much else to recommend it beyond permission to drink. Candidate for most sordid and steamy dive in town is the compulsory stop-in-after-the-Forum **Triñanes,** a Spanish restaurant (don't eat here) cater-corner from that Kentish Town hall of rock. Its earlier-evening flamenco nights can actually be pretty authentic and fabulous. The most genuine, diviest late-night bar is one you can't really visit without an invitation—it's at Bayswater's **Commodore** hotel, where the hippest not-too-famous bands stay, and drink all night if that's the sort of thing they do.

Two-step, waltz, salsa, and boogie... If you want to make like Fred and Ginger, there aren't that many places to go. All the regular dances are in hotels, and the three best are, unsurprisingly, found in three of the best hotels: **Claridges**, the **Savoy**'s River Restaurant, and the Terrace at the **Dorchester**. All have dinner dances with prix-fixe menus, inclusive of cover, and all but the Savoy hold the events on Friday and Saturday nights only (till 1 a.m.); the Savoy does it every night but Sunday. Tunes tend to be more Sinatra than Strauss at all of the hotel hops. Latin dance is getting all popular, meanwhile. Several places follow the same pattern of an early-evening class for the gringos to prepare for the night of nonstop salsa. Check the listings for these, though the Islington tapas bar, **La Finca**, and the West End **Bar Rumba** have all been running them for some time. Teddy boys and girls, ska and rock-steady fans, jivers and rockers have two places to go: **Gaz's Rockin Blues**, which is probably Soho's longest-running "one-nighter" club, or the **100 Club**, which, at press time, was holding its chief R&B night Mondays. Medium to large venues to rock out in include the north London **Forum** and the central **Astoria**. Even hipper than those are the **Brixton Academy** in the wilds of South London, and **Subterania,** ditto in the West.

Where to be invited by members... **Groucho** thinks it's the center of the publishing/TV/publicity/literary world, and, unfortunately, it's right. After about 10 years, the irreverent club that's secretly establishment still has what it takes, to the extent that if you yourself move in these worlds, you'll find it more challenging to avoid Groucho than to be invited. A place with a rep you'll have more trouble entering is near-legendary **Annabel's**, which is a surreal mix of early-Jackie-Collins-novel discotheque and black-tie supper club. Yes, rollicking royals really do drop in on occasion, and a glass of champagne costs 20 quid. Less predictable, and even older, is the wonderfully housed **Chelsea Arts Club**, with its gardens, bedchambers, dimly lit dining, and its snooker tables in the bar. It's disreputable by design, but really is often full of pissed sculptors taking their clothes off, having fist fights, or simply falling over. Among newer clubs, the **Soho House** has found its niche after its first few years. It's for the end of the Groucho crowd with shorter skirt, higher alcohol tolerance, bigger drug habit, louder mouth, and more likely to be in movies 'n' videos than books 'n' newspapers. If you're gorgeous to the rest of the world, as well as to each other, and make a living from this, head to the **Met Bar**. Another, loucher, warmer choice for you beauties is the cash bar at the casbah, **Momo**.

Jazz standards... This week's big name in town will be found at **Ronnie Scotts**, where the cover charge seems less exorbitant since everywhere else has caught up. **Pizza Express** is in a similar mainstream-but-musically-hip vein to Ronnies, but serves far better pizza. Meanwhile, there is no food, little atmosphere, but great music (depending on who's on, of course) at the **Queen Elizabeth Hall** and **Purcell Room** at the South Bank, where you'll catch the bigger, or more staid, folk. For the absolute coolness of the cutting edge, you'll need to leave downtown and go north to the **Jazz Café,** in sunny Camden Town, or northeast to the Stoke Newington **Vortex**. Higher quality than most, though way out in Barnes, is the riverside **Bull's Head**.

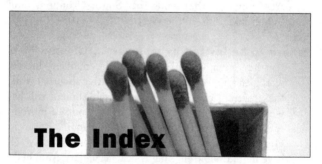

The Index

All Bar One. Why are we listing this chain? Because all couple dozen are clean, well-lighted places. This is the Leicester Square one... *Tel 0207/747–9921. Leicester Sq. WC2, Leicester Sq. tube stop.*   **(see p. 185)**

Annabel's. Whatever the opposite of a dive is, this members-only *boîte* is it. Nobs, snobs, and hoorays (braying, chinless Hooray Henry is the Sloane Ranger's brother) are those members. Surprisingly, it can be a blast.... *Tel 0207/ 629–1096. 44 Berkeley Sq. W1, Green Park tube stop. Members only.*   **(see p. 189)**

Astoria. Very central, at the top of Oxford Street, this big hall has a pleasantly louche vibe, for wrecks in their twenties to see bands on the up.... *Tel 0207/434–9592. 157 Charing*

Cross Rd. WC2, Tottenham Court Rd./Leicester Sq. tube stop. Open late. Cover charge. **(see p. 189)**

Atlantic Bar and Grill. See Dining.

Babushka. A dark, atmospheric bar just north of Portobello Road. Check out the chocolate-flavored vodkas. Live DJs and a function room upstairs.... *Tel 0207/727–9250. 41 Tavistock Crescent, W11, Westbourne Park tube stop.* **(see p. 188)**

Bar Italia. See Dining.

Bar Rumba. A conveniently located West End place that offers a free salsa class before the bargain (at press time, Tuesday night) "Salsa Pa'Ti".... *Tel 0207/287–2715. 36 Shaftsbury Ave. W1, Piccadilly Circus tube stop. Cover charge.* **(see p. 189)**

Barcelona. A divey Spanish-ish bar with tapas; useful for being Soho central and managing to stay open late.... *Tel 0207/287–9932. 17 Old Compton St. W1, Leicester Sq. tube stop. Open late.* **(see p. 188)**

Beach Blanket Babylon. As a bar, restaurant, and a place to meet fellow twenty–thirties, this gothique Portobello joint rocks on weekends. *Tel 0207/229–2907. 45 Ledbury Rd. W11, Notting Hill Gate tube stop.* **(see p. 186)**

The Beat Bar. Small, velvet-draped bar located in the middle of Portobello Market. Live DJs change daily. *Tel 0207/792–2043. 265 Portobello Rd. Ladbroke Grove tube stop.* **(see p. 188)**

The Bricklayers Arms. Much frequented by artists—excellent weekend breakfasts, hearty food. Do not dress up! The look is deconstructed to the point of apocalyptic. If you're lucky, you might be sneered at by a prize-winning artist.... *Tel 0207/739–5245. 63 Charlotte Rd. EC2, Old St. tube stop.* **(see p. 187)**

Brixton Academy. A huge hall in South London's reggae-culture neighborhood tends to be very hip and pretty young, and has bands playing most nights, as well as club events.... *Tel 0207/924–9999. 211 Stockwell Rd. SW9, Brixton tube stop. Open late. Cover charge.* **(see p. 189)**

NIGHTLIFE | THE INDEX

Mondays.... *Tel 0207/631–1353. 16 Chenies St. W1, Goodge St. tube stop.* **(see p. 187)**

The End. Banging tunes from the best sound system in London—not for the old or the faint of heart.... *Tel 0207/419–9199. 18 West Central St. WC1, Tottenham Court Rd. tube stop.* **(see p. 186)**

Fabric. Three floors, 2,000 capacity, big-name DJs, residents and guests, and DTPM, the famous gay Sunday night out—oh my lord, the mind boggles. A must.... *Tel 0207/490–0444. 77A Charterhouse St. EC1, Farringdon tube stop.* **(see p. 187)**

La Finca. This tapas bar/restaurant has salsa classes and dance nights in its upstairs club.... *Tel 0207/837–5387. 96 Pentonville Rd. N1, Angel tube stop. Cover charge; waived for diners.* **(see p. 189)**

...& Firkin. They are everywhere, these firkin Firkins, and all featuring puns like that one, brewed-on-premises pints of Dogbolter, stripped-pine floorboards, and student types. The first microbrewery pubs in London, long since bought out by the big boys.... *Everywhere.* **(see p. 186)**

First Out. The name is exact—if you're walking into Soho from Oxford Street, and are gay, the relaxed, friendly coffee cafe/bar is the first landmark.... *Tel 0207/240–8042. 52 St. Giles High St., WC2, Tottenham Court Rd. tube stop.* **(see p. 186)**

Fleadh. Finsbury Park's annual Celtic music fest is pronounced "flah," and is practically guaranteed to feature Van Morrison, Sinead O'Connor, and whichever Pogues have still got functioning livers.... *Tel 0208/963–0940. Finsbury Park tube stop. Mid-June. Admission charged.* **(see p. 186)**

Forum. A well-loved and well-frequented former ballroom in the north hosts medium-famous, medium-hip bands, usually for the twenties set, though older performers do attract older kids.... *Tel 0207/284–2200. 9–17 Highgate Rd. NW5, Kentish Town tube stop. Cover charge.* **(see p. 189)**

Gaz's Rockin Blues. One of this town's oldest one-night-per-week clubs, Gaz (son of blues man John) Mayall's friendly

R&B, ska and rock 'n' roll Thursdays are still going strong.... *Tel 0207/437–0525. St. Moritz, 159 Wardour St. W1, Tottenham Court Rd. tube stop. Cover charge.* **(see p. 189)**

Golborne House. Relaxed, informal, and very cool. The new jewel in the West London drinking crown. Come, relax, and just hang (the food's not bad either).... *Tel 0208/960–6260. 36 Golborne Rd. W10, Westbourne Park tube stop.*

(see p. 188)

Great Eastern Dining Rooms. Often crowded after-work pub/bar/restaurant. No dress code, but often frequented by lots of suits. Located in the heart of the Eastern drinking zone.... *Tel 0207/613–4545. 54 Great Eastern St. EC2, Old St. tube stop.* **(see p. 187)**

Groucho. You can't get in unless you know a member, but this is so integral to the life of the London intelligentsia (drinking division) that it can't be left out.... *Tel 0207/439–4685. 45 Dean St. W1, Leicester Sq. tube stop.* **(see pp. 186, 189)**

Hanover Grand. At press time, very hip, but by now who knows? Another one-nighter host, this one's a West End, two-tier wonderland of swanky decor and heaving dance floor.... *Tel 0207/499–7977. 6 Hanover St. W1, Oxford Circus tube stop. Open late. Cover charge.* **(see p. 186)**

Heaven. A venerable and vast (mostly) gay dance club under the arches behind Charing Cross has the boomingest bass, and laser lights that give you the bends.... *Tel 0207/930–2020. Off Villiers St. WC2, Charing Cross tube stop. Open late. Cover charge.* **(see p. 187)**

Home Bar. This, the most fashionable of the East London watering holes, is, at press time, extending its dining facilities and doubling in size. Maybe it'll be less dark and hot too—great for the twentysomethings.... *Tel 0207/684–8618. 100 Leonard St. EC2, Old St. tube stop.* **(see p. 187)**

Jazz Café. A converted bank in downtown Camden hosts the hottest combos from all over, and consistently swings. It's worth getting tickets in advance, and booking a table if you're having dinner.... *Tel 0207/916–6060. 7 Parkway NW1, Camden Town tube stop. Cover charge.* **(see p. 190)**

Jerusalem Tavern. In the most happening media folks' nabe is this remade Georgian. It was from here the Knights of St John set out on the Crusades. Kind of... *Tel 0207/490–4281. 55 Britton St. EC1, Farringdon tube.* **(see p. 186)**

Market Bar. A Portobello institution—all Gothic candles and flowing locks (dreadlocks, that is). It's great for a quick drink to escape the market crowds and offers good Thai food upstairs as well.... *Tel 0208/460–8320. 240 Portobello Rd. W11, Ladbroke Grove tube stop.* **(see p. 188)**

Match Bar. Ultra-styled cocktail bar that serves food as well. Ideally located for preclub drinks (Turnmills and Fabric are 'round the corner).... *Tel 0207/250–4002. 45–7 Clerkenwell Rd. EC1, Farringdon tube stop.* **(see p. 187)**

Met Bar. Members-and-hotel-guests-only scene. The place is titchy, overpriced, and overrated, but if a crowd wedged firmly up its own ass is your cup of tea, this is the place for you. Oh, and the doorstaff are rude as well. Smashing.... *Tel 0207/447–1000. Metropolitan Hotel, Old Park Lane, W1, Hyde Park Corner tube stop. Open late.* **(see p. 190)**

Momo. Unless you're a member, you'll have to dine in the restaurant upstairs to gain entrance to this mosque-lamped, mud-walled slice of Old Morocco, and even then you can only eat before you eat. Bit tight, really, but nice.... *Tel 0207/434–4040. 25 Heddon St. W1, Piccadilly Circus tube stop. Open late.* **(see p. 190)**

Notting Hill Arts Club. This dance club on Notting Hill Gate is open late. Friendly staff and a varied menu of cool sounds. Phone for details, but check out Thursday's Brazilian Love Affair and Sunday's Lazy Dog.... *Tel 0207/460–4459. 19 Notting Hill Gate, W11, Notting Hill tube stop.* **(see p. 188)**

Notting Hill Carnival. A two-day street party of genuine Island vibes, heaving merengue-ing crowds, sound stages, parades, curried goat, Red Stripe, and ganja.... *No phone. August bank holiday. Centered around the Westway, Portobello Road, Ladbroke Grove tube stop.* **(see p. 186)**

100 Club. A venerable dive that concentrates on rock and jazz, blues and R&B, with live bands and dance nights.... *Tel*

NIGHTLIFE   THE INDEX

0207/636–0933. 100 Oxford St. W1, Oxford Circus tube stop. Cover charge. **(see p. 189)**

The Paradise Bar. Chilled hangout bar with restaurant out back and dancing till 12 (sometimes) upstairs.... *Tel 0208/ 969–0098. 19 Kilburn Lane, W10, Ladbroke Grove tube stop, then 52 bus north.* **(see p. 188)**

Pharmacy. Conceptual artist Damian Hirst (he of the bisected cow)`opened this ultra-cool conceptual bar a few years back.... *Tel 0207/221–2442. 150 Notting Hill Gate, W11, Notting Hill tube stop.* **(see p. 188)**

Pizza Express. A big jazz venue, as well as London's best pizzas. This tends to host mainstream performers.... *Tel 0207/ 437–9595. 10 Dean St. W1, Tottenham Court Rd. tube stop. Cover charge.* **(see p. 190)**

Ronnie Scotts. London's best-known and most-loved jazz venue is missing the late, great saxophonist Ronnie, but is still hosting hot line-ups.... *Tel 0207/439–0747. 47 Frith St. W1. Leicester Sq. tube stop. Open late. Cover charge.* **(see p. 190)**

Royal Vauxhall Tavern. Just an old south London pub that happens to have hosted drag shows all its life, and still does so.... *Tel 0207/582–0833. 372 Kennington Lane, SW8, Oval tube stop.* **(see p. 187)**

The Shoreditch Electricity Showrooms. Open-plan bar that shows films on Tuesday night and major sports fixtures (generally soccer and rugby only!) on a projection screen. Good fun, strange name.... *Tel 0207/739–6934. 39a Hoxton Sq. N1, Old St. tube stop.* **(see p. 187)**

Soho House. Another members-only Soho haunt of media types, more the TV, movie sort than its rival's, Groucho's, hacks.... *Tel 0207/734–5188. 40 Greek St. W1, Leicester Sq. tube stop. Members and guests only.* **(see p. 189)**

Subterania. A groovy duplex dive beneath the Westway, in Notting Hill, hosts happening bands, and late-late clubbing for twentysomethings.... *Tel 0208/960–4590. 36 Acklam Rd. W10, Ladbroke Grove tube stop. Open late. Cover charge.* **(see p. 189)**

THE INDEX

NIGHTLIFE

333 Club. Three floors of varied music and a hip, grungy crowd. Dance, sweat, and meet.... *Tel 0207/739–1800. 333 Old St. EC1, Old St. tube stop.* **(see p. 187)**

Triñanes. Where everyone goes when turfed out of the Forum, across the street. The tapas—let alone the Spanish entrées—are not why, but the flamenco performers are a weekend plus.... *Tel 0207/482–3616. 298 Kentish Town Rd. NW5, Kentish Town tube stop. Open late.***(see p. 188)**

Turnmills. Famous venue for Trade (nine-year-old gay after-hours club) is also worthwhile on other nights. If you like your music hard, Trade is a must, straight or gay.... *Tel 0207/250–3409. 636 Clerkenwell Rd. EC1, Farringdon tube stop.* **(see p. 187)**

Vortex. Serious jazz buffs should make the trek out to Stokey—a residential neighborhood, with Asian/vegetarian restaurants and some good pubs—for the cutting edge of the London scene.... *Tel 0207/254–6516. 139–141 Stoke Newington Church St. N16, Stoke Newington BR.* **(see p. 190)**

Westbourne. Wrap your shades 'round your head and pose like your life depends on it. The large terrace is a must in summer, but the bar will be a scrum—watch out.... *Tel 0207/221–1332. 101 Westbourne Park Villas, W2, Royal Oak tube stop.* **(see p. 188)**

William IV. Gorgeous on Sundays—the sun streams through the windows, the food is delicious, and the place is filled with children playing. Grab a saggy leather armchair and snooze with a beer—or four.... *Tel 0208/969–5944. 786 Harrow Rd. NW10, Kensal Green tube stop.* **(see p. 188)**

The Yard. This gay-oriented Soho cafe-bar does, indeed, have a little courtyard for coffee or beer, as well as two floors of bars that buzz by night.... *Tel 0207/437–2652. 57 Rupert St. W1, Piccadilly Circus tube stop.* **(see p. 186)**

Ye Olde Cheshire Cheese. Ye original hokey tourist hostelry, with sawdust-strewn floors and great blackened beams to bang your forehead on, but it's been open for over three centuries, so go anyway.... *Tel 0207/353–6170. 145 Fleet St. EC4, Blackfriars tube stop.* **(see p. 185)**

Closed weekends

THE INDEX

NIGHTLIFE

enterta

7

nment

As we are only too
aware, what
London is most
famous for is
theater. Well, is its
snob reputation
deserved?

The scope and bravery of the best theater companies here is certainly wide and sometimes innovative, too—although the very newest in physical theater tends to come from elsewhere in Europe. Those European companies visit London, though, so you end up with the best of all worlds: indigenous high-brow, Shakespeare, West End (London's Broadway), home-grown experimental, and imported avant-garde. Look out for the June London International Festival of Theatre (LIFT) for concentrated doses of Catalan mimes and French nouvelle clowning. Crossover genres like physical theater (Théâtre de Complicité are masters of this), new circus (look for Ra Ra Zoo and Archaos), narrative dance (Yolanda Snaith), and comedic performance (Rose English, for instance) are worth seeking out here if you're a true fan of living theater, and not just worshiping at the shrine of the traditional proscenium arch and three acts. Not that there's anything wrong with the **National Theatre** and the Royal Shakespeare Company....

If theater sends you to sleep, London's got plenty of music, from opera to jazz and all points in between; dance, ballet to aforementioned experiments; and comedy (this is the home of *Monty Python* and *Absolutely Fabulous*) to keep you amused. There are even sports.

Sources

At the risk of sounding like an infomercial, we have to give the estimable *Time Out* another plug here. If you bought only one "what's on" guide, this would be it—the nearest thing to having a clued-in Londoner on your team (which, naturally, is an even better way into the mysteries of this town). The second-best source of entertainment information is the *Evening Standard;* more especially its weekly "Hot Tickets" magazine—free with the paper on Thursdays. Both those publications give plenty of background to their listings, so you'll get a feel for what's hot at this moment.

Getting Tickets

The best way to get theater tickets is to go to the box office of the theater itself, or to call it with your charge card at hand. There's nothing wrong with ticket agents, like **First Call** (0207/420–0000) or **Ticketmaster** (0207/413–3321), unless you hate to pay the reasonable booking fee, and they do come up trumps for major rock gigs or for when you're having a theater orgy and want to book several shows. If that's you, **Keith Prowse** can be called before you leave home, at the

New York office (212/398–1430 or 800/669–8687). If you're planning a theaterfest, are a control freak, and want to do it all yourself, send for the *Complete Guide to London's West End Theatres* (£9.95 + p&h from the Society of London Theatre, Bedford Chambers, The Piazza, Covent Garden, WC2E 8HQ, tel 0207/836–3193), which has seating plans and booking information for all the West End houses. If you're cheap, broke, or smart, wait till you're in London and line up at the indispensable **Half Price Ticket Booth** (no phone) on the southwest corner of Leicester Square, which has tickets for later the same day at about 25 theaters (Mon.–Sat. 1–6:30 for evening shows; Tues.–Sun. from noon for matinees. Cash only; £2 service charge). Traditionally, theaters have been dark on Sundays, but there has been a recent smattering of Sunday performances, so check the listings. Hotels—including those with a dedicated theater desk—charge a bigger fee than the phone bookers and are only worth using if you're lazy, loaded, or longing to see Lloyd Webber's latest, in which case the best of them (**The Savoy**, the **Athenaeum**, the **Dorchester**...) may come up with the impossible, pricey, ticket. Those shows, predictably, are the most likely to harbor a crop of **scalpers** outside (known as ticket touts here). Just say no. Never buy from a guy furtively brandishing a fistful of tickets—common sense will tell you when there's someone with a legitimate extra one. If you feel that you must deal with a scalper, you should know that by law the tout must tell you the face value of the ticket at the time of sale so you can see how much he's marking it up, and be warned that it will be more than generous. Know the top prices of the show you want to see and remember that very few are regularly sold out. Every single theater keeps at least one row of **house seats** back till the last possible moment (for emergency oversales and unexpected situations) plus a dozen or two **returns**. Policies on how these are dispensed vary, but be prepared to stand in line, possibly in the morning, probably an hour before curtain, with no guarantee of success. On the other hand, you may find yourself in the stalls (orchestra) at the newly renovated Royal Opera House for a song (an £85+ seat for about £22). Failing that, if it's a big new show, you don't want to spend your vacation in line, and money's no object, check out the **classified ads** in the *Standard* for sort-of-legitimate scalpers who bought blocks of tickets and are unloading them at a premium. This is also your only hope for major sporting events, like the FA Cup Final (Football Association), or the late rounds of the men's singles, center court, Wimbledon. Apart from those, the toughest London ticket to acquire is the season's hottest fringe production (often called **Off–West End** in imitation of New York's off-Broadway appellation).

The Lowdown

The West End and the Nationals... "West End" refers to the 50-odd mainstream houses, most of which are in that neighborhood, with a few exceptions. The weird thing about West End is its ever-closer resemblance to New York's Broadway, with productions transferring back and forth across the Atlantic like so much stock from the Gap. To be fair, though, downright West End disappointment usually arises from a combo of overinflated expectations, a large dent in the pocketbook, and a bad pick. The London *Les Miserables* (nicknamed by some "The Glums") or any of the 53 Lloyd Webber monstrosities—sorry, monster hits—will please you as much as a high-school production of *Fiddler on the Roof*, if you hate musicals. Look for the houses that pitch their brow higher—like the **Haymarket**, the **Aldwych**, the **Arts**, the **Cambridge**, the **Comedy**, the **Garrick**, the **Old Vic**, and more. The easiest, safest way to go is to select from the current season at the **Royal National Theatre** or the **Barbican Arts Centre**. The latter is where the Royal Shakespeare Company (RSC) has made its home. Many screen stars—from Ralph Fiennes to Patrick Stewart—earned their stripes on this legitimate stage, and an RSC production practically comes with a warranty. The other guaranteed ticket is to the South Bank Centre's **Olivier** or **Lyttelton**. Less so the South Bank's "theatre-in-the-round" studio, the **Cottesloe**, where embarrassing juvenilia alternates with exciting edge-of-the-seat new talent.

On the fringe... The fringe denotes all the other theaters—about the same number again. It's where the exciting stuff is—where the much-vaunted British reverence for the stage is still at large. The best of the ones known nowadays as Off–West End do theater as it might have been in its premovie heyday—with passion, conviction, infectious adoration of the medium. Those with the best track record for supplying chills of awe are the

Almeida, the **Bush**, the little **Gate**, the **Riverside**, the **Donmar Warehouse** (actually West End, but nobody remembers), the **Greenwich** and the increasingly yummy **Young Vic**. The Almeida demands a trek north, but this place hardly ever misses—it's worth it. Others often worth traveling for include the **Theatre Royal Stratford East**, the **Battersea Arts Centre**, that beauteous old music hall the **Hackney Empire**, and the Kilburn **Tricycle**. Don't overlook the **Royal Court Theatre Upstairs** or the **Lyric Studio**, which are the factory outlets of their West End selves, mounting works experimental, debut, or in the round, while the theater at the redoubtable **Institute of Contemporary Arts** is exactly as it sounds—avant-garde, yet slightly worthy. Many is the show we've endured here in the name of art.

Way out on the fringe... With little fringe places, usually secreted above pubs, behind cafes, or way out in the sticks, you're on your own. Quality, degree of professionalism, amount of scenery, size of audience—everything is so utterly variable that generalization would be foolish and misleading. If they're good enough for long enough, they get sucked into the Off–West End list, like the Gate, the Bush, and the Almeida's neighbor, the original pub theater, the **King's Head**. However, there are a few pub joints that enjoy a good reputation: The Battersea **Grace Theater at Latchmere Pub**, **Jackson's Lane** up north, the Chelsea **Man in the Moon**, and the Islington **Old Red Lion**, for instance, are long-standing. We've also cried real tears and/or laughed till we were sick at the **Canal Café Theatre** (in lovely Little Venice—a plus), though this may have been serendipitous, and can in theory happen in any London fringe theater.

Verdi to Schnittke... As it seems to be everywhere these days, opera is big in London. A first night at the **Royal Opera House** is once more a hot ticket, as the renovation of the Opera House for the millennium is complete. During its dark period, the Royal Opera was a moved feast, appearing mostly at the Barbican Theatre, but also in whichever auditoria could take it. Every bit as good as the Royal Opera is the English National Opera, which lives at the **Coliseum**, off Trafalgar Square, wand hich is also looking at a major move, or a renovation. As far as repertoire is concerned—and assuming that all resumes much as it was before the intermission—the main differences between the two houses are that the ENO costs less to see and their performers sing in English. The Royal Opera gets more of the ultimate stars, and projects "surtitles" over the stage. The ENO is far more likely to mount Philip Glass or Schnittke or Janacek, while the House will be first with your Wagner. Another theater with an opera program is the Islington **Sadler's Wells**, which is where to find the D'Oyly Carte, founded by the Englishissimo Gilbert and Sullivan, and still churning out *The Yeomen of the Guard*, *The Pirates of Penzance,* et al., plus other people's operettas. If the music is not your top priority—although the standard is rising each year—then don't pass up the **Holland Park Open Air Theatre**, wherein little companies stage full-scale productions of *La Traviata* and *Tosca*—and *The Yeomen of the Guard*—accompanied by the bedtime screeches of peacocks and a Technicolor sunset.

Mozart to Martinu... Indigenous world-famous orchestras and ensembles include the Royal Philharmonic Orchestra—which plays at home in the **Royal Festival Hall**—and the less glamorous London Symphony Orchestra, which lives at the **Barbican Arts Centre** with the English Chamber Orchestra. You'll find a lot of Henry Purcell and Thomas Tallis around—not just because they're English, but because Baroque is in vogue. As for venues...a lot goes on in a few places. Between them, the **South Bank Centre** and the **Barbican** have most of the major recitals and concerts sewn up, the former with its set of three halls of diminishing size—the **Royal Festival Hall**, the **Queen Elizabeth Hall**, and the **Purcell Room**. Other than these there's the glorious **Wigmore Hall**, behind Oxford Street, and the aforementioned (in Diversions) **Albert Hall**, which is most remarkable for the wonderful summer series of Henry Wood Promenade Concerts, or Proms. Good for a gentle evening is a recital at one of these two historic houses: Holland Park's **Leighton House** and Hampstead's **Burgh House**.

Pew music... Some of the major classical music venues, and certainly the most numerous, are churches. A few, like the leader of the pack, **St. John's Smith Square**, are deconsecrated; others, including the other big cheese, **St. Martin-in-the-Fields**, retain their pasture, and operate a double life as house of entertainment/house of God. (The latter spawned the famous Baroque ensemble, the Academy of St. Martin-in-the-Fields, by the way.) Others of the genre include several churches in the city, like **St. Giles in the Barbican** and Wren's **St. James's Garlickhythe**, plus the Piccadilly Wren with the plastic spire (OK, fiberglass); **St. James's Southwark Cathedral** is a major venue, and look out for the program at Nicholas Hawksmoor's **Christ Church Spitalfields,** because the building's as glorious as the music. There's a very good festival there in June and September. Concerts in churches are big bargains—and often they're entirely free, especially at lunchtime.

The dance... This city's up there with the best, in both the classical and young choreographers departments. The ballet is biggest and glossiest when given by the Royal Ballet, formerly at the **Royal Opera House** and soon to enter its brand-new purpose-built home. Stars they own include Irek Mikhamedov and Darcey Bussell, but visiting feet dance here, too, as they do at the other big ballet place, **Sadler's Wells**, where there's also flamenco and tango and whichever specialty dancers are dropping by. If you prefer newer stuff, look out for dance festivals, like the summer Dance Umbrella, the springtime Spring Loaded and the Islington Dance Festival; get the program from **The Place**, which is the center of new dance.

Ha ha ha ha... Comedy is huge, and growing, and places to see it are legion. The one that kicked off the thing called alternative comedy, which became the mainstream in the '80s (and still is), was the **Comedy Store**. Since way before *Monty Python*, Britain has had a special affinity for comedy, but we will attempt no explanation of the scene, nor of the British sense of humor. You'll have to figure it all out yourself, using *Time Out*'s exhaustive comedy listings. **Jongleurs** has three spots, and counting, and hosts incredibly popular, and therefore pretty reliable, line-ups. Look out for anything with the brand name Perrier stamped on it—the sparkling-water people give awards to the best performers on the Edinburgh Festival Fringe. Killing them on TV are Vic Reeves, Bob Mortimer, Paul

ENTERTAINMENT | THE LOWDOWN

Whitehouse, and Charlie Higson of *The Fast Show*, which you can see live at Labatts Apollo, if you hit the right season. Totally recommended.

Jolly good sports... On the whole, Londoners like watching other people do sports more than they like exerting themselves. One of the best sports to watch is football (soccer). London has three clubs in the elite Premier League. Catch **Spurs** (Tottenham Hotspurs) at **White Hart Lane**, or **Arsenal** or **Chelsea** at their respective grounds. Rumors about football hooliganism have been greatly exaggerated, although it is true that Chelsea fans like to chant "You're going home in a London ambulance" to the opposing side's fans. By comparison, cricket is as genteel as the afternoon tea that stops play at 4 p.m. See the quintessential English game at **Lords** or **The Oval**. On the violence scale, rugby falls somewhere in between. The game's like grid-iron without padding; the players are known for singing ditties with filthy lyrics ("rugby songs") in the showers and for their large quadriceps. It's an upper-class sport played at public (read exclusive, private) school, and also the passion of the entire Welsh nation. The 13-a-side professional game's Rugby League Final is played at **Wembley Stadium**; the purists' preferred (it's a bit like American League/National League favoritism) 15-a-side amateur Rugby Union, a.k.a. rugger, is played at **Twickenham**. What everybody wants during the last week of June and first week of July is **Wimbledon** tickets. Well, sorry, but those are allocated on a lottery system in January. However, during the first week, it's a cinch to see grand-slam, big-shot players up close on the outer courts.

The Index

Albert Hall. See Diversions.

Aldwych. A West End theater.... *Tel 0207/416–6003. The Aldwych WC2, Covent Garden tube stop.* **(see p. 202)**

Almeida. Possibly London's best Off–West End theater; it's always exciting, once you've tracked it down.... *Tel 0207/ 359–4404. Almeida St. N1, Angel tube stop.* **(see p. 203)**

Arsenal Football Club. Emotions run high for all the soccer teams, but Arsenal fans may be the most fanatical of all.... *Tel 0207/704–4000. Avenell Rd. Highbury N5, Arsenal tube stop. Season runs Aug.–May.* **(see p. 206)**

Arts Theatre. A West End theater.... *Tel 0207/836–2132. 6 Great Newport St. WC2, Leicester Sq. tube stop.*
(see p. 202)

Barbican Arts Centre. This major arts center's two theaters are home to the Royal Shakespeare Company, its auditorium to the London Symphony Orchestra and English Chamber Orchestra.... *Tel 0207/638–8891; 24-hour info: music 0207/638–4141, RSC 0207/628–3351. Silk St. EC2, Barbican/Moorgate tube stop.* **(see pp. 202, 204)**

Battersea Arts Centre. A.k.a. the BAC—a long way out, but often worth it.... *Tel 0207/223–2223. Lavender Hill SW11, Clapham Junction BR.* **(see p. 203)**

Burgh House. An elegant Hampstead chamber-music venue.... *Tel 0207/431–0144. New End Square NW3, Hampstead tube stop.* **(see p. 204)**

Bush. Off–West End venue with sometimes controversial

tastes.... *Tel 0208/743–3388. Shepherds Bush Green W12, Goldhawk Rd. tube stop.* **(see p. 203)**

Christ Church Spitalfields. Nicholas Hawksmoor's church is being renovated, but it still gives concerts.... *Tel 0207/ 377–0287. Commercial St. E1, Aldgate East tube stop.* **(see p. 205)**

Cambridge. A West End theater.... *Tel 0207/494–5080. Earlham St. WC2, Covent Garden tube stop.* **(see p. 202)**

Canal Café Theatre. Its Little Venice waterside location is a bonus; there's a late cabaret after the play.... *Tel 0207/ 289–6054. Bridge House, Delamere Terrace W2, Warwick Ave. tube stop.* **(see p. 203)**

Chelsea Football Club. Wear dark blue to see a match at the most geographically accessible London soccer ground.... *Tel 0207/385–5545. Stamford Bridge, Fulham Rd. SW6, Fulham Broadway tube stop.* **(see p. 206)**

Coliseum. Home of the English National Opera.... *Tel 0207/ 632–8300. St. Martin's Lane WC2, Charing Cross tube stop.* **(see p. 203)**

Comedy Store. The first—and if not the best, at least one of the most reliable—of the funny clubs.... *Tel 0207/344– 0234 (info), 0207/344–4444 (credit card reservations). Oxendon St. SW1, Piccadilly Circus tube stop.* **(see p. 205)**

Comedy Theatre. A West End theater, not a comedy club.... *Tel 0207/369–1731. Panton St. SW1, Piccadilly Circus tube stop.* **(see p. 202)**

Cottesloe. See National Theatre.

Donmar Warehouse. Is it West End? Is it Off? Is it fringe? Cabaret? Who cares—this central place nearly always has something good on.... *Tel 0207/369–1732. 41 Earlham St. WC2, Covent Garden tube stop.* **(see p. 203)**

Garrick. A West End theater.... *Tel 0207/494–5085. Charing Cross Rd. WC2, Leicester Sq. tube stop.* **(see p. 202)**

Gate. This tiny, ambitious, and well-known theater has been around forever.... *Tel 0207/229–0706. 11 Pembridge Rd. W11, Notting Hill Gate tube stop.* **(see p. 203)**

The Grace Theater at Latchmere Pub. Above the Latchmere pub in Battersea is this very good fringe theater.... *Tel 0207/794–0022. 503 Battersea Park Rd. SW11, Clapham Junction BR.* **(see p. 203)**

Greenwich Theatre. A West End theater, far from the West End.... *Tel 0208/858–7755. Crooms Hill SE10, Greenwich BR.* **(see p. 203)**

Hackney Empire. A loverly old theater in the East End, where a lot of comedy happens—also plays and music.... *Tel 0208/985–2424. 291 Mare St. E8, Hackney Central BR.* **(see p. 203)**

Haymarket Theatre Royal. A West End theater.... *Tel 0207/ 930–8800. Haymarket SW1, Piccadilly Circus tube stop.* **(see p. 202)**

Holland Park Open Air Theatre. The cutest stage in town is in the ruins of a Jacobean mansion.... *Tel 0207/602– 7856. Holland Park W8, Holland Park tube stop. April–Aug.* **(see p. 204)**

Institute of Contemporary Arts (ICA). The theater at the Institute of Contemporary Arts stages performance pieces, lectures, dance and bizarre hybrids of same.... *Tel 0207/930– 3647. The Mall SW1, Charing Cross tube stop.***(see p. 203)**

Jackson's Lane. A place in the north, mainly for dance, usually nonindigenous, with some comedy and experimental theater. A veggie cafe offers a community feel.... *Tel 0208/ 341–4421. 269 Archway Rd. N6, Highgate tube stop.* **(see p. 203)**

Jongleurs. Eight venues nationwide, with two in London, that consistently round up *funny* comedians, at least judging by the popularity. This one has a picturesque canalside setting.... *Tel 0870/787–0707. Dingwalls Building, Middle Yard, Camden Lock NW1, Chalk Farm tube stop.* **(see p. 205)**

THE INDEX

ENTERTAINMENT

King's Head. A very long-standing pub theater; at this one you can drink during the play.... *Tel 0207/226–1916. 115 Upper St. N1, Angel tube stop.* **(see p. 203)**

Leighton House. Hear chamber music in Victorian splendor.... *Tel 0207/602–3316. 12 Holland Park Rd. W14, Kensington High St. tube stop.* **(see p. 204)**

Lords. The hallowed turf of British cricket since 1811.... *Tel 0207/289–1611. St. John's Wood Rd. NW8, St. John's Wood tube stop.* **(see p. 206)**

Lyric. It's a West End theater, though it's in Hammersmith.... *Tel 0208/741–2311. King St. W6, Hammersmith tube stop.* **(see p. 203)**

Lyric Studio. The experimental version of the above.... *Tel 0208/741–2311.* **(see p. 203)**

Lyttelton. See National Theatre.

Man in the Moon. Another pub fringe theater, this one in Chelsea.... *Tel 0207/351–2876. 392 Kings Rd. SW3, Sloane Sq. tube stop, then the 11 or 22 bus.* **(see p. 203)**

National Theatre. The South Bank Centre's trio of theaters (Olivier, Lyttelton, Cottesloe) are the playgrounds for the occasionally star-flecked, ever-changing, nearly always brilliant Royal National Theatre Company.... *Tel 0207/452–3000. South Bank SE1, Waterloo tube stop.* **(see p. 202)**

Old Red Lion. Here's yet another pub theater in Islington, this one conveniently close to the tube stop.... *Tel 0207/837–7816. 418 St. John's St. N1, Angel tube stop.* **(see p. 203)**

Old Vic. West End, but off the path, this theater stages consistent crowd-pleasers.... *Tel 0207/928–4397. Waterloo Rd. SE1, Waterloo tube stop.* **(see p. 202)**

Olivier. See National Theatre.

The Oval. The not-quite-as-hallowed-as-Lords-turf of British cricket.... *Tel 0207/582–6660. Kennington Oval SE11, Oval tube stop.* **(see p. 206)**

The Place. This is the place for contemporary dance—practically the center of the world for it.... *Tel 0207/387–0031. 17 Duke's Rd. WC1, Euston tube stop.* **(see p. 205)**

Purcell Room. See South Bank Centre. **(see p. 204)**

Queen Elizabeth Hall. See South Bank Centre. **(see p. 204)**

The Riverside Studio. Hidden by the Thames near Hammersmith Bridge is this happening arts complex.... *Tel 0208/237–1111. Crisp Rd. W6, Hammersmith tube stop.* **(see p. 203)**

Royal Court. This West End theater made its name on ground-breaking programming (e.g., Osborne's *Look Back in Anger*).... *Tel 0207/565–5000. Sloane Square SW1, Sloane Sq. tube stop.* **(see p. 203)**

Royal Court Theatre Upstairs. The still-groundbreaking studio version of the above stages all new plays.... *Tel 0207/565–5000.* **(see p. 203)**

Royal Festival Hall. See South Bank Centre. **(see p. 204)**

Royal Opera House. Just reopened after massive refurbishments, the companies have returned to the fold from their different locales across London.... *Tel 0207/304–4000. Bow St. WC2, Covent Garden tube stop.* **(see pp. 203, 205)**

Sadler's Wells. This Islington theater is best known for dance, but also transfers European theater and music productions.... *Tel 0207/863–8000. Rosebery Ave. EC1, Angel tube stop.* **(see pp. 204, 205)**

St. Giles in the Barbican. A City church with a classical concert program.... *No phone. Fore St. EC2, Barbican tube stop.* **(see p. 205)**

St. James's Garlickhythe. See Diversions.

St. James's Piccadilly. See Diversions.

THE INDEX

ENTERTAINMENT

St. John's Smith Square. BBC Radio often broadcasts concerts from this deconsecrated church, the major minor concert hall.... *Tel 0207/222–1061. Smith Square SW1, Westminster tube stop.* **(see p. 205)**

St. Martin-in-the-Fields. Beautiful church, beautiful music. See if you can catch the Academy of St. Martin-in-the-Fields on its home turf.... *Tel 0207/839–8362. Trafalgar Square WC2, Charing Cross tube stop.* **(see p. 205)**

South Bank Centre. The center of mainstream-but-still-good—often really good—theater (see National Theatre, above), and classical music at the three concert halls (Royal Festival and Queen Elizabeth Halls, Purcell Room).... *Tel 0207/960–4242. South Bank SE1, Waterloo tube stop.* **(see p. 204)**

Southwark Cathedral. See Diversions.

Theatre Royal Stratford East. This Off–West End theater is hit or miss, since it stages a lot of brand-new work and young playwrights' stuff. When it hits, it's great.... *Tel 0208/534–0310. Gerry Raffles Square E15. Stratford tube stop.* **(see p. 203)**

Tricycle. This well-loved Off–West End theater almost closed due to lack of funds but now thrives again.... *Tel 0207/ 328–1000. 269 Kilburn High Rd. NW6, Kilburn tube stop.* **(see p. 203)**

Twickenham. The Rugby Union valhalla where the Pilkington Cup is fought in early May.... *Tel 0208/892–8161. Whitton Rd., Twickenham Middlesex. Twickenham BR. Season runs Sept.–Aug.* **(see p. 206)**

Wembley Stadium. The FA (Football Association) Cup Final is fought here, as is the Rugby League (as opposed to the Union) Silk Cut Trophy. Since you'll never get tickets to either, go see another match at this 70,000-seater.... *Tel 0208/902–0902. Wembley Middlesex HA9, Wembley Park tube stop.* **(see p. 206)**

White Hart Lane. Home of the Spurs—the Tottenham Hotspur footy team.... *Tel 0208/365–5050. 748 High Rd. N17, Turnpike Lane tube stop.* **(see p. 206)**

Wigmore Hall. This lovely, recently restored concert hall behind Oxford Street has a really accessible program.... *Tel 0207/ 935–2141. 36 Wigmore St. W1, Bond St. tube stop.* **(see p. 204)**

Wimbledon. For a chance at tickets to the tennis tournament, write with a SASE from Aug. to Dec. For information, call 0208/944–1066 (not during the tournament). *All England Lawn Tennis & Croquet Club, Box 98, Church Rd., Wimbledon SW19 5AE, Southfields tube stop.*

(see p. 206)

Young Vic. An excellent Off–West End theater with two auditoria.... *Tel 0207/928–6363. 66 The Cut SE1, Waterloo tube stop.* **(see p. 203)**

hotlines & other basics

Airports... The one you'll almost definitely land at is **Heathrow**. The best way into town from there is undoubtedly the new **Heathrow Express,** leaving for Paddington from 5 a.m. until midnight every 15 minutes, with a journey time of 15 minutes; tickets are £12. Otherwise, it is a 40- to 60-minute journey by tube. Take the Piccadilly Line for just over £3 to central London. By changing lines, you can get virtually anywhere without rising above ground, but if you have heavy bags, the sometimes endless walks between lines could be a drag. The other cheap way into town is the **Airbus**. Both routes, A1 (to Victoria) and A2 (to Russell Square) depart all four terminals every 15 to 30 minutes, take about an hour, and cost £6 one way. The buses run 5 a.m.–8 p.m.; the tube 5:30 a.m.–midnight (Sun. 7 a.m.–11:30 p.m.); after that you'll have to take a **taxi**, for around £35, plus tip. One more lesser-known option: Tell the information desk you want a **minicab** into London. They keep a secret list of local firms, with whom a trip into central London is more like £20–25.

There's a slim chance your flight will land at the other main London airport, **Gatwick,** or even at the newest facility, **Stansted**. The **train** is the best way into town from either: The **Gatwick Express** leaves for Victoria Station every 15 minutes (every 30 minutes between 1 a.m. and 5 a.m.), for around £10 one-way, and takes 30 to 40 minutes. The **Stansted Express** leaves for Liverpool Street every 15 minutes, for £11 one way; this service operates from 6 a.m. until midnight. Whichever airport you leave from, you'll pay a **Departure Tax** of £10 per person on your airline ticket.

Baby-sitters... Both the **Nanny Service** *(tel 0207/935–3515, 6 Nottingham St. W1)* and **Universal Aunts** *(tel 0207/738–8937, P.O. Box 304 SW4ONN)* are tried and trusted.

Buses... Those red double-deckers, synonymous with London, are the cheapest tourist attraction in town. During rush hour (8–9:30 a.m. and 4:30–6 p.m.) it's best not to hop on a bus if you're in a hurry; otherwise it's a scenic, if roundabout, way to travel. By no means are all buses double-deckers, but all are hailed the same way—by waiting at the concrete post with a flag-like sign on its top. If the sign is red, it's a "request stop," and you stick out your arm; otherwise the bus stops automatically (unless there isn't room on it). An oblong sign lower down the post illustrates the routes of the buses that stop there, but also check the destination sign in front of the bus, since many fail to run the whole route. Fares are assessed on the same system as for the tube (see below), and **Travelcards** are valid for both modes of transportation. Show your card or pay your coins to the conductor (who often doubles as the driver) and get free bus maps from **Travel Information Centres** at main tube stations.

Car Rental... We strongly advise you not to drive in London. You have to do it on the left, use a stick shift, and park. If you must rent a car, though, your own driver's license is all you'll need (though you could also get an International Driver's Permit from AAA). You'll find **Alamo** *(tel 800/327–9633)*, **Avis** *(tel 800/331–1212)*, **Budget** *(tel 800/527–0700)*, and **Hertz** *(tel 800/654–3131)* at the airports and at other locations in London, charging somewhat higher rates than you may be used to, with unlimited mileage at around £60 to £80 per day for a midsize, plus tax, insurance, and extras like collision damage waiver. You don't have to reserve in advance.

Climate... The infamous climate is as unpredictable as you've heard. Summer 1999 (like 1975) saw a 90-degree-plus heat wave, for instance, while 1997 saw the hottest August since records began, and the wettest June since

1860, and snow is available during an occasional February, but then absent for three straight years. Unless you hit those extremes, you can pretty much count on **rain**— often a soaking, dark-sky drizzle that can go on for days— and mild temperatures, on the cool side (40–50 degrees F) from November through March; hovering around 70 degrees from June to September. For the official London weather forecast, dial 0839/500–951*.

Consulates and Embassies... The **U.S. Embassy** is at 24 Grosvenor Square W1A 1AE, tel 0207/499–9000; the **Canadian High Commission** is nearby, at 1 Grosvenor Square, W1, tel 0207/258–6600.

Currency... Pounds sterling and pence are the money here, with notes in denominations of £5, £10, £20, £50, and £100; coins in 1p, 2p, 5p, 10p, 20p, 50p, £1, and £2 sizes. The exchange rate hovers around the £1=$1.50 mark.

Dentists... The best bet for emergency dental work is **Guys Hospital** (*tel 0207/955–4317. St. Thomas St. SE1*), which is central and has the longest hours: Mon.–Fri. 8:45–3:30; Sat., Sun. 9:30–5. If your abscess blows up at dinner, trek to **King's College Hospital** (*tel 0207/737–4000. Denmark Hill, SE5*), open 6–11 p.m. daily. There is no charge.

Doctors... Doctors on 24-hour call: tel 07000/372–255. Central London hospitals with 24-hour emergency rooms are: **Charing Cross** (*tel 0208/846–1234, Fulham Palace Rd., Hammersmith W6*); **Guys** (*tel 0207/955–5000, St. Thomas St. SE1*), and **St. Thomas's** (*tel 0207/928–9292, Lambeth Palace Rd. SE1*), plus the north **London Royal Free** (*tel 0207/794–0500, Pond St. Hampstead, NW3*).

Electricity... Different from home, it's 220-volt, 50-cycle AC (alternating current), instead of 110-volt, 60-cycle AC, and the wall outlets accept three-prong plugs. Adapters or transformers are necessary.

Emergencies... Dial 999 (it's a free call) from any phone for police, fire department, or ambulance.

Festivals and Special Events...

Many of the annual exhibitions, special events, and commercial festivals take place at the Earls Court Exhibition Centre and the Kensington Olympia. For information on what's coming up (food, cars, skiing), call the Earls Court box office at 0207/373–8141. Tickets can be booked.

January: **1**, The **London Parade**—this year called the Millennium Parade London—has cheerleaders, floats, marching bands, and the Lord Mayor of Westminster.

12:30 to 3 p.m. Westminster Bridge—Berkeley Square. **Early–mid-month, London International Boat Show** *(tel 01784/473377; Earls Court, Warwick Rd., SW5)*. Europe's largest.

February–March: **London Arts Season** packages the arts, with bargain-priced tickets and special events *(tel 0207/563–3188—number works for Arts Season only)*.

March: **Camden Jazz Festival,** for 10 days in north London *(tel 0207/860–5866)*. **British Antique Dealers' Association Fair** *(tel 0207/589–6108; Duke of York's Headquarters, King's Rd., Chelsea SW3)*.

April: **Oxford & Cambridge Boat Race on the Thames** and the **Flora London Marathon** *(tel 0207/620–4117; Box 1234, London SE1 8RZ)*, see Diversions for both.

May: **Chelsea Flower Show** *(tel 0207/344–4343; Chelsea Royal Hospital, Swan Walk, 66 Royal Hospital Rd., SW3)* **Football Association FA Cup Final** *(tel 0208/900–1234; Wembley Stadium)*.

June: **Trooping the Colour**—the queen's birthday parade on the 4th *(tel 0207/414–2497; Horse Guards, Whitehall. Ticket Office, Headquarters, Household Division, London SW1A 2AX. Send SASE Jan. 1–Feb. 28 for tickets)*.

June–July: **LIFT (London International Festival of Theatre**); tel 0207/490–3964. **Wimbledon Lawn Tennis Championships** *(tel 0208/946–2244; Church Rd., Wimbledon SW19 5AE)*.

July: **Hampton Court Palace Flower Show** *(tel 0207/630–7422; East Molesey, Surrey)*.

August: **Notting Hill Carnival** *(Portobello Rd., Ladbroke Grove, All Saints Rd.)*. Bank Holiday weekend—the big Caribbean extravaganza.

July–September: **Henry Wood Promenade Concerts** (the Proms) *(tel 0207/589–8212; Royal Albert Hall, Kensington Gore SW7 2AP)*.

November: **5, Guy Fawkes Day.** The day when the lack of success of a 1605 attempt to blow up the Houses of Parliament is commemorated with fireworks and bonfires on which effigies of Mr. Fawkes are incinerated. Lord Mayor's Show. Band, floats, razzmatazz (Guildhall to the Royal Courts of Justice), a fair in Paternoster Square, fireworks on the Thames *(tel 0207/606–3030)*.

December: Christmas tree in Trafalgar Square, many carol-singing sessions; lighting ceremony.

Gay & Lesbian Hotlines... London Lesbian & Gay Switchboard *(tel 0207/837–7324)*, 24-hour info and advice; **London Lesbian Line** *(tel 0207/251–6911; Tues.– Thurs. 7–10 p.m., Mon., Fri. 2–10 p.m.).*

Holidays... New Year's Day (Jan. 1), Easter (Good Friday, Easter Monday), May Day Bank Holiday (first Mon. in May), Spring Bank Holiday (last Mon. in May), August Bank Holiday (last Mon. in Aug.), Christmas Day & Boxing Day (Dec 25–26).

Hotel Hotline... The London Tourist Board's credit-card accommodation booking service *(tel 0207/932–2020).*

The Internet... The Internet business is booming in London. Most hotels now take bookings via the Internet. Some museums and other attractions also have information in cyberspace. Some useful sites: www.londonmillenniumcity.com (London Tourist Board information site); www.dome2000.co.uk (site for tickets and information on the Y2K folly's spectaculars); www.whatsonwhen.com (worldwide listings, not confined to London, on one-off events, gigs, bizarre festivals, and happenings).

Newspapers... London drowns in newsprint. The daily broadsheets, or "Qualities," are: the *Times*, the *Guardian*, *The Independent*, *The Daily Telegraph*, and the *Financial Times*, while the awful, but entertaining, tabloids are the *Mirror*, the *Mail*, the egregious *Sun* and even worse *Star*. There is also the valuable evening paper, the *Standard*, out weekdays before lunchtime. Sundays offer a mountain that keeps you occupied all day: the broadsheet *Sunday Times*, *Observer*, *Independent on Sunday*, and *Sunday Telegraph*, and the tabs, the *Sunday Mirror*, *Mail on Sunday*, the *People*, the *News of the World* and—the father of American *Enquirer*-type trash—the unbelievable *Sunday Sport*. Don't be surprised by its high nipple count.

Opening & Closing Times... **Banks**, Mon.–Fri. 9:30–4 or 5:30 in some branches, plus Sat. morning in some cases. **Shops**, typically Mon.–Sat. 9–6, with many now open Sun. **Pubs**, Mon.–Sat. 11 a.m.–11 p.m. (some shut 3–5:30 p.m.), Sun. noon–10:30 p.m. (some shut 3–7 p.m.). **Museums**, average opening hours are Mon.–Sat. 10–6, Sun. 2–5, but always check, especially during holiday periods. **Post offices**, Mon.–Fri. 9–5:30, Sat. 9–1.

Parking... You've already been warned not to drive, but if you insist, know that parking is hell, thanks to the usual meters and restrictions, and also the dread "Denver Boot," or wheel clamp—an immobilizing device administered by independent operators, which costs about £120 to get removed. **NCP (National Car Parks)** lots are open throughout London, but they fill up quickly and they're expensive—£10 for 3 hours in most places, and up to £15 in others. Parking **on the street** is no less expensive, nor easy. Meters take varying amounts, anywhere from 5p to £1, and it must be in coin; 20p will usually buy between 6 and 20 minutes of time, depending on location.

Passports & Visas... U.S. and Canadian citizens need a valid passport to enter the U.K. for stays of up to six months.

Pharmacy... Get late-night drugs from **Bliss** *(5 Marble Arch W1; tel 0207/723–6116; open daily 9 a.m.–midnight).*

Postal Service... Mailboxes are rather attractive scarlet cylinders with the times of collection posted on the front. Get stamps from post offices, many newsagents, and shops. Rates at press time are: 43p for airmail letters (up to 10g) to the U.S., postcards 35p; within Britain, 26p for letters, 20p for second class and post-cards. The post office at **Trafalgar Square** *(tel 0207/930–9580; 24–28 William IV St. WC2)* keeps long hours: Mon.–Sat. 8–8.

Radio Stations... There are five national radio stations: **1FM**, 98.8FM (mainstream pop music, with some more interesting stuff, including John Peel's great indie and alternative show Tues.–Thurs. at 10:10); **Radio 2**, 89.1FM (easy listening); **Radio 3**, 91.3FM (classical, some talk); **Radio 4**, 93.5FM, 198/720AM (talk, news, game shows, drama. A beloved national institution, especially *The Archers*—a 30-year-old radio soap about country folk); **Radio 5**, 693m AM (the new one—sports, talk), plus the **World Service**, 648m AM. The principal London stations are: **Capital FM**, 95.8 (pop), **Kiss FM**, 100FM (dance/club music; probably the hippest station in town), **JFM**, 102.2FM (jazz), **Classic FM**, 101.6 (AOR classical), **GLR**, 94.9FM (talk, music), **Virgin**, 105.8FM (pop and rock music), **London News**, 97.3FM, **Magic,** 105.4FM (easy listening and golden oldies—ironically, rather hip), and **Talk,** 1053AM (like an only slightly more civilized aural Jerry Springer).

Standards of Measure... England is supposed to be metric, like the rest of Europe, but you'll see as many feet and inches, pounds and ounces, as meters and centimeters, kilos, and grams. Human weight is given in stones and pounds; one stone=14 lbs. Clothing sizes: For women, increase one size for English wear across the board; men's suit and shirt sizes are the same. Clothing sizes tend to vary wildly anywhere, however. Shoes are often sold in European sizes. For men: European 41=U.K. 7=U.S. 8. For women: European 41=U.K. 7=U.S. 10.

Subways... See **Tubes.**

Taxes... Value Added Tax (VAT) adds 17.5 percent to many purchases, and is often refundable. U.K. departure tax is £10 per person (see **Airports**, above).

Taxis... Hail one when the orange "For Hire" light on the roof is lit. An empty one may stop even if its light is off, since drivers sometimes use this method to screen passengers at night. London cabbies are among the best in the world—they all have an encyclopedic grasp of London's geography, having passed an exhaustive exam called "The Knowledge." Of this they are justly proud; don't insult your driver by offering directions. Metered fares are £1.40 for the first 528 yards, rising by 20p per 264 yards or 54 seconds, plus surcharges as follows: after 8 p.m., 40p; after 12 a.m., 60p; Sundays and holidays, 60p; Christmas and New Year's, £12. There are also charges for dogs, and if the driver must put a passenger's bag next to him.

Unlicensed taxis, called minicabs, must be booked by phone or in person at the office. Most hotels and restaurants keep numbers of local services, and will call one for you. You can also call 0800/654–321 (free) for instant connection to your nearest minicab office. Fares are about 25 percent lower than for black cabs.

Telephones... Public phones are either those familiar scarlet boxes or else nondescript booths; either accept coins, or prepaid BT (British Telecommunications) cards, and/or credit cards. **Coin phone boxes** accept 10p as the minimum payment. **Cardphones** take BT Cards, which you can buy in units from 10 (£1) to 100 (£10) and more from newsagents and general stores. Slot in the card, and a display shows how much time is left; the card is returned when you replace the receiver. **Credit cards** are used by swiping the magnetic stripe. The British ring is a double chirrup; repeated short beeps mean the line is busy, and a continuous beep means the number is "unobtainable"—either it's cut off or you dialed the wrong prefix. All London numbers are changing. From Jan. 1, 2000, the system is as follows: the 01 and 02 prefixes denote normal rates; 03, 08, and 09 prefixes denote special rates (for example: 0800=free; 0345=local rate; 0839=50p per minute); the 07 prefix denotes a cellular phone number. London numbers all begin with 020.

Numbers that were 0207 are now 0207; 0181 numbers have become 0208. When in London, drop the 020 and call an 8-digit number beginning in 7 or 8. Standard rate: Mon.–Fri. 8 a.m.–6 p.m.; cheap rate: 6 p.m.–8 a.m. and weekends. The international access code is 00; for the international operator, credit card, or collect calls, dial 155. For international directory inquiries, dial 153; domestic is 192. For the operator, dial 100. Hotels often whack on a surcharge, so consider using a U.S. calling card. Some access numbers are: **AT&T USA Direct** *(tel 0500/890–011)*; **MCI Call USA** *(tel 800/444–4444)*; and **Sprint Express** *(tel 800/877–4646)*.

Tipping... Hotels and restaurants often add a 10 to 15 percent service charge automatically, so think before you pay twice. Don't tip theater ushers or bartenders. Do tip: washroom attendants (about 20p in the saucer), taxi and minicab drivers (15 percent), porters and bellhops (£1 per bag carried), doormen (£1 or £2 for hailing cabs, etc.), concierges (at your discretion, for exceptional services like procuring difficult theater tickets or dinner reservations), hairdressers, beauty parlor technicians, etc. (15 percent).

Tours... Sightsee on an open-topped double-decker bus with **Original London Sightseeing Tours** *(tel 0208/877–1722; April–Oct. daily 9 a.m.–7 p.m.; Nov.–March 10–5. Board at Trafalgar Square or Green Park tube outside the Ritz Hotel)*, which follow four different routes over 70 stops, including all the greatest hits. Tickets last 24 hours and cost £12 adults, £6 kids. Buses make about 21 stops, at which you can get on and off at will. The best walking tours are led by **The Original London Walks** *(tel 0207/624–3978)*. **City Walks** *(tel 0207/700–6931)* and **Streets of London** *(tel 0208/346–9255)* are also reliable. Customized tours are given by cabbies with "The Knowledge," in **Black Taxi Tours of London** *(tel 0207/289–4371)*, or, if you want to leave London, by **British Tours** *(tel 0207/734–8734)*.

Travelers With Disabilities... Hotlines include the **Artsline** *(tel 0207/388–2227)*, for advice on accessibility of arts events, and the **Holiday Care Service** *(tel 0129/377–4535)* for help with accommodations questions. **London Transport** has a **Unit for Disabled Passengers** *(tel 0207/222–5600)*, which includes the **Stationlink** service, a wheelchair-accessible "midibus" between nine BritRail stations and Victoria Coach

Station. **RADAR** (the Royal Association for Disability and Rehabilitation) *(tel 0207/250–3222; 12 City Forum, 250 City Rd., London EC14 8AF)*, publishes travel information for the disabled in Britain.

Tubes... The London subway is the fastest way to get around—usually. There are 12 lines, plus the Docklands Light Railway, which may be on maps already (in pale green). They all run Mon.–Sat. 5:30–12:30 a.m., Sun. 7 a.m.–11:30 p.m. approx., and the average waiting time is 5 to 10 minutes. **Tube fares** are assessed in zones, with the price rising according to how many of the six you pass through. The most expensive way to travel is by single ticket (90p–£3.40). Better: Get a **Travelcard** (from £3.30/day, £1.90 for children), valid all day from 9:30 a.m. for tube and bus, or an **LT Card** (from £4.80, children £2.40), without time restrictions. For Weekly and Monthly Travelcards, you need a photo, as you do for a **Visitor's Travelcard**, which you get in the U.S. from BritRail Travel International (tel 212/382–3737; 1500 Broadway, New York, NY 10036) (3, 4, or 7 days for $25, $32, or $49; $11, $13, or $21 for children), which includes discount vouchers to London sights. You can be fined on the spot for traveling without a valid ticket.

Visitor Information... Contact the **British Tourist Authority**. New York: tel 212/986–2200 or 800/462–2748; 551 5th Ave., Suite 701, New York, NY 10176. Chicago: tel 312/787–0490; Suite 1510, 625 N. Michigan Ave., Chicago, IL 60611. Los Angeles: tel 213/628–3525; World Trade Center, 350 S. Figueroa St., Suite 450, Los Angeles, CA 90071. Atlanta: tel 404/432–9635; 2580 Cumberland Pkwy., Suite 470, Atlanta, GA 30339. Toronto: tel 416/925–6326; 111 Avenue Rd., 4th Floor, Toronto, Ontario M5R 3J8 Canada.

The city's main **Tourist Information Centre** is at Victoria Station Forecourt, Mon.–Sat. 8–7, Sun. 8–5; others are at Heathrow Airport (Terminals 1, 2, and 3), and department stores Harrods and Selfridges, all open to personal callers only. For phone information, you will pay premium rates (60p/min. at all times, plus any hotel/payphone surcharge) for the **LTB's Visitorcall** phone guide. To order free cards listing all of its services, call 0207/971–0026. For information on goings-on in the next three months, call 09064/123–401.